Toward a Jewish Theology of Liberation

Toward a Jewish Theology of Liberation

The Challenge of the 21st Century

MARC H. ELLIS

Third Expanded Edition

Baylor University Press
Waco, Texas USA

Cover Design: Steven Day/Joan Osth

This is the third edition of *Toward a Jewish Theology of Liberation* by Marc H. Ellis originally published by Orbis Books, Maryknoll, NY: first edition in 1987, second edition in 1989.

The Library of Congress has cataloged the hardback edition as follows:

Library of Congress Cataloging-in-Publication Data

Ellis, Marc H.
  Toward a Jewish theology of liberation : the challenge of the twentieth-first century / Marc H. Ellis.— 3rd ed.
      p. cm.
  Includes bibliographical references and index.
  ISBN 1-932792-00-7 (hardcover : alk. paper)
  1. Holocaust (Jewish theology) 2. Judaism—United States. 3. Jews—United States—Attitudes toward Israel. 4. Liberation theology. 5. Judaism and social problems. 6. Arab-Israeli conflict—Religious aspects—Judaism. I. Title.

  BM645.H6E44 2004
  296.3—dc22

                                        2004003214

The ISBN-13 for the paperback edition is 978-1-60258-345-0

Printed in the United States of America on acid-free paper

Marc Ellis has written a book for people who want to think. Challenging our conventional ideas, he forces us to reconsider our assumptions regarding Jewish identity and politics. What emerges is a fascinating and original reconfiguration of some of the most hotly debated political and religious topics today.

—Susannah Heschel, Eli Black Chair in Jewish Studies,
Dartmouth College and author of *Abraham Geiger and the Jewish Jesus*

Marc Ellis's *Toward a Jewish Theology of Liberation* is a seminal work. It is not only a brilliant piece of Jewish dissident writing but a moral, impassioned call for reflection and justice that should be read by Jews and non-Jews alike. There is no doubt this book will become the standard among scholars for decades to come.

—Sara Roy, Senior Research Scholar,
Center for Middle Eastern Studies, Harvard University

Ellis argues against current political policies based on Jewish vulnerability, with the Holocaust as the chief lens, and issues a prophetic call for contemporary Jews to return to the liberation theology embedded in the Exodus, seeking justice for all.

—Rabbi Elliot N. Dorff, Rector and Distinguished Professor of Philosophy,
University of Judaism

October 25, 2000

Dear Consul,

I met you at the dinner put on by Baylor University and the Conference for Christians and Jews. I am the son of Marc Ellis.

I would like to express my deepest anger for what you said, which was both unfounded and untrue. In your speech, you went on about how the Palestinians have all the rights that the Israelis have. This is in no way true. Until you stop pointing tanks and helicopter gun ships at the Palestinians, do you really expect them to feel security that you won't bomb them into oblivion?

You are still monitoring everything that they are doing. You are cutting them off to the world, by building walls around their territories, and are scaring them into irrational violence with the violence that you too are partaking in. How can you, as a member of the Israeli government, sleep at night, knowing that you as a people are firing bombs, firing missiles, at defenseless innocent Palestinians. What you are doing is pressing your heel against the throats of people who can't do anything to defend themselves!

How can you rationally say that Yassir Arafat is solely responsible for all of this warfare? Who called off the peace process? Not Arafat alone.

So while the Palestinians are of course not little angels in this conflict, the Israelis are, like the Palestinians, not free of blame. If you are too ignorant to step out of your position for one second and look at the situation as a whole, and see that the Israelis are using brute force to oppress a people then I don't think that you can be helped.

I noticed that you made reference to the Bible. Didn't the Lord Our God, *Adonai*, tell us to be kind to the stranger, because we were once strangers in the land of Egypt? You are now undermining the "Name of God," as I see it.

A question was brought up: "Why don't the Jordanians just accept the Palestinians?" How incredibly unthought out, and un-educated, is this question? That's like saying to all Latinos in the United States, "Get out of the United States and go to Latin America." What isn't understood, is that they weren't born in Latin America. They were born in the United States; and who are we to tell them that they can't live there?

I understand that Israel is a democracy. If you say that, that you are forcing Palestinians to move out because you are more militarily advanced than they are, you create a totalitarian government, much like that which was created in Germany in the 1930's. You, in essence, are saying that whoever has the most powerful thugs, Gestapo, Army, or secret police, should rule regardless of their political views. This is exactly what led to the suffering of so many fellow Jews and others. This, also, is what's happening to the Palestinians even as you read this, only on a smaller scale.

I don't know how you really support your views, except for the fact that Israel is more powerful than the Palestinians, and therefore should rule over them, which is of course just down right stupid for anyone to think this, much less an entire nation.

Thank you for your time, and I would greatly appreciate a letter back, as I am trying to find out the truth.

Sincerely,
Aaron Ellis

September 4, 2004

My Precious Son Aaron,

I began this book many years ago as you were coming to life. With your letter I feel a sense of completion, as if somehow I have finished my task. I see now that the prophetic voice will never be silenced.

I have been faithful as a Jew. Yet I am part of a failed generation.

I wish you the wisdom and the perseverance to succeed in your struggles. But above all I hope for you the strength to be faithful.

Always search for the covenant. The covenant is among peoples that are foreign to you and in places you are not supposed to be.

Practice revolutionary forgiveness in your personal and public life. Avoid bitterness even against those who persecute you.

Work tirelessly to break the cycle of violence and atrocity. Always speak for those outside. Never be silent in the face of injustice. Never use the historic suffering of our own people to cause suffering to others. It demeans those who suffer today. It demeans our journey as a people.

Above all do not despair. Trust that your word and your testimony will be heard. It is not too late.

My Loving Father,

Just as your life comes full circle, I have competed this book and finished my life's work. As with Aaron's letter, I experience a sense of completion. I hope that you have this same feeling with regard to me, your son. Know that your gentle and kind spirit, your concern and humor, will always be with me. As you wrote to me on my fiftieth birthday: "I feel very blessed."

Contents

Foreword

by Desmond Tutu

The world owes a great deal to the Jews. I know that I certainly do. My identity as a believer would be nonexistent without my particular antecedents. I thank God that I am a spiritual descendant of God's friend, Abraham. My ministry and witness have been undergirded and informed by the imperatives and the verities expounded in the Hebrew Bible which forms the Old Testament of our Christian Bible. I would have been at a loss to justify my opposition to the injustice and viciousness of apartheid had I not been able to refer to the teachings of the Torah and the proclamations of the prophets.

Without the Jews and all that they have given to the world in the realm of morality and the standards and values that they have proclaimed concerning human conduct, we would all have been much impoverished. It is almost bizarre that I have first to establish my credentials and my *bona fides* before I can speak about this book, though they have said about self-justification that your friends do not need it and your enemies do not believe it. It seems that I am following the trite cliché: "Some of my best friends are. . . ." But it is nonetheless necessary, as I shall show. I am at present a member of the board of directors of the Shimon Peres Peace Centre in Tel Aviv (as are several other Nobel Peace laureates). I am a patron of the Holocaust Centre in Cape Town. The chairs of the Boards of the Desmond Tutu Peace Centre in Cape Town and of the Desmond Tutu Peace Foundation in New York are both Jews. When Leah and I were ill simultaneously in Atlanta, our neighbour across the road from us used to ply us with food parcels left on our doorstep and she has ever since become our Jewish momma.

I am constrained to do this in the hope that I can forestall any charges of anti-Semitism that some might be tempted to level at me for what they may consider to be unacceptable criticism in what follows. My apprehension is not baseless. In 1989 I went to the Holy Land to be with our fellow Anglicans at Christmas. On that occasion I visited Yad Vashem, the Holocaust Memorial. When I emerged, the media asked for my impressions. I said it was a devastating testimony to our capacity for being inhuman to one another and reminded us of something we should never forget. I then added that my Lord who was a Jew would have asked, "but what about forgiveness?" We were staying at St George's Close. On the following morning after my visit to Yad Vashem, there was graffiti on the wall opposite St George's Cathedral reading, "Tutu is a black nazi pig."

On another occasion, I was sharply critical of the Israeli government's collaboration on several levels with the apartheid regime. Some in the United States Jewish community picketed me as anti-Semitic when I attended the inauguration of Mayor David Dinkins. I have been pilloried on other occasions as anti-Semitic, hence the need to establish my credentials. I might add that although white South Africans had humiliated and oppressed and harassed us, I have never been anti-white. I have without apology certainly been "anti" the injustice and oppression that the whites practiced, and will, pray God, be so always firmly opposed to injustice and oppression wherever.

I write this foreword as someone who loves the Jewish people as I do others. I pray that we can all make the important distinction between the Israeli government and the Israeli or Jewish people; that criticism of the Israeli government is not therefore inevitably criticism of Jews as such. The Israeli government is made up of fallible human beings as are all governments. They cannot thus be above criticism unless they have been exalted to the position of gods. I criticized the Reagan administration pungently for its policy of constructive engagement with the South African apartheid government. No one ever thought to accuse me of being anti-American. I have denounced the war against Iraq as immoral and suggested that Mr. Bush and Mr. Blair should apologize. I have not thereby been accused of being anti-American or anti-British.

The Jews suffered unimaginably during the Holocaust and the Christian church, in so far as it encouraged and condoned this unspeakable horror and colluded with its perpetrators, deserves all the opprobrium and condemnation heaped on it. Western countries must also accept that they were culpable. The Jews deserve all that could be done in the way of reparations, whilst we all know that no amount of reparations could ever begin to make up in any but the most inadequate and symbolic way for one of the worst examples of our inhumanity to one another.

In many ways, therein lies the rub: the Jews suffered so deeply, so traumatically at the hands of others. They were humiliated, they were dispossessed, they were driven from their homes. Their human dignity was callously trodden underfoot by the powerful and the arrogant. They were rendered nonentities. Others decided for them, others discussed them. They were objects, really just things that the powerful manipulated as they wished; they were ciphers. If all this is true—and I contend most emphatically that it was so and worse—then my anguish is deepened even more when I ask, "How could it be that people who experienced such untold suffering could now in their turn through the Israeli government treat others as abominably as they were treated? How could those who were made refugees, so soon be able to make other hapless people refugees?"

Is it possible to forget so soon? To some extent, I can answer that it is possible to do so because I have seen it happen in my own country. Those who in the anti-apartheid struggle were so magnanimous and altruistic, ready even to die if it would advance the cause of freedom for others, have in a very short space of time jettisoned their noble ideals and are self-serving and even corrupt after the demise of apartheid. So it is possible. And yet. . . . The fifth book of Moses repeatedly exhorts Israel to remember and not to forget what the Lord has done for her lest she is tempted to become unfaithful and go whoring after other gods. But a second reason for remembering is that they had been slaves and aliens and that should be the motive for them to treat slaves and aliens compassionately and mercifully.

As a black South African I remember most of what has happened to us: the forced population removals involving nearly 3 million people; people pointing out what were formerly their homes, which had been confiscated and were now owned by whites; the Pass laws that severely restricted our movement in the land of our birth; the humiliations and harassments at police road blocks and checkpoints; the balkanization of South Africa into unviable Bantustan homelands—broken up into non-contiguous settlements like so many pieces of different jigsaw puzzles where we were meant to enjoy a travesty of the privileges and rights of citizenship in what were client states, and meant to be client states of a powerful white overlord who determined who should represent us in a dialogue of the unequal.

It is a nightmare from which I want to be awakened when I see most of this and more replicated in the Holy Land with the addition of a wall of partition that gobbles up Palestinian land and leaves the Palestinians humiliated, powerless and despairing . . . and seething. What fertile soil for producing bitter, resentful suicide bombers. I have condemned the outrage of suicide bombers as also the terrorism of Israeli reprisals of demolishing family dwellings in collective punishment.

I want to see Israel continue as a sovereign state with internationally recognized borders, an Israel which is not resented by so many in the Middle East and increasingly alienating many others elsewhere who accepted the two-state solution when there was the possibility of a truly viable, sovereign Palestinian state side by side with Israel. In South Africa, the Muslims and Jews have had a good relationship. The situation in the Middle East is changing that relationship there, as in other parts of the world—a tension has developed between these two communities. We do not want that. In our country, some of the foremost stalwarts of our struggle have been Jewish, and we value enormously their continuing contribution to the success of our racial experiment of the rainbow nation. We do not want that subverted by developments in the Middle East.

God, so the Bible attests, will not be mocked forever. This is a moral universe and all the arrogantly powerful who treat God's favourites—the widow, the orphan and the alien—harshly will get their comeuppance. Israel may have won a total victory but it may be pyrrhic. We learned in South Africa that you cannot get true security from the barrel of a gun. We used to say to white South Africans, "You will never be free until we blacks are free." So, Israel will not be truly free and secure until the Palestinians are truly free and can establish viable structures of government with credible and uncorrupt leaders.

Liberation theology speaks to the downtrodden, the poor, the vulnerable, the powerless and voiceless ones. It is a paradox to have a liberation theology for the powerful unless it is to call the powerful to heed the warnings and teachings of their antecedents. Look to the rock from which you were hewn.

My anguish for a long time has been the relative silence from the spiritual leadership of the Jewish community. It is not easy to speak when you may be labeled self-hating and are helping to encourage a climate for another holocaust. I am in anguish as I watch this great people having their being eroded by the arrogant use of power. "Where is thy brother?" must be a haunting question, as it seems the people may become like Esau who sold his birthright for a mess of potage.

This book has assuaged my pain to a considerable extent because it says, as it has been saying since the first edition, the voice of prophecy has not been silenced in the Jewish community.

We will all be the poorer if that voice is not heeded, but how wonderfully enriched if it is heeded and Israel becomes truly Israel—the Chosen People of God for the sake of God's world, a light to the nations.

I pray, I cry for that to be so. Amen. Thank you God for Marc Ellis.

by Gustavo Gutiérrez

In the Bible we recognize two central commandments: the necessity to remember and the rejection of idolatry. Forgetfulness and idolatry are, as a consequence, the two most relevant transgressions of the believer in the God of the Bible. Forgetfulness because it deprives history of its meaning and direction, and because it hides the relationship to the other and to one's self; and idolatry because it exonerates the people from the responsibilities inherent in their freedom.

Marc Ellis's book *Toward a Jewish Theology of Liberation* (1987) offers a powerful link to these two proscriptions in our time. This link to the present is renewed with the publication of this third edition, in which the author takes into account more recent developments in the Israeli-Palestinian conflict and post-September 11th world. In these pages, Ellis offers a new and important contribution to the fecund theological trend that he has embarked on since the first edition of his work.

In the biblical worldview, memory is not principally—and certainly not exclusively—a relationship with the past; its primordial bond is with a present that projects itself forward. The past is there, but to offer depth to the moment that the believer lives. If memory is evoked, it is because of its current validity. The memory in the Bible goes beyond the conceptual and aims for a certain behavior, a practice, if you will, that works toward changing both social and personal conditions. To remember is to take into account, or to take care of, somebody or something. It evokes action, for without action memory loses meaning and direction, becoming a mere initiation of itself in a type of intellectual gymnastics.

"The history of the Jewish people is filled with anguish and struggle," Ellis argues. It is a walk of suffering (in which the Christian world has an historic responsibility); but, at the same time, it emerges as a "paradigm of liberation that forms the heart of the Jewish experience," which inspires both within and beyond the Jewish people, efforts for justice and freedom. Hence, an excruciating question is posed: "Why is it that a people that has contributed so much to the world has often received such scornful treatment in return?"

To look for an answer to this query requests an appeal to memory. Memory offers more than history. Memory is not history—if we understand the latter to be a simple tale of past facts—and, certainly, is more than an actualization of what occurred. It is, in the Bible, a sign of comprehension that makes "of history a theophany," a revelation of the God that calls us to life and rejects any sort of unjust death. It places us in every moment before the Deuteronomistic alternative: "See I set before you this day life and prosperity, death and adversity . . . blessing and curse. Choose life—if you and your offspring would live."

The memory of a God who liberates and demands the establishment of justice and righteousness, and the memory of the suffering of a people, among which the horrors of the Holocaust are especially prominent, grasps times and subverts the forgetfulness and cynicism that have accumulated over the years. The memory of God and suffering converts the past to an always new, exigent, and creative present that leads to the God of life. This God demands an engagement with the poor and a struggle toward the construction of a more just and fraternal world.

However, the historical process does not move toward those objectives without obstacles. "The choice between fidelity and betrayal arises from the history of our people," Ellis asserts; and he explains more specifically, amplifying the horizon: "but the fidelity to our own values and history is intimately connected to the struggles of liberation of others." The sense of the other offers fidelity its more authentic sense and this is concretely the scope of our history. Indeed, in the Bible there is a continuous, strong, and at the same time painful, position on the situation that currently confronts the Jewish and Palestinian people.

Dissident opinion exposes itself to criticism and isolation, but that is intrinsically attached to the memory of one's own people. This leads Ellis to affirm that the "brokenness of our past is betrayed, our political empower made suspect when others become our victims." A provocative affirmation to be sure, but it emerges, at least partially, from the contrast between the contribution of the Jewish people to humanity and the diverse reactions that Jews have experienced in history.

Ellis's understanding is strong: memory is fidelity; memory offers identity and liberates us from our isolation. In the end, memory opens us to the other.

The rejection of idolatry is the other fundamental commandment. Idolatry is, in the final analysis, rejection of the living God. This God demands certain behavior of the people, while consistently calling them to freedom. Idolatry is the risk that each religious person should confront; its origins lie in resting our confidence in something or someone who is not God, or it is to play within the ambiguity of proclaiming God, and at the same time, to look for other sources of support. This is what happens with money and power: when abused, it leads to the oppression of the other. This was the impetus for the harsh criticism by the prophets.

Ellis does not see his own people free of this danger today. He writes: "In religious terms, the inability to see the connection between our own suffering and the suffering of the other may be related to a contemporary form of idolatry, an ancient Jewish insight that, like the Exodus and the prophets, has atrophied in the contemporary Jewish community." He fears that since September 11th, the Jewish community has adopted new idols. His reflections on the threat of idolatry are, in one way or another, valid beyond his own community to other religious groups, including Christianity.

In relation to the Israeli-Palestinian conflict, Ellis pays special attention to the idolatry of empowerment and the violence derived from it. *Toward a Jewish Liberation Theology* does not believe in these methods, and Ellis questions aspects of Jewish empowerment in the United States. He understands Jewish empowerment as a defensive reaction to the historic suffering of the Jewish people, but holds that there are other ways to experience and utilize that empowerment. It is necessary to recognize and comprehend, Ellis says, with the courage that is manifest in all his work, that "by simply applying pre-Holocaust and Holocaust categories to the contemporary world we close our eyes and ears to the pain and possibility of the present." Fixation about the past, then, is in opposition to memory and an invitation to idolatry.

To the prophets, the gods of idolatry are tied to violence. Much blood has been shed because of profit and power motive and we see it each day in the international arena. Ellis advocates for peace and mutual understanding, and for solutions that work under the principles of justice and compassion. For that, a prophetic voice is required, and a prophetic voice demands a perspective derived from close contact with reality. In a different way, the prophecy reminds us of the danger when the utopian ideal and quest for justice loses its horizon. Ellis raises the question, "Will the Jewish prophetic voice survive Jewish empowerment?" His book is an act of faith that the prophetic voice has yet much to tell us.

There is much more in Ellis's book. He reflects on the connections between a Jewish liberation theology and other theologies of liberation. Respectful as he is of the individual essence of each, Ellis acknowledges and underscores the reciprocal influences among the different theological lines: "A Jewish theology of liberation encourages dialogue with other liberationist theologies and communities in a gesture of humility and solidarity." Ellis pays particular attention to the contribution of Naim Ateek, a Palestinian and Anglican priest, whose work, *Justice and Only Justice: A Palestinian Theology of Liberation*, emerges, along with Ellis's work, within the crucible of Jewish power. This provides Jews insight into the consequences of the power they wield. The same reality is considered from two points of view that find themselves in completely diverse traditions, but that work toward the same objective of justice and peace.

Ellis's narrative belongs alongside those theological narratives that are and ought to be discussed. This is an unquestioningly vigorous and important work, passionate for justice, rooted in a strong love for his people, and with a deep sensitivity to other human communities. Thus

Toward a Jewish Theology of Liberation is an important contribution to theology, to all liberation theology, and, as is true for any reflection, deeply rooted in the earth. It represents with force the need for justice in our cruel and sorrowful world, especially in these uncertain days.

Introduction

The history of the Jewish people is filled with anguish and struggle. More often than not, the defining motif of Jewish life has been exile, forced wandering, and lament. And yet, through this travail the Jewish community has bequeathed much to the world: a developed monotheism, a prophetic social critique, an awareness of God's presence in history, and the foundation of two other world religions, Christianity and Islam.

As important as these contributions are for the Jewish community, of which I am a part, the paradigm of liberation that forms the heart of the Jewish experience, the dynamic of bondage confronted by the call to freedom, has been appropriated by other struggling peoples throughout the ages. The songs of African slaves in nineteenth-century America calling on God for freedom echo the lamentations of the Jews in Egypt. The Exodus tradition, articulated in the writings of Latin American liberation theologians, again emerges within the struggle of Latin Americans for justice.

To cite these contributions of the Jewish people is to pose a fundamental contradiction of world history, one posed often but answered only weakly. Why is it that a people who have contributed so much to the world have often received such scornful treatment in return? Why is it that, historically, Jews have been considered more problematic than principally contributing to Western religious and intellectual heritage? And why is it that, in these allegedly enlightened times, a people born of suffering are sometimes doubted and dismissed, as if the world should have no concern for a people's long and difficult history?

The paradox of achievement and suffering is only part of Jewish history. To be sure, the overwhelming motif of wandering and exile flows from a fidelity to covenantal truths and values, an innocence often rewarded with brutality. On the other hand, the Jewish community's struggle to be faithful to those values has been shadowed by the reality of betrayal, for in advancing our own interests, we have been slave merchants and masters, supported corrupt kings and governments, and even at times oppressed one another.

Today, in Israel and in the Jewish community in North America, policies and alliances increasingly resemble those historically used to oppress our own people. On the Israeli side, one need only mention the recently-concluded occupation of parts of Lebanon and the continuing subjugation of West Bank and Gaza Palestinians; just as horrific are the relations Israel maintained with South Africa and Israel's military assistance to the murderous governments of El Salvador and Guatemala in previous decades.

In America the mainstream Jewish community continues to support Israeli policies toward Palestinians almost without hesitation. It often uses its power to suppress those Jews and non-Jews who dissent from those policies. Relations between American Jewry and the poor and oppressed of America remain strained, and Israel's ambivalent courtship of fundamentalist Christians, in exchange for their support of Israel, continues.

It is not too much to say that these developments threaten the very ethical witness of the Jewish people. A crossroads appears, which calls us to fidelity to our values, though it may yet tempt us to betrayal of those values.

The choice between fidelity and betrayal arises from the history of our people, guided as we are by the image of "enslaved ancestors," as Walter Benjamin once wrote. To be faithful to our ancestors, particularly those who have struggled, suffered and died in the Holocaust, is to be attentive to their cries, which must guide us. But fidelity to our own values and history is intimately connected to the struggles for liberation of others; the brokenness of our past is betrayed, our political empowerment made suspect, when others become our victims.

Poised between Holocaust and political empowerment, we in the Jewish community find it increasingly difficult to articulate a witness consonant with our past. The thunderings of expansionist Israelis and of neoconservative American Jews witness to the haunting possibility of a Judaism lost. Other Jews, often less articulate and removed from centers of power, are caught within this dialectic, fearing to speak, yet distinctly uncomfortable with the direction our community is taking. Still others, intellectuals and activists within Israel and America, actively oppose the paths already chosen by the institutional representatives of the Jewish community. Yet how, in our post-Holocaust world, do we articulate these feelings and opposition? And who is to name betrayal and fidelity?

Although there is no corner on truth here and the risks for the Jewish community are great, the discussion cannot continue to be censored. Every community has patterns of fidelity and betrayal, points of paralysis and breakthrough, and the Jewish community is no exception. Patterns move us beyond the incidental and isolated example to movements toward and away from the central ideals of the community, ideals forged in historical struggle and affirmation. In history final resolutions are impossible. What becomes important is the direction in which a community moves.

However, at certain times in history the community reaches a crossroads it cannot seem to articulate or acknowledge. This is the point of paralysis where rational thought, even the wisdom of one's tradition, seems to falter. The community drifts; the rhetoric drones on; judgment becomes clouded. Paralysis is less an evil than an indicator that the community needs to review its inner dynamic and its relations with other communities.

Questions surface. Does our present situation, if pursued, lead us to justice and renewal, or to emptiness and oppression? Are our discussions addressing the values and witness we are called to live, or are they covering over a hope we refuse to face because of its difficulty? Some historical situations might demand accentuation of particular values and the de-emphasis of others, and there are, no doubt, times when the community is simply bereft of values, exhausted, as it were, by history's travails. Are we willing to admit this state so we can begin the process of renewal?

If we come to understand points of paralysis, the possibility of breakthrough increases. Of course, the problem is that patterns of fidelity and betrayal occur in the mix of history, and the lessons of history are often as ambivalent as they are terrifying. Proponents and opponents, prophets and villains appear at every turn, defined by angles of vision and experience that depend on various propensities and points of view. What to one faction is a breakthrough may be to the other an apocalypse. This is the dilemma in which the Jewish people of America and the state of Israel— the two most articulate and politically powerful Jewish communities— presently find themselves.

To say that the questions raised by this situation are controversial is an understatement. The deep hurt of the Jewish people, our historical and contemporary sense of isolation, our feeling of being adrift in a hostile world: these are intensely subjective memories and emotions which spring from our history. To speak publicly on issues of the Holocaust and Israel in a critical manner is to court suspicion and raise the specter of treason. The result may be excommunication from the Jewish community, or worse, the accusation that one is supporting the climate for another holocaust. But the difficult questions remain, and the movement of our lives and community, toward fidelity or betrayal, lies before us.

This book is one attempt to address the crisis that confronts us. It has had three incarnations, and the context of each is important.

Toward a Jewish Theology of Liberation was first published in 1987 and came into being as the result of several visits to Israel. My first visit took place in 1973 as part of my junior year abroad. Stationed in London for the year, I had several holiday opportunities to travel, going first to the Soviet Union and later to Israel.

I went to Israel alone, as no one on my study program thought it important enough to divert from more fun holidays on the beaches of France or Morocco. In some ways I was fulfilling a challenge that my Hebrew teacher had provided me some years earlier. It was in 1968, right after Israel's victory in the Arab-Israeli war that lasted only six days, that my teacher was brought to Israel to witness the "miracle" of its birth, development and recent victory.

When he returned, he spoke to me of its physical beauty and of the emotional ties he felt with Israel. I listened intently. Some weeks earlier I had read an article in a national news magazine on the Palestinian refugees created during that war. As the article pointed out, it was the second refugee crisis that the Palestinians had faced, the first coming within Israel's 1948 war for independence.

As I knew nothing about either refugee crisis—in Hebrew school we were taught only about the miracle of Israel and nothing about the Palestinians—I asked about these "Palestinians" and whether he had met any of them. I was quite naïve and asked the question without any agenda. The response was so strong that I was startled. Almost shouting, my Hebrew school teacher couldn't contain himself: "How could you know anything about Israel; you have never been there!"

Indeed I had not, but went the first chance I had. And there I discovered, as he had, the beauty of the land. I also discovered Palestinians who were within Israel proper and Palestinians in the territories conquered by Israel in the 1967 war. To be honest, their culture was foreign to me and the old city of Jerusalem, then Arab in population and culture, was intriguing, but difficult for an American Jew like myself.

I was not drawn to Arab culture, at least as I observed it from an outsider's perspective, but I recognized that they were a people indigenous to the land. The Israelis I met were European in background, and it was clear that they had imported themselves into the Middle East and were dominant over the indigenous Palestinians. Again, like most Jews of my generation, I did not know the history of the conflict, but I was simply stunned by the evident inequality. Here Jews were not integrated into the culture, as Jews in America; they were over the Palestinians and did not want to be integrated. Lacking the historical knowledge and coming from America, it was difficult for me to understand the situation intellectually. However, I was quite uneasy from the start. Without being able to identify or name it, something was profoundly wrong.

Like most Jews, I experienced the 1967 war as positive for my Jewish identity. When Israel won so quickly and decisively, I felt stronger, more assured. Jewish identity had never been problematic for me at all; as a child, I savored my Jewishness as I still do today. And with all the travails and disappointments that have come in my life from my struggle to be faithful as a Jew, there has never been one day when I would trade my Jewish identity for another. The 1967 war simply highlighted the positive self-image I already possessed.

The reality of war was, of course, unknown to me, and the celebration of Israel's victory with the sometimes crude jokes that circulated in the Jewish community about the Arab incapacity for war strike me today as silly and sad. Often the ultimate joke is on the victor.

While this journey to Israel in 1973 startled me, what was I to say about what I had seen? With what language could I speak and to whom would I speak? There was another complication. My travel to Israel took place in October, and the Yom Kippur war started while I was there. Being in the midst of war is a story in itself, but suffice it to say that the anxiety of my parents for my safety and their relief when I reported back to London safe and sound limited the discussion of what I had experienced.

I welcomed the chance to return in 1984 and then again in 1986 when I met and traveled with Palestinians for the first time. Sitting in Palestinian homes with parents and children, eating their food and sleeping in their homes, introduced me to the human face of a tragedy that was still unfolding. From their villages, towns and cities, I saw the Jewish settlements being built. The settlements were in the occupied territories, usually on hills overlooking—indeed dominating—the Palestinian villages below; they were built on the land rather than from it, and they looked liked nothing less than fortresses.

The occupation was in full swing and I saw many Israeli soldiers, on and off duty, carrying their guns the way I later carried a briefcase. It was a world being transformed right before my eyes. I noticed that Jerusalem was changing: the sanitation had improved markedly and it was much more comfortable for me to visit. In the decade since I had been there the Old City especially was becoming a Jewish city. The Palestinians were being systematically pushed out.

It was from these travels that this book originally took hold in my mind. Something was terribly wrong in Israel, but I also felt things changing in America as well. The liberal Jewish community in which I had grown up was still liberal in rhetoric, but increasingly conservative in its activities. A recent book on neoconservatives in America had been published, and, as I read it, I noticed how many Jews were among their leading intellectuals.

I was making connections, and as I began to write, the relationship between what I had witnessed in my travels to Israel and the increasingly neoconservative nature of Jewish leadership and intellectual life was becoming clearer. Jewish life was changing and it had to do with the Holocaust, with Israel and the increasing orientation of the Jewish community around these events. In America our affluence was now assured, and we were becoming assimilated into American culture and power.

But was this the right direction for us to take? Did it serve our best interests? More importantly, I asked whether this direction of Jewish life fit the teachings I had absorbed during my early Hebrew school years. I had begun at an Orthodox Hebrew school and then attended and became a *bar mitzvah* within the Conservative movement of Judaism. Was the assumption of power, with less and less compassion for the victim, the Jewish identity I had been taught to love and cherish?

The answer was clearly no. But again, the difficulty of finding a voice with which to speak. The people who had taught me seemed to have no difficulty with the transition I was seeing and experiencing within the Jewish world. If they did, they did not share it with me. From what place could I argue? Like most Jews of the time, I was ignorant of the history of Israel and the Palestinians. I was also ignorant of the long line of dissenting voices that I recall in these pages.

What is even more interesting and tragic is that what I found while writing my book in 1986–87 is still unknown to most Jews and indeed to most Jewish leaders. Rabbis are not exceptional in this regard; for the most part they are unqualified to speak on the topic of Israel at all. They simply mouth the propaganda that is given to them, a trend that was only beginning in the 1970s and has continued in its overwhelming reach today.

My book was written in a hurry, with a passion that I now revisit. As I wrote, I searched for information, for writers on all sides of the issues, for a perspective that was Jewish in the way that I know Judaism, a compassionate Judaism that is now passing from history.

I felt alone in this search and writing. Yet the publication of the book decreased my aloneness because I began to meet other Jews who had been feeling some of the same emotions and felt, like I did, that we were the only Jews with these feelings.

Soon after the publication of the book, the first Palestinian uprising began. I remember it clearly, December 1987, and the outbreak of violence against Palestinians that followed. Palestinians were demonstrating for their right to a state alongside of Israel, but they were met with a violence that even now seems petty and narrow-minded. And many Jews in America felt that way as well.

For about a month the Jewish world stood on a precipice as if we were at the crossroads of Jewish history. A decision had to be made and eventually it was: were we to become a conqueror as we had been conquered? Once we were denied our dignity. Would we now deny dignity to another people?

It was then that a new edition of my book was commissioned. The text of the book remained the same; the cover and the subtitle changed. I added an Afterword. Originally the cover was blue, with the only illustration being a Star of David. In the second edition I changed the cover. The Star of David was now smaller and placed next to a Palestinian scarf, a *kefiah*, which had become a symbol of the Palestinian movement. Jews were not alone in the land and I illustrated the need to share the land with a shared cover. The subtitle was also important—"The Uprising and the Future"—and it was a shortened version of the title of the Afterword, "The Palestinian Uprising and the Future of the Jewish People." By 1989 I realized what I had only glimpsed a short time before, that we were on the verge of becoming everything we loathed about our oppressors and that only by embracing those whom we had displaced would there be any Jewish future worth bequeathing to our children.

I write now from another vantage point, over a decade and a half later, with many books and lectures on this subject, and travels around the world behind me. And yet, what I wrote in 1987 contains the essence of what I have developed even more radically in the ensuing years. The many foreign-language translations of this book convinced me of the need to write and learn more.

As I learned, I began my next book, *Beyond Innocence and Redemption: Confronting the Holocaust and Israeli Power*. I wrote that book as the second edition of *Toward a Jewish Theology of Liberation* was published. In many ways it is an extension of that book and represents a more learned approach to the subject matter at hand. For this third edition, I have combined parts of both books, integrating them and bringing both up to date. Thus, I have added additional material written during the 1990s and still more that has been written for this edition.

As with the first and second editions, I complete this third revision within a new context. The second Palestinian uprising, beginning in 2000, and the introduction of Israel's use of helicopter gunships and targeted assassinations—as well as the building of the Wall of Separation that cuts into and runs the course of the West Bank, effectively ghettoizing the Palestinian population and once again expanding the borders of Israel—have raised the stakes of this history for both Jews and Palestinians. Ostensibly built to limit the possibility of Palestinian suicide bombers reaching Israel, the extent, sophistication and permanence of the wall leaves little doubt as to its real goals and consequences.

As I write these words, I wonder if we have already come to the end of the Israeli-Palestinian conflict. I wonder, too, if we have thus come to the end of Jewish history, at least as it embodied an ethical witness to the world.

So, in doing this revision, I have had mixed feelings.

On the one hand, *Toward a Jewish Theology of Liberation* is a youthful attempt to tackle a difficult and enormous issue. Though many see this book as being about Israel and Palestine, it really addresses the question of what it means to be Jewish. It is an attempt to enter Jewish history at a time of crisis, a crisis not unlike ones that Jews have faced in the past and with the same tremendous consequences. Whatever its flaws and limitations, writing it helped define and shape my fidelity as a Jew. Everything else that I have written is a footnote to this book.

On the other hand, I have been deeply distressed, I might even say depressed, at how relevant and fresh this material remains. Though an author should be overjoyed that books written more than a decade ago are still relevant, I feel just the opposite. In general, none of the warnings I sounded have been acted upon and, in reality, almost everything is now worse. The Jewish tradition has not responded to the crisis, nor has Jewish leadership. The plight of the Palestinians is far, far worse than it was then, and the trajectory that I warned about—the trajectory of injustice and the loss of the Jewish ethical witness—has come to pass. The relevance of this book is therefore a profound problem, at least for me. I fear that it might even be more relevant in the years to come.

The challenge of the 1980s and 1990s has not been met. Will we meet that challenge in the first decades of the 21st century? I have revisited, integrated, and updated this book with the hope that by 2010, I can declare my own writing important only in having faced a crisis and turned toward the direction of justice and compassion. *Toward a Jewish Theology of Liberation* would then be seen as important for its day, now to be considered along with other Jewish writing of the time to be part of a positive change in Jewish history.

I am not confident of this verdict. The hour is very late, perhaps too late.

One more autobiographical note. Originally, I featured two quotes at the opening of the book, one from Etty Hillesum, a Jewish victim of the Holocaust, and one from Michael Lerner, a contemporary Jewish dissenter. Both figures are discussed at length in the book and both quotes are also cited there.

I have replaced these quotes with two items: the first, a letter that my oldest son, Aaron, sent to a member of the Israeli consul from Houston after the official delivered a speech at my university in October 2000, just a month into the second Palestinian uprising. It was the day after the speech that Aaron sent me his letter via email from his high school. He had written the letter in about half an hour between the time I dropped him off at school and the time I arrived at my office. Within the hour I had a prearranged meeting with the consul. It was then that I handed him Aaron's letter.

Aaron's letter is beautiful and moving, succinct and powerful. It provided me with a hope for the future. The Jewish prophetic voice will never die.

It also reminded me that it was during his birth year that I originally wrote this book. It was as if I was writing it for a future, for my own son, and now my son has come of age. He represents a possible future for the Jewish people. He is not alone.

I have never written for my critics, or even to convince the unconvinced. I write simply as a testimony, and for those who find in this testimony part of their own.

When he wrote his letter, Aaron was fourteen years old, a year past the typical age to become a *bar mitzvah*. Yet, because of the exilic condition of Jewish dissenters, that time passed without his formal initiation into the responsibilities of the covenant. Through Aaron's study with me and his interaction over time on an intellectual and spiritual level with ordained rabbis, as well as theologians and activists from diverse geographic and religious traditions, he has achieved that status well beyond what the mere formality of religious ritual confers. I have included my hope for him next to the letter he wrote, a great gift for my life.

Chapter 1 begins with the Holocaust and the pain and vision that issue from it. Theology that emerges from the Holocaust is crucial, for, to a large extent, it responds to a consensus within the Jewish community. Controversial in its origins, Holocaust theology began in the 1960s and continued its original and provocative journey through the 1980s. Though its originality has waned, the power of Holocaust thought and reflection remains. It is central to the Jewish conversation and crucial to our understanding and perspective of the world. But the Holocaust also moves beyond the Jewish community. In many ways, Jewish thinkers understand that the Holocaust represents a watershed event in the political and religious history of the world. The unsettling impact of the Holocaust persists in the 21st century precisely because it has a particular and universal impact.

A central theme of Chapter 2 is Jewish political empowerment in Israel and America and the theological rationale that undergirds it. At the same time, certain persons are trying to assess the ethical cost of this empowerment, something to which Holocaust theologians initially gave little thought. We find a debate over the relationship of political empowerment and ethical concern—a debate that flourished in the 1980s and began to challenge the Jewish consensus on our sense of innocence and redemption, in relation to our historical journey. For some Jewish theologians, like Rabbi Irving Greenberg, the Jewish community has entered a new era of history, one in which Jewish empowerment has become a sacred obligation. For others commentators, such as Roberta Strauss Feurlicht and Earl Shorris, empowerment presents the danger of losing the ethical compass that distinguishes the Jewish ethical tradition. It is an understatement to feel that understanding the cost of empowerment is crucial for the future of the Jewish community and its ethical witness in the world. In the end empowerment represents a challenge to the Jewish community after the Holocaust. Is the lesson of the Holocaust Jewish empowerment without restraint, or is it the continuing struggle toward an *interdependent* power, where "never again" applies to Jews and all the peoples of the world?

Chapter 3 suggests that alternative views of the Holocaust and Israel are important for Jews to consider so as to gain a different vantage point on contemporary Jewish life. These alternative views are historical in nature, some emerging in the 1940s and continuing into the 1980s and beyond. Though it is largely forgotten today, before and just after the establishment of the state of Israel in 1948 there was a wide spectrum of Jewish opinion on the assumption of state power and what that assumption might mean to the Jewish future. Similarly, the way that the Holocaust is often used in public discourse today has occasioned Jewish dissent. There are those who believe that the lessons of the Holocaust need re-evaluation. Like the dissent toward Israel and its policies, those who defy Holocaust "orthodoxy" are often unknown in the Jewish world. The recovery of these voices is important so a broader and more balanced view of contemporary Jewish life can be accessed.

As the voices are recovered, we find that a tradition of dissent exists and in Chapter 4 I outline the broad parameters of that dissent, especially in relation to Israel. What is evident here is a continuing concern for Jewish ethics in the most difficult of circumstances. I delve deeper into the conflict over Zionism and the structural readjustment that took place in that passionate debate. When that debate came to an end in the 1960s, the discussion shifted to Israel's policies vis-à-vis the Palestinian people, especially with the Israeli occupation of the West Bank and Gaza after Israel's victory in the 1967 Arab-Israeli war.

The issue of the settlements originates here, as well as that of the behavior of Israel as an occupying power over the Palestinians. Jewish responses to the first Palestinian uprising in 1987 are featured here, as they occasion the arrival of new and vibrant dissenting voices in America and Israel. Also crucial is the signing of the Oslo Accords and the subsequent assassination of Prime Minister Yitzhak Rabin in 1995. The chapter ends with Jewish responses to the second Palestinian uprising, which began in 2000. What we find throughout this time period is a striking and increasingly vocal debate within the established Jewish community and even among Jewish intellectuals who emphasize the Holocaust and Israel as central to the Jewish future.

Chapter 5 features the evolution of another distinctive Jewish tradition, but one that has taken on a strange and ominous twist. Here, we encounter the Jewish liturgy of destruction that has traditionally helped Jews place contemporary Jewish suffering in the broad sweep of Jewish history, thereby gaining strength and perspective to resist oppression. Has that tradition been expanded today to include the Palestinian people? Is Palestinian suffering at the hands of Jews, and the recognition of that suffering as intimate to the Jewish future now an obligation for Jews? Has the liturgy of destruction now become inclusive of Palestinian suffering, and does this inclusivity point a way forward for Jews and Palestinians together? Though they are focused on Israeli policies toward the Palestinians, the frame of reference is increasingly that of the Holocaust. In fact, more than a few references in the evolving literature of that time harken back to the Holocaust and even invoke it as a strange and disturbing metaphor. In the beating back of the Palestinian uprisings and the Palestinian desire for a state of its own, alongside Israel, are Israelis and their Jewish supporters in America becoming like those who oppressed us in the past?

Chapter 6 is an excursion outside the Jewish community to Christian liberation movements that paradoxically (i.e., despite Christianity's long history of abuse and oppression of the Jewish people) carry forth the tradition of the Exodus, of the prophets, and the refusal of idolatry that we bequeathed to the world. The question posed here is whether we will show solidarity with those struggling for justice and, in so doing, recover our own history and witness. The Holocaust is again discussed, now in the broader framework of other suffering peoples, and the issue of Jewish contributions to that suffering are brought to the fore. Can we bond with those who are suffering today if we do not look honestly at the history we are creating? To enter into solidarity with suffering peoples, however, we need to look again at our own history, especially in relation to the Holocaust and to the state of Israel. Crucial here is the voice of an evolving Palestinian theology of liberation that was pioneered by Naim Ateek, an Anglican priest and theologian, in the 1990s.

Jewish responses to these theologies of liberation are varied and might be building blocks of a community response in the future. Suggested here is the need to wrestle with liberation theologies from around the world and to listen to the witness of diverse Jews like Etty Hillesum and Martin Buber. Another possibility is envisioning Jerusalem as the broken middle of Israel/Palestine rather than as the triumphant city of a dominant power. To so revise Jerusalem will require a confession on the part of the Jewish people and the practice of revolutionary forgiveness. This forgiveness moves beyond piety and symbols and places at its heart the question of justice. Could confession and the practice of justice bring forth a reconciliation of these two estranged peoples?

From the preceding discussion, the themes of contemporary Jewish life that have surfaced are brought together in Chapter 7 in a new framework. The dialectic of the Holocaust and political empowerment, confronted by renewal and solidarity as the way to recover our history and witness, is the path of liberation for Jews. Liberation cannot avoid the difficult questions, and this chapter seeks to move beyond Holocaust theology to a prophetic theology or a Jewish theology of liberation. Such a theology represents a willingness to enter the danger zones of contemporary Jewish life and examine the liberal rhetoric and activity that protect our recently acquired affluence and power. The aim is to help create, in concert with others, an atmosphere in which the deepest parts of our tradition can speak in the language of fidelity.

September 11th seems another watershed event, and I end the book with some thoughts on the meaning of this event for Jewish history. In many ways the event itself has been used to consolidate the trends in the Jewish community toward the embrace of power. Certainly the Arab and Islamic elements of the September 11th attacks have been cited in the need to protect America, Jews. and Israel from this threat. Yet. though the dangers are real, the questions I raise have to do with the direction of our politics and religiosity. For the violence suffered is part of the violence perpetrated.

Are we as Jews doomed to exist within a cycle of violence and atrocity in which we now also participate? Or is there a way to end this cycle? At times, walls, like the Wall of Separation that is being built by Israel to surround and enclose Palestinians on the West Bank, may seem the best protection for a community.

But permanent walls are also an illusion. If September 11th proved anything it is this: that only with an interdependent empowerment are we safe and secure. Instead of walls of separation we need movements of justice and compassion that reach out to the suffering and the displaced of our world, a population—within Palestine and around the world—that has grown considerably since the first edition of this book.

I am grateful for many individuals over the years for their support. I would like to thank Gustavo Gutiérrez and Desmund Tutu for writing forewords of meaning and depth. And to Sara Roy, Susannah Heschel, and Rabbi Elliot Dorff for endorsing my efforts in these pages. Also a thank you to my graduate students: Robert Smith for assisting in the production of this volume and Santiago Slabodsky for communicating with Gustavo Gutiérrez and for the translation of his foreword.

Though this third edition of *Toward a Jewish Theology of Liberation* is dedicated to my older son, Aaron, I renew and deepen my dedications in the first and second editions: to my parents Herb and June Ellis, to my wife Ann, and to our youngest son, Isaiah, who, like Aaron and his biblical namesake, embodies the prophetic. A special word to my father who now suffers from Parkinson's disease: Your gentle and kind spirit, your concern and humor, will always be with me. It is deep inside of me. I am grateful for my mother and her continuing support over the years. A special word to my wife, Ann: You have been with me through the most difficult moments, in the birthing of this book and during the years of persecution. I am grateful for your loving presence. Isaiah, you are special beyond words. Your mother and I love you dearly.

For me personally the new edition of *Toward a Jewish Theology of Liberation* brings me full circle. For now the before and after, the many words and battles of the past, and those to come, rest in these words before you, the reader. With all their flaws and limitations these words define my own journey and destiny. They are my own words; they are part of my people's story.

CHAPTER I

A Shattered Witness

One cannot understand the Jewish community today without a sense of its past, for it was born in struggle and hope. Geographically, the beginnings of the Jewish community obviously lie in ancient Egypt and Canaan, as is recalled in the Hebrew Scriptures. The experience of slavery and liberation, though, repeated time and again in Jewish history, marks the last two thousand years as a time of movement in exile rather than of liberation.

To withstand intense communal suffering repeatedly, it is necessary to take seriously both the community's history and its promise of freedom. Interpretation of events becomes crucial, even consuming: at the heart of Jewish life is the dialectic of slavery and liberation, a paradox to be thought through in each generation.

For contemporary Jews, the overwhelming experience of suffering is the Jewish Holocaust, the death of six million Jews and the attempted annihilation of our entire people. Interpretation of the event is omnipresent, though insights are diverse and often controversial. One might say that the Holocaust is the formative event for the Jewish community of today and provides the framework from which the struggle to be faithful to our values takes shape.

To delve into the Holocaust world is to be surrounded with the agony of a people on the threshold of annihilation. Survivors' accounts and histories include testimonies of both survivors and perpetrators of the Holocaust. All point to the same incredible reality: a Kingdom of Death built by the Nazis to consume an ancient people—quite simply, to eliminate all Jews from the face of the earth.

Within the Holocaust Kingdom, Jews from all over the world struggled to understand, survive and even to resist actively the Nazi goal of annihilation. Existing on the other side of history in ghettos, concentration camps, and death camps, these Jewish voices provide the memories and context for contemporary Jewish life.

The witnesses are diverse and poignant, and to hear their voices is difficult; they sound like discordant notes rather than a melody. The struggle to live is challenged by the desire to die; resistance is countered by helplessness. The sense of isolation and abandonment is omnipresent. They are witnesses from another world.

The desire to die is perhaps the most difficult for us to affirm. The situation, however, calls us to an understanding. A Jewish mother of Eastern Europe relates her story of survival as a prayer for death. She and others had been herded onto a field, sprayed with machine-gun fire, and buried in a pit with those dead and dying.

> And yet with my last strength I came up on the top of the grave, and when I did, I did not know the place, so many bodies were lying all over, dead people; I wanted to see the end of this stretch of dead bodies but I could not. It was impossible. They were lying all over, all dying; suffering, not all of them dead, but in their last sufferings; naked; shot, but not dead. . . . I was searching among the dead for my little girl, and I cried for her—Merkele was her name—"Merkele!" There were children crying "Mother," "Father"—but they were all smeared with blood and one could not recognize the children. I cried for my daughter. I was praying for death to come. I was praying for the grave to be opened and to swallow me alive. Blood was spurting from the grave in many places, like a well of water, and whenever I pass a spring now, I remember the blood which spurted from the ground, from that grave. I dug with my fingernails, but the grave would not open. I did not have enough strength. I cried out to my mother, to my father, "Why did they not kill me? What was my sin? I have no one to go to." I saw them all being killed. Why was I spared? Why was I not killed?[1]

In the face of evil, helplessness was often the order of the day. Women who became pregnant in the camps were sent to their death as punishment for the ultimate affirmation of life: conceiving new life. And women who somehow concealed their pregnancy and gave birth found their babies drowned by Nazi guards before their eyes.

Mothers were often asked by the authorities to select which of their children would be spared and which would be sent to their death. Thus, the givers of life were forced to become accomplices in the murder of their own children.

These horror stories are hardly random tales. The death of Jews was logically and legally planned. Mass death was systematic; sporadic murder was in fact discouraged. The extermination of the Jews came about through a complex series of acts that started by defining who was a Jew. Since the Nazis defined Jews as a racial type rather than as a people with professed beliefs, categorization did not come easily. Lineage was traced, the mixture of other "races" through intermarriage ascertained and judged. Finally, a decision was rendered.

Once a person was defined as a Jew, personal property and rights of citizenship were withdrawn; thus, Jews were instantaneously rendered poor and stateless. At the outset this required laws and decrees, transfers of property and employment, and a plan to relocate those who were now, by definition and ability, outside of German society. From that point the outcome was predictable, even logical, within the Nazi framework: elimination.

This plan necessitated an intricate system of transportation and receiving facilities for the vast numbers of those now dislocated. Indeed, the elimination of the Jews had become a system requiring the cooperation of every sector of German society. As Richard Rubenstein writes, "The bureaucrats drew up the definitions and decrees; the Churches gave evidence of Aryan descent; the postal authorities carried the messages of definition, expropriation, denationalization and deportation; business corporations dismissed their Jewish employees and took over 'Aryanized' properties; the railroads carried the victims to their place of execution."[2]

Through all of this suffering, the feeling of isolation and abandonment reigned. The Western world's failure to accept Jewish refugees and to develop a policy of Jewish rescue, including the refusal to destroy the death camps so as to cripple the capability of the Nazis to continue their slaughter, has now been amply documented. Even the question of whether the Western powers and the populace at large knew of the atrocities has been investigated and answered affirmatively.

Canada, which had been advertising for settlers for over a hundred years, illustrates the Western policy. A reporter went to a government official and asked if the doors of the country were going to be opened to Jewish refugees. The official responded that Canada did not want too many Jews. The reporter then asked, "How many is too many?" The response: "None is too many."[3]

But well before the retrospective studies were concluded, the victims already understood their abandonment. As Alexander Donat, a survivor of Treblinka, records:

In vain we looked at that cloudless September sky for some sign of God's wrath. The heavens were silent. In vain we waited to hear from the lips of the great ones of the world, the champions of light and justice, the Roosevelts, the Churchills, the Stalins, the words of thunder, the threat of massive retaliation that might have halted the executioner's axe. In vain we implored help from our Polish brothers with whom we had shared good and bad fortune alike for seven centuries, but they were utterly unmoved in our hour of anguish. They did not show even normal human compassion at our ordeal, let alone demonstrate Christian charity. They did not even let political good sense guide them; for after all we were objectively allies in a struggle against a common enemy. While we bled and died, their attitude was at best indifference, and all too often friendly neutrality to the Germans. Let the Germans do this dirty work for us.[4]

This is the legacy left after the end of World War II. The event is so overwhelming that it took nearly two decades to name it the Holocaust. Its meaning remains even more problematic, and Jewish theologians are left with this difficult task.

Over the years essentially four basic positions on the meaning of the event have emerged, represented by four major Jewish thinkers: Elie Wiesel, writer and survivor of the Holocaust; Richard Rubenstein, for many years a professor of religious studies at Florida State University; the late Emil Fackenheim, formerly a professor of philosophy at the University of Toronto; and Irving Greenberg, a rabbi and founder of the National Jewish Center for Learning and Leadership in New York City.

One point, at least, is agreed upon: fidelity to the Jewish people in the present lies in grappling with this experience of destruction and death.

The Witness of Elie Wiesel

Elie Wiesel's fundamental struggle to be faithful is found in the recounting of the story itself. Through fiction, essays, and public talks, Wiesel has spent a lifetime trying to put into words the indescribable, to articulate the unimaginable as an expression of his fidelity to the experience of the victims.

All those uprooted communities, ravaged and dissolved in smoke; all those trains that criss-crossed the nocturnal Polish landscapes; all those men, all those women, stripped of their language, their names, their faces, compelled to live and die according to the laws of the enemy, in anonymity and darkness. All those kingdoms of barbed wire where everyone looked alike and all words carried the same weight. Day followed day and hour followed hour, while thoughts, numb and bleak, groped their way among the corpses, through the mire and the blood. And the adolescent in me, yearning for faith, questioned: Where was God in all this? Was this another test, one more? Or a punishment? And if so, for what sins? What crimes were being punished? Was there a misdeed that deserved so many mass graves? Would it ever again be possible to speak of justice, of truth, of divine charity, after the murder of one million Jewish children? I did not understand, I was afraid to understand. Was this the end of the Jewish people, or the end perhaps of the human adventure? Surely it was the end of an era, the end of a world. That I knew, that was all I knew.[5]

From the first, he knew that, as a survivor, he was called to witness. What eluded him was how to answer that call.

I knew that the role of the survivor was to testify. Only I did not know how. I lacked experience, I lacked a framework. I mistrusted the tools, the procedures. Should one say it all or hold it all back? Should one shout or whisper? Place the emphasis on those who were gone or on their heirs? How does one describe the indescribable? How does one use restraint in recreating the fall of mankind and the eclipse of the gods? And then, how can one be sure that the words, once uttered, will not betray, distort the message they bear? So heavy was my anguish that I made a vow not to speak, not to touch upon the essential for at least ten years. Long enough to see clearly. Long enough to learn to listen to the voices crying inside my own. Long enough to regain possession of my memory. Long enough to unite the language of man with the silence of the dead.[6]

Yet Wiesel's task is to find a voice for the voiceless and to keep alive a memory that is always on the verge of extinction. The task of remembrance is, in a sense, more important than an answer to the meaning of suffering, because for many there is no answer.

For Wiesel, the question of belief undergoes a traumatic reversal in the death camps. Coming from a religious home, Wiesel as a young boy experiences the shattering of his faith soon after arriving at Auschwitz.

Never shall I forget that night, the first night in camp, which has turned my life into one long night, seven times cursed and seven times sealed.

Never shall I forget that smoke. Never shall I forget the little faces of the children, whose bodies I saw turned into wreaths of smoke beneath a silent blue sky.

Never shall I forget those flames which consumed my faith forever.

Never shall I forget that nocturnal silence which deprived me for all eternity of the desire to live.

Never shall I forget those moments which murdered my God and my soul and turned my dreams to dust. Never shall I forget these things, even if I am condemned to live as long as God Himself. Never.[7]

From that moment on, Wiesel struggles with two apparently irreconcilable realities—the reality of God and the reality of Auschwitz. As Robert McAfee Brown comments in his *Elie Wiesel: Messenger to All Humanity*, "Neither seems able to cancel out the other, and yet neither will disappear. Either in isolation could be managed— Auschwitz and no God or God and no Auschwitz. But Auschwitz and God, God and Auschwitz?" At Rosh Hashanah, the Jewish new year, Wiesel records his reaction when ten thousand inmates repeat the Jewish prayer "Blessed be the Name of the Eternal":

Why, but why should I bless Him? In every fiber I rebelled. Because He had had thousands of children burned in His pits? Because He kept six crematories working night and day, on Sundays and feast days? Because in His great might He had created Auschwitz, Birkenau, Buna, and so many factories of death? How could I say to Him: "Blessed art Thou, Eternal, Master of the Universe, Who chose us from among the races to be tortured day and night, to see our fathers, our mothers, our brothers, end in the crematory? Praised be Thy Holy Name, Thou Who hast chosen us to be butchered on Thine altar"?[8]

And later, at the hanging of three inmates, one of them a child, someone behind Wiesel asks, "Where is God? Where is He?" As the chairs are toppled and the three victims swing with the ropes around their necks, the prisoners are marched by at close range.

The two adults were no longer alive. Their tongues hung swollen, bluetinged. But the third rope was still moving; being so light, the child was still alive. . . .

For more than half an hour he stayed there, struggling between life and death, dying a slow agony under our eyes. And we had to look him full in the face. He was still alive when I passed in front of him. His tongue was still red, his eyes not yet glazed.

Behind me, I heard the same man asking: "Where is God now?"

And I heard a voice within me answer him: "Where is He? Here He is—He is hanging here on this gallows. . . ."[9]

Through the experience of the death camps an innocence that cannot be recovered is lost. The world has changed, and so has faith. Prayer is replaced by memory: memory is a prayer articulated in solemn silence. For those who remain within the "fiery world of Holocaust," the fires of the crematorium still smolder; the skeletons remain as they were, piled high and naked. Wiesel's mission is simply put: "Anyone who does not actively engage in remembering is an accomplice of the enemy. Conversely, whoever opposes the enemy must take the side of his victims and communicate their tales, tales of solitude and despair, tales of silence and defiance."[10]

The reliability of remembrance can hardly be assumed, because so much has been stripped away. Testimony itself becomes naked, and the tradition, with its layers of symbol and word no longer, is available. Wiesel uses a Hasidic tale to describe the situation.

When the great Rabbi Israel Baal Shem-Tov saw misfortune threatening the Jews it was his custom to go into a certain part of the forest to meditate. There he would a light a fire, say a special prayer and the miracle would be accomplished and the misfortune averted.

Later, when his disciple, the celebrated Magid of Mezeritch, had occasion, for the same reason, to intercede with heaven, he would go to the same place in the forest and say, "Master of the Universe, listen! I do not know how to light the fire, but I am still able to say the prayer," and again the miracle would be accomplished. Still later, Rabbi Moseh-Leib of Sasov, in order to save his people once more, would go into the forest and say: "I do not know how to light the fire, I do not know the prayer, but I know the place and this must be sufficient." It was sufficient and the miracle was accomplished.

Then it fell to Rabbi Israel of Rizhyn to overcome misfortune. Sitting in his armchair, his head in his hands, he spoke to God: "I am unable to light the fire and I do not know the prayer; I cannot even find the place in the forest. All I can do is to tell the story, and this must be sufficient."

And it was sufficient.[11]

A Broken Covenant

The stories of the dead coalesce in a different way. The challenge of Auschwitz is not simply to remember, but to investigate its meaning, in all its religious and historical dimensions. The religious dimension is complex, relating to a belief in a God of history, to the tradition within which Jews place themselves, and to the leadership of the Jewish community. Richard Rubenstein sees all three aspects as contributing to the death of six million, and each as thus negated in the Holocaust event.

The omnipotent, benevolent God of history is shown to be a farce in the face of the systematic death of the innocent. God, indeed, is a culpable figure, for belief in their chosenness (a belief inculcated by God) supported Jewish acquiescence in the events around them, sure as they were that they would be preserved amid the destruction. The tradition that posits suffering as an integral part of this special relationship with God is also called to accountability, for it did not provide the foundation for clarity of thought, nor for armed resistance to human evil.

Stressing wandering and suffering as an affirmation of Jewishness, the tradition encouraged passivity in the face of annihilation. At the same time, some Jewish leaders embodied a belief in God *and* compliance with those authorities who sought annihilation of all Jews. Jewish councils in Europe presided over the ghettos, provided all basic services to the people (including the policing of the ghetto), and fulfilled Nazi orders, even to the point of organizing the evacuation of Jews to the death camps.

Jewish compliance with such authorities is critical to Rubenstein's understanding of the failure of Jewish tradition in the face of annihilation, a compliance intimately connected with Jewish history. According to Rubenstein, the last time the Jews had taken up arms against an enemy was during the Judeo-Roman Wars of 66–70 and 131–135 of the Common Era. On both occasions, they fought valiantly and lost disastrously.

Those who counseled surrender became the religious and political leaders of the Jewish people. As Rubenstein writes, "The religious leaders of the European Diaspora for almost two thousand years were the spiritual heirs of the Pharisees and rabbis who rose to political and religious dominance only after they had been selected by the Romans as their 'loyal and non-seditious agents.'" Thus, Diaspora Judaism began in military defeat and survived by developing a culture of surrender and submission.

The heir of that tradition, rabbinic Judaism, helped to shape and condition Jewish responses for two thousand years. Despite secularization and emancipation, the Jewish community continued to "respond to overlords as had those who had surrendered to the Romans." Instead of armed resistance, they sought to avert hostile action by bribery, petitions for mercy, appeal to ethical sentiments, or flight. In fact, the organized Jewish community was a major factor in preventing effective resistance. "Wherever the extermination process was put into effect, the Germans utilized the existing leadership and organization of the Jewish community to assist them. It was not necessary to find traitors or collaborators to do their work. The compliance reaction was automatic."

There was some sporadic resistance to the Germans, the most spectacular being the 1943 Warsaw Ghetto uprising, but this was the exception. The overwhelming majority of Jews did not resist. "They had been conditioned by their religious culture to submit and endure. There was no resort to even token violence when the Nazis forced Jews to dig mass graves, strip, climb into the graves, lie down over the layer of corpses already murdered and await the final coup de grace." This submission was the final chapter in the history of a cultural and psychological transformation begun by the rabbis and Pharisees almost two thousand years earlier.[12]

For Rubenstein, those three factors—the failure of God, Jewish tradition, and Jewish leadership—signal the end of Jewish life as we know it. To persevere in pre-Holocaust patterns of Jewish life is to indulge a fantasy that portends a repetition of the Holocaust event. Yet, this failure moves beyond the Jewish community; the Holocaust represents the severing of the relationship between God and person, God and community, God and culture. The lesson of the Holocaust for Rubenstein is that humanity is alone, and that there is no meaning in life outside of human solidarity.

The Holocaust also throws into question the possibility of human solidarity, for it introduces systematic mass death as a permanent possibility of the increasingly powerful state. Secular society is characterized by a bureaucratic rationality that renders entire populations superfluous, in a time when population increases exponentially. In other words, just as more persons come into the world, their social and political importance is diminished—a situation that often leads to mass executions.

For Rubenstein, a moral and political landmark in the history of Western civilization was achieved by the Nazis in World War II; the systematic, bureaucratically administered extermination of millions of citizens or subject peoples is now one of the capacities and temptations of government. In effect, Auschwitz has enlarged our conception of the state's capacity to do violence. "A barrier has been overcome in what for millennia had been regarded as the permissible limits of political action. The Nazi period serves as a warning of what we can all too easily become were we faced with a political or an economic crisis of overwhelming proportions. The public may be fascinated by the Nazis; hopefully, it is also warned by them."[13]

Thus, the secular world born of the death of religious belief promises little more, or perhaps even less, to human flourishing and advance. In sum, one sees a tragic impasse: the religious world collapses of its own inadequacy, and the modern world devours its own children.

Rubenstein's understanding differs from Wiesel's in significant ways. Wiesel's overall sensibility is in story: the recounting of the horror and a willingness to remain in the tension of belief, though silent and unnamed. The way to prevent another holocaust is to preserve the memory of the first. For Rubenstein, the tension of belief is broken and holocaust continues unabated. The need now is to create a political sensibility within the Jewish community, and outside of it, that responds to the social, economic, and political crises of modern life. If Wiesel's fidelity is found in remembering suffering, Rubenstein's is defined by his refusal to accept indiscriminate evil as an attribute of divinity and by his emphasis on the necessity of human solidarity in a de-sacralized world.[14]

The Commanding Voice of Auschwitz

The thought of Emil Fackenheim finds a middle ground between Wiesel and Rubenstein. For Fackenheim, the Holocaust is a challenge to both faith and secularism as found in the Jewish context. The midrashic framework of interpretation, which sees present experience as continuous with the past and therefore counterposes the two to lend depth to interpretation and mystery, breaks down in the cataclysmic event of the Holocaust.

Root experiences, such as the Exodus, are challenged and overturned as clarity of faith is diminished. However, the secular option is also challenged, because the secular Jew was also singled out for annihilation. Even in claiming status as a born Jew, the secularist gives testimony to the survival of the Jewish people. "For a Jew today merely to affirm his Jewish existence is to accept his singled-out condition; it is to oppose the demons of Auschwitz: and it is to oppose them in the only way in which they can be opposed—with an absolute opposition. Moreover, it is to stake on that absolute opposition nothing less than his life and the lives of his children and the lives of his children's children."[15]

After Auschwitz, the Jew who claims affiliation with the Jewish people is a witness to endurance, because Jewish survival is a dangerous and holy duty. In another sense, this identification as Jew after the Holocaust offers humanity survival and testimony in an age jeopardized by nuclear confrontation. Fackenheim rules out two possibilities as authentic responses to the Holocaust: abandoning Jewish identification with poor and persecuted peoples, and using identification with the world to flee from Jewish destiny.

Ultimately, in the event that one must choose between two suffering peoples, the Jew must identify with the Jewish people. This identification is the essence of the commanding voice of Auschwitz. Fackenheim writes that "Jews are forbidden to hand Hitler posthumous victories. They are commanded to survive as Jews, lest the Jewish people perish. They are commanded to remember the victims of Auschwitz lest their memory perish. They are forbidden to despair of man and his world, and to escape into either cynicism or otherworldliness, lest they cooperate in delivering the world over to the forces of Auschwitz. Finally, they are forbidden to despair of the God of Israel, lest Judaism perish."[16]

The commanding voice of Auschwitz is heard today because the command to survive was heard within Auschwitz. The Nazi logic of destruction was irresistible, and yet, for Fackenheim, it was resisted. This Nazi logic is a novum in human history, the "source of an unprecedented, abiding horror." But resistance to it on the part of the most radically exposed is also a novum in history, and it is the "source of an unprecedented, abiding wonder."

For Fackenheim, to hear and obey the commanding voice of Auschwitz is a possibility today because the hearing and obeying was a reality in the death camps. Fackenheim cites Pelagia Lewinska, a survivor of the Holocaust, as illustrating this commanding voice.

> At the outset the living places, the ditches, the mud, the piles of excrement behind the blocks, had appalled me with their horrible filth. . . . And then I saw the light! I saw that it was not a question of disorder or lack of organization but that, on the contrary, a very thoroughly considered conscious idea was in the back of the camp's existence. They had condemned us to die in our own filth, to drown in mud, in our own excrement. They wished to abase us, to destroy our human dignity, to efface every vestige of humanity. . . . From the instant when I grasped the motivating principle. . . it was as if I had been awakened from a dream.... I felt under orders to live. . . . And if I did die in Auschwitz, it would be as a human being. I would hold on to my dignity.[17]

Fackenheim's fidelity to the experience of Holocaust places him with neither Wiesel nor Rubenstein, yet close in some ways to both. Like Wiesel, Fackenheim remains in the dialectic of faith, but he moves beyond story and recognizes that contemporary Jewish life, in its diversity, is the locus of fidelity and that a new midrashic framework has emerged, counterbalancing annihilation and survival. On the one hand, this framework is shaken by the Holocaust and must be articulated lest the people perish through cynicism and assimilation. The present Jewish

community thus becomes a witness to the world of survival and perseverance, and it is in this activity that the story of evil is remembered. On the
other hand, Fackenheim refuses Rubenstein's secular option because
even secular Jews are within and testify to Jewish survival.

The Jewish community is neither split nor irretrievably broken in
any ultimate sense; Jewish life continues in an altered and more urgent
form. The option that Rubenstein offers, to see the Holocaust as a
broader experience of the twentieth century, is neither denied nor
affirmed; Fackenheim is propelled by the singularity of the Jewish experience, both in slaughter and in survival.

Moment Faiths

In an important way, Irving Greenberg encompasses the previous interpretations of the Holocaust and moves beyond them. Greenberg per-
ceives the Holocaust both as an indictment of modernity, because of
modernity's false universalism and the evil perpetuated under its reign,
and as a critique of the Jewish and Christian religions, because they contributed to powerlessness and hatred. Both modernity and religion have
not only contributed to the Holocaust; they have essentially passed over
its challenge in silence. The message of the victims—to halt the carnage
and to reevaluate the dynamics of social and religious life—has fallen on
deaf ears.

The recovery of the story and of the meaning of Holocaust, then, is
essential to the redirection of modern life. However, this redirection can
occur only if the brokenness is acknowledged. For the past two centuries
an allegiance has been transferred from the "Lord of History and
Revelation" to the "Lord of Science and Humanism," but the experience
of the death camps asks whether this new Lord is worthy of ultimate loyalty. "The victims ask that we not jump to a conclusion that retrospec-
tively makes the covenant they lived an illusion and their death a gigantic
travesty."[18]

At the same time, nothing in the record of secular culture justifies its
claim to authority, especially insofar as it provided the setting for mass
death. According to Greenberg, the victims ask us above anything else
"not to allow the creation of another matrix of values that might sustain
another attempt at genocide." The experience of the past and the possibility of the future urges resistance to the absolutization of the secular.

To refuse to absolutize the secular does not, however, allow an escape
into the religious sphere. After Auschwitz, we can speak only of "moment
faiths," instances when a vision of redemption is present, interspersed
with the "flames and smoke of burning children," where faith is absent.
Greenberg describes these "moment faiths" as the end of the easy

dichotomy of atheist/theist and of the unquestioned equation of faith with doctrine.

After the Holocaust, the difference between the skeptic and the believer is frequency of faith, not certitude of position. The rejection of the unbeliever by the believer is literally the denial or attempted suppression of what is within oneself. To live with moment faiths is to live with pluralism and without the superficial certainties that empty religion of its complexity and often make it a source of distrust for the other.

The dialectic of faith is illustrated in contemporary Jewish experience by the establishment of the state of Israel; and Israel, like the Holocaust, takes on an aspect of a formative experience as well. "The whole Jewish people is caught between immersion in nihilism and immersion in redemption," Greenberg suggests, and fidelity in the present means to remain within the dialectic of Auschwitz (the experience of nothingness) and Jerusalem (the political empowerment of a suffering community).

If the experience of Auschwitz symbolizes alienation from God and from hope, the experience of Jerusalem symbolizes the presence of God and the continuation of the people. Burning children speak of the absence of all human and divine value; but the survival of Holocaust victims in Israel speaks of the reclamation of human dignity and value. "If Treblinka makes human hope an illusion, then the Western Wall asserts that human dreams are more real than force and facts. Israel's faith in the God of History demands that an unprecedented event of destruction be matched by an unprecedented act of redemption, and this has happened."[19]

It is Greenberg's understanding that the victims of history are now called to refuse victimhood as meaning fidelity to the dead, although he adds the proviso that to remember suffering propels the community to refuse to create other victims. According to Greenberg, the Holocaust should not be used for triumphalism, and its moral challenge must be applied to Jews as well. He uses the example of religious Jews who use the Holocaust to unjustly malign other religious groups and who are thereby tempted into indifference at the Holocaust of others (cf. the general policy of the American Orthodox rabbinate on United States Vietnam policy). Greenberg also addresses those Israelis who are "tempted to use Israeli strength indiscriminately (i.e., beyond what is absolutely inescapable for self-defense and survival)." This risks "turning other people into victims of the Jews." Neither faith nor morality can function without serious twisting of perspective," Greenberg concludes, "even to the point of becoming demonic, unless they are illuminated by the fires of Auschwitz and Treblinka."[20]

As we can see, within Greenberg's theological perspective, the dialectic of Holocaust and political empowerment is crucial: the first expressed in Auschwitz, symbol of nothingness; the latter in Jerusalem, portent of redemption. But Greenberg's dialectic is broader and more nuanced: the experience of the death camps is a critique of false religion and of theological language, as well as of political and technological developments within the modern secular world. It enjoins us to do acts of loving kindness and to refuse that matrix of values and institutions that support genocide.

Israel, as a manifestation of political empowerment, is a symbol of fidelity to those who perished. The counterpoint is the possibility that Israeli values and power may undermine that very sign Israel seeks to be to the Jewish community and the world. If, for Greenberg, the dialectic of Holocaust and political empowerment is the foundation of the struggle to be faithful, both poles of the dialectic are shadowed by the haunting possibility of betrayal.

The Holocaust as a Universal Crisis

In the contemporary Jewish experience, then, fidelity to the Holocaust revolves around the themes of remembrance, critique, and affirmation, all three sought within a broken world. Complexity and diversity are recognized, and, though the crisis engendered by the Holocaust demands unambiguous answers, such answers are not easily attained.

The emergence of the state of Israel is an example of this difficulty. From the vantage point of the Holocaust, the political empowerment of the Jewish community cannot be denied as an essential form of fidelity to the dead. Empowerment, though, especially in the form of a state, places the community in an obvious dilemma: the desire to nurture life and community is often frustrated by the demands of national security in a hostile environment. We are also beginning to learn that entry into history as a powerful community can lead to either fidelity to, or abuse of, the formative event that is the justification for the community's existence. Having emerged from the prospect of annihilation, the Jewish community has entered a present that offers both fruitful possibility and danger. The formative event of the Holocaust can serve to legitimize or to critique power; what we do with that event will determine how the desire to be faithful works itself out concretely in history. The road taken will be the ultimate criterion of fidelity, for if the struggle to be faithful is open to the future, it is yet constrained by the memory of the suffering.

For the Christian, the Jewish Holocaust is no less challenging. Whether in Nazi Germany, Poland, or dozens of other countries, the persecutors were often Christians. Though it is inappropriate to label any of these movements authentically Christian, the symbolic formation and reservoir of hatred that allowed Jews to be isolated, and finally destroyed, owes much to a millennium of Christian anti-Semitism. If this were not enough, the institutional Church, at that great moment of crisis, sought self-preservation rather than the commitment demanded to mend a history covered with blood. However, there were Christians willing to place their lives in jeopardy to provide refuge from evil. Though small in number, this witness allows the question of the validity of Christian faith and activity to remain before us today.[21]

Unfortunately, few Christians have contemplated the haunting difficulty raised by the Jewish Holocaust: What does it mean to be a Christian when Christian understandings and actions issued in the death camps of Nazi Germany?

The first response of those who have authentically confronted this evil is to ask forgiveness of the Jewish people and to seek forgiveness from Jesus, himself a Jew, whose essential message of love was betrayed. The second response is to remain in dialogue with the experience of Holocaust as a formative event for Christians as well. For to recognize the reality of the death camps and of Christian complicity involves a questioning of the authenticity of Christian faith and activity.

Only by realizing and admitting how their own conduct denied true Christianity can Christians both salvage and reconstruct their faith. Only by entering into the nothingness of the death camps can a contemporary Christian way of life become authentic. This is what Johannes Metz, the German Catholic theologian, means when he writes, "We Christians can never go back behind Auschwitz; to go beyond Auschwitz is impossible for us by ourselves. It is possible only together with the victims of Auschwitz."[22]

What of those born Jewish or Christian whose faith has been torn away within or in response to the Holocaust? The experience of dislocation and death has caused a great crisis in belief. The response is either a passion to transform the world so as to prevent injustice and indiscriminate torture or, more often, a numbness and passivity resulting in cynicism. Is it not correct to say that, just as the Jewish and Christian sensibilities are found wanting in the Kingdom of Death, so, too, is the humanist tradition that carries the secular hope of the twenty-first century?

As noted earlier, it is the very advances of modern life that contributed to the building and activities of the death camps. Like the two major religious traditions of the West, Judaism and Christianity, the humanist tradition became immersed in a formative event that challenged its interpretation of life. While some can remain in the framework that includes both faith and human concern, vast numbers of people cannot continue in that dialectic and are now either passively accepting their fate or consciously, through cynicism and power, causing others to suffer. For those divorced from religious sensibilities, can the Holocaust help them form an active and reflective orientation toward the world in which we live?

These difficult questions must await further clarification. Jewish thinkers are courageous in their ability to face the unknown, although in a sense they have no choice but to face the darkness. Whatever their conclusions, grappling with the horrific signals the desire to be faithful to the experience of the Jewish people. As a whole, Christians and humanists have not honestly addressed the terror of systematic annihilation and what it means for their faith and their world-view. For many, the experience of the Jews is too bothersome to contemplate or is relegated simply to the dustbin of history, as if an enterprise 1,900 years in the making, which issued in its most horrific form only decades ago, is already archaic.

Of course, difficulties glibly addressed or passed over in silence do not disappear, but await rediscovery and interpretation. Awaiting clarity, we travel a path of ignorance toward a destination unknown, a destination that, more often than not, becomes recognizable in the form of nightmare.

CHAPTER 2

The Cost of Empowerment

Immersion in the Holocaust event represents a critique of contemporary religion and humanism, in both the theoretical and the practical realms; it demands a rethinking of where we have come from and where we are going. In one sense, the Holocaust is a Christian and Western inheritance, and its victims cry out for justice. Yet, in another sense, the Jewish community carries forth this memory and, therefore, has a special task: to be faithful.

The Jewish writers analyzed earlier pose the question of fidelity in the stark terms of the Holocaust memory, the survival of a decimated people, and Jewish political empowerment in the state of Israel. The price now, however, seems prohibitive. The rise of the neoconservative movement in North America, with its visible and articulate Jewish component, initially exemplified by Norman Podhoretz, editor of *Commentary* magazine, Irving Kristol, coeditor of *The Public Interest,* and now Jews like Paul Wolfowitz, the Deputy Secretary of State, as well as the ascendancy to power in Israel of religious and secular expansionists, exemplified by recent prime ministers Benjamin Netanyahu and Ariel Sharon, begins to cloud the horizon.

Jewish political empowerment is confronted by the marginalized populations of North America and the Third World. An ever-growing, displaced Palestinian people challenges the integrity of the state of Israel. The desire to remain a victim is evidence of disease; yet, to become a conqueror after having been a victim is a recipe for moral suicide.

It is not too much to claim that the acquired values of the Jewish people, discovered and hammered out over a history of suffering and struggle, are in danger of dissipation. In our liberation, our memory of slavery is in danger of being lost. This loss would allow us to forget what it means to be oppressed. Yet, to forget one's own oppression is to open the possibility of becoming the oppressor.

Within the Jewish community the discussion is heated, often framed in terms of struggle rather than debate. Many of the bed-rock issues facing Jews today were articulated in the 1980s following the foundational writing of the Holocaust theologians in the 1970s. Though sometimes dated in particular references and events, the mainline argument remains relevant today. Representative voices of this heated struggle are Irving Greenberg, Nathan and Ruth Ann Perlmutter, Earl Shorris, and Roberta Strauss Feuerlicht.

The voices are starkly disparate: views of our history, perceptions of our future are sometimes diametrically opposed. That the future of our people is in jeopardy is clear, as is the fact that one or the other's view might lead to disaster.

The Third Era of Jewish History

Irving Greenberg's more recent analysis of contemporary Jewish life illustrates this struggle for survival and witness in the theological realm. Having named the Holocaust and its implications, Greenberg embarks on an ambitious, perceptive, and troubling exploration of what he labels "the third great cycle" in Jewish history. While Greenberg attempts to address the difficult realities of Holocaust and empowerment, the limitations of his analysis define the task of Jewish theologians to come.[1]

For Greenberg, Jewish history can be divided into three eras: the biblical, the Rabbinic, and the present, still unnamed, but which emphasizes the hiddenness of God or Holy Secularity.

The biblical era represents the formation of the Jewish people, particularly their liberation from slavery and the developing covenantal relationship between God and the people. This was not an easy era by any means. For Greenberg, the difficulty of the period lay in trying to uphold covenantal values in the context of Jewish political sovereignty. When the leaders of the people failed in this task, the prophets arose.

Along with the development of the cultic priesthood surrounding the Temple, the biblical era was marked by a high degree of divine intervention. God's presence in the Temple was the cultic counterpart of prophecy. God spoke directly to Israel through the prophets, and at Jerusalem the divine could be contacted. Thus, for Greenberg, the biblical period represents a growing sense of mission, with divinity and holiness being expressed in cult and prophecy: Jewish leadership reflects the "active intervention of the divine in Jewish life as well as the struggle to live with the tensions between the covenant and realpolitik."

The destruction of the Second Temple and the crushing defeats of the Jews in 70 and 135 of the Common Era generated a major crisis of faith and meaning in the Jewish people that ultimately ushered in the Rabbinic era. The tremendous loss of life, the sale of thousands of Jews into slavery, and the triumph of Rome, despite the conviction of the Jewish people that God alone should rule Israel, deepened the questions. "Was there not God? Had God been overpowered by the Roman gods? Had God rejected the covenant with Israel and allowed his people and the Holy Temple to be destroyed? Were the traditional channels of divine love, forgiveness and blessing now closed to the Jewish people?"[2]

The destruction of the Temple was devastating, for many could no longer envision Judaism without the Temple. At the same time, what was left of Jewish sovereignty disappeared as physical dispersion was complemented by increasing exposure to the cosmopolitan sophistication of Hellenic culture. The rabbis responded by emphasizing Torah study. By internalizing the teachings and values of God's way, Jews were thus able to compensate in part for the absence of the Temple and the loss of national sovereignty.

Greenberg sees the rabbis as engaged in a fundamental theological breakthrough: as manifest divine presence and activity were being reduced, the covenant was actually being renewed. Instead of rejecting the Jews, God had called them to a new stage of relationship and service. In the view of the rabbis, God had withdrawn and become more hidden to allow humans more freedom and a higher level of responsibility, even of partnership, in the covenant, albeit in a newly secular world.

To be sure, a world in which God is more hidden is a more secular world. It is paradoxical that it is within this secularization that the synagogue emerges as the central place of Jewish worship. Greenberg contrasts the Temple, where God was clearly manifest and holiness was visible and concentrated in one place, and the synagogue where a more hidden God could be encountered only through effort and prayer. "The visible presence of God in the Temple gave a sacramental quality to the cultic life of the sanctuary," Greenberg writes. "Through the High Priest's ministrations and the scapegoat ceremony, the national sins were forgiven and a year of rain and prosperity assured. In the synagogue, the community's prayers are more powerful and elaborate than the individual's but the primary effect grows out of the individual's own merits and efforts. One may enter the synagogue at all times without the elaborate purification required for Temple entrance because sacredness is more shielded in the synagogue." God spoke in the Temple directly through prophecy while God does not speak in the synagogue. According to Greenberg, "The human-divine dialogue goes on through human address to God. Prayer, which we view today as a visibly sacred activity, was by contrast with the Temple worship, a more secular act. Prayer became the central religious act because of the silence of God."[3]

The rabbis represent a more secular leadership than do priests or prophets. Priesthood was inherited and ritually circumscribed; the rabbis achieved their status through learning, and their sacramental duties were no different from those of the average Jew. If prophets spoke the unmediated word of God, the rabbis used the record of God's instruction to help guide the community in the present. In fact, for the rabbis, prophecy ended with the destruction of the Temple and the exile. How could there be prophecy if God had withdrawn? "Prophecy is the communicative counterpart of splitting the Red Sea," Greenberg writes. "Rabbinic guidance is the theological counterpart of a hidden God."[4]

The characteristics of the Rabbinic era thus come into view. The rabbis were able to interpret the meaning of Jewish fate, to assure the people that the covenant was not broken, to broaden the understanding of and participation in holiness. In essence, they interpreted the meaning of the new Jewish condition of powerlessness and exile and created a unity out of a condition of relative political powerlessness. The hiddenness of God, the synagogue as institutional center, and leadership by the rabbis gave coherence to the second era of Jewish history.

The Third era of Jewish history begins with the Holocaust and the crisis of faith and meaning that follows. The covenant of redemption is shattered, and the individual and communal response to that shattering, especially in the building of the state of Israel, is shaping the third era. The third era starts with a series of questions: "Does the Holocaust disprove the classic teaching of redemption? Does Israel validate it [the classic teaching of redemption]? Does mass murder overwhelm divine concern? How should we understand the covenant after such a devastating and isolating experience?"

For Greenberg the answer lies in activities that heal the brokenness of the Jewish people rather than in a spoken theology. Jews are called to a "new secular effort to recreate the infinite value of the human being," Greenberg writes, and in this effort to testify to the hope that a hidden relationship to God's presence still exists. Ultimately it is a call to a new level of covenantal responsibility.

> If God did not stop the murder and the torture, then what was the statement made by the infinitely suffering Divine Presence in Auschwitz? It was a cry for action, a call to humans to stop the Holocaust, a call to the people Israel to rise to a new, unprecedented level of covenantal responsibility. It was as if God said: "Enough, stop it, never again, bring redemption!" The world did not heed that call and stop the Holocaust. European Jews were unable to respond.

World Jewry did not respond adequately. But the response finally did come with the creation of the State of Israel. The Jews took on enough power and responsibility to act. And this call was answered as much by so-called secular Jews as by the so-called religious. Even as God was in Treblinka, so God went up with Israel to Jerusalem.[5]

To be sure, the new covenantal mandate challenges more traditional understandings of Jewish faith, for the rabbinic world of synagogue and prayer is no longer adequate. The move from powerlessness to power represents a decisive change in the Jewish condition. The resources, energy, and spirit necessary to create a Jewish state flow in a novel direction. Building the earthly Jerusalem comes first, and the "litmus test of the classic religious ideas becomes whether they work in real life and whether a society can be shaped by them."

For Greenberg the movement toward power is historically inescapable in the face of the Holocaust; Jewish powerlessness is immoral, for it is no longer compatible with Jewish survival. Since the power needed for survival in the contemporary world is available only to sovereign states, achieving power in Israel reaches the level of sacred principle. According to Greenberg, "Any principle that is generated by the Holocaust and to which Israel responds . . . becomes overwhelmingly normative for the Jewish people." Arguing about how power is used is acceptable if the argument does not threaten the Jewish possession of power. How to use the power is the critical point, but endangering the power is the unforgivable sin. In an era oriented by the Holocaust and Israel, such a denial is the "equivalent of the excommunicable sins of earlier eras: denying the Exodus and the God who worked it in the biblical age or denying the rabbis and separating from Jewish fate in the Rabbinic era."[6]

At the same time, Greenberg understands that power, being pragmatic and results-oriented, will test the ability of the tradition to advance values and community. Can Jewish ideals be actualized in the world, or are they empty spiritual generalities? Pragmatism rather than the prophetic, compromise rather than perfection, will be the norm in the third era.

This shift to pragmatism and compromise signals the end of the traditional Jewish presence on the radical end of the political spectrum, a presence that reflected not only the community's humanitarian concerns, but also its lack of power. The use of power involves compromise and conservation as well as reform and perfection. Guilt and partial failures are inevitable.

Despite the fact that power corrupts, it nonetheless must be assumed. For Greenberg, then, the test of morality is a relative reduction of evil and improved mechanisms of self-criticism, correction, and repentance.

"There is a danger that those who have not grasped the full significance of the shift in the Jewish condition will judge Israel by the ideal standards of the state of powerlessness, thereby not only misjudging but unintentionally collaborating with attempted genocide. Ideal moral stances applied unchanged to real situations often come out with the opposite of the intended result."

This new pragmatism allows the "occasional use of immoral strategies to achieve moral ends," and Jews must accept this as the price of empowerment. However, in Greenberg's view, power must constantly be challenged by the memory of our powerlessness lest we become hardened to the suffering of others. It is precisely the memory of the Holocaust that has enabled Israel to be a "responsible and restrained conqueror."

The practical application to the plight of the Palestinians follows. For Greenberg the ideal would be maximum self-governance for Palestinians and Arabs as a check on Jewish abuse. However, this arrangement can be accepted only if it does not threaten the existence and security of the Jewish people. "To yield autonomy without overwhelming proof of Palestinian desire to live in peace is to invite martyrdom and morally reprehensible death by genocide. The Palestinians will have to earn their power by living peacefully and convincing Israel of their beneficence or by acquiescing to a situation in which Israel's strength guarantees that the Arabs cannot use their power to endanger Israel."[7]

The Third era of Jewish history poses two fundamental shifts: the movement from the sacramental to secularity, and from hiddenness and powerlessness to empowerment. Though most obvious in Israel, this Third era is no less present in the Diaspora. Despite their minority status, European and North American Jews have become increasingly politically active. This activity, according to Greenberg, arises out of the lessons of the Holocaust and the example of Israel, as well as out of the desire to prevent a repetition of the Holocaust and to preserve Israel. Active involvement, rather than "invisibility," represents a fundamental shift in Diaspora self-consciousness: though many may elect to remain in the Diaspora rather than settle in Israel, Greenberg believes that psychologically we are coming to the end of exilic Judaism.

The end of almost two thousand years of exilic Judaism poses the final aspect of the Third era, the emergence of new Jewish institutions. The primary Third-era institutions arise within and exist to support Israel. The Knesset and the Israeli defense forces are prime examples of institutions that deal pragmatically and competently with contemporary Jewish life. Israeli welfare agencies and private organizations also serve this function in Israel and increasingly in the Diaspora. "Kibbutzim and other settlements absorb Diaspora Jews seeking Jewish expression; problem children are sent to Israeli institutions and orphans to Youth Aliya villages. Israeli universities and *yeshivot* have become important centers for foreign Jewish students."

The Israeli Holocaust memorial center, Yad VaShem, represents a new sacred institution of the Third era. Though government-sponsored and historical rather than mythic, it provides a place where the memory of the Holocaust is preserved and where acts of mourning can be publicly expressed. For Greenberg, Yad VaShem illustrates classic religious values in masked fashion: martyrdom, sacrifice, heroism, saintliness, and continuity. The same is true of Beit Hatefutsot, the Diaspora Museum, which, Greenberg maintains, is not really a museum but a "liturgical recounting and reenacting of the Jewish experience in the Diaspora presented in a secular, pluralist, hidden religious fashion."[8]

The Jewish Federation and United Jewish Appeal are examples of Third-era institutions in America because they achieved preeminence by responding to the post-Holocaust/Israel reality. Though critics question the religious content of these institutions, Greenberg believes they have tapped both the moral resources of the Jewish community and that community's desire for survival and empowerment. Their message: "You can respond to the worthlessness of Jewish life in the Holocaust by testifying through giving money to rehabilitate Jewish lives." At the same time, political representation of Jewish interests has increased, both within the Federation and the Appeal and in direct lobbying groups such as the American Israel Public Affairs Committee (AIPAC).

Still, American Jews seem uncomfortable with politics, preferring philanthropy and sometimes invisibility. Thus, in Greenberg's view, America's Jewish political culture is far less mature than that within Israel. Liberalism and universalist rhetoric, with their refusal to admit of group interests and conflicts, have limited American Jewry's political development. Greenberg wants to promote the growth of Jewish political activity in the United States through networks of Jewish political action. These include the working principle "permanent interests, not permanent friends" and policy recommendations such as upgrading AIPAC and establishing Jewish Political Action Committees (PACs) to further Jewish interests domestically and especially in relation to Israel. Not only are Jewish interests promoted, but the danger is lessened that American Jews who lack experience in governance will play a righteous prophetic role vis-à-vis Israel—that is, "hold it to an unreal moral standard one it could live up to only by endangering its survival."[9]

Implicit in this political view is the notion that the security of Israel is directly linked to the exercise of United States influence and power and that American Jews have a grave responsibility for influencing the United States toward that goal. In the 1970s and early 1980s, in the shadow of Vietnam and the Yom Kippur war, disillusionment steered American

Jewish opinion toward peace initiatives that evidenced a strong idealism in foreign policy and hence a great reluctance to use military force to accomplish foreign-policy objectives. In Greenberg's view, this idealism underestimated the role of power in creating peace: "Good will is truly a force in human society and foreign affairs."

But for Greenberg, good will operates primarily in the framework of a balance of power—preferably with rewards for good (i.e., peaceful) behavior and punishment for bad (i.e., counter-peaceful) behavior. "The emphasis on good will translated into one-sided pressure for concessions from the West; fortunately, for Greenberg, the American arms build-up, the stationing of medium-range missiles in Europe, and the Strategic Defense Initiative in the 1980s redressed this balance, and the 'proper process of reward and punishment started up again.'"[10]

Those who promulgate anti-American or anti-Israeli policies must now be wary of the consequences. For Greenberg the renewal of American power illustrated in the 1980s by increasing pressure on the Russians in Afghanistan, by the expansion of rebel forces in Angola, by the U.S. support of the Contras in Nicaragua and by the U.S. withdrawal from UNESCO, portended a breakthrough in the Middle East, as does the military action in Afghanistan and Iraq after the September 11th assault on the World Trade Center and the Pentagon. Israeli strength and perseverance and American power are the two major keys to peace to the Middle East; and the American Jewish community, in its lobbying for aid to Israel as well as in its support for the American intervention, plays a pivotal role in securing peace.

The newly forming political attitudes and alliances of American Jewry are seen by some as Judaism without religious content or as a "checkbook Judaism" that substitutes financial support for religious obligation. But for Greenberg the relationship between Third-era institutions in America, the memory of the Holocaust, and the survival of Israel moves beyond these labels.

Though some believe that the Jewish Federation's power is a function of their superior access to money, Greenberg argues that they are able to attract money only because they transmit meaning and values and can bestow status. The United Jewish Appeal offers donors access to Israeli officials, considered to be on the front line of Jewish self-defense. It is the combination of social appeal and theological and historical relevance that makes this kind of involvement so important.

At the same time, one of the Federation's recruiting mechanisms has been tours to Israel and Eastern Europe that recall the roles of the Holocaust *and* of Israel and validate philanthropy and Jewish political self-defense. Greenberg believes that beneath these levels of historical consciousness is "a sense that the covenant and destiny of the Jewish people is being continued through this vehicle. The continual media attention to Israel, even the obsessive focus on condemning Israel in the United Nations, is often seen by givers as the secularized version of the Jew's role as a 'light unto the nations' or as the chosen people, singled out and standing alone, testifying to a world mired in the status quo of power politics and oppression."[11]

Third-era institutions in their secularity and response to empowerment eclipse those institutions that characterized the Rabbinic era, especially the centrality of the synagogue. "By continuing to proclaim the evident sacredness of God and of its own place as it did before the Holocaust and rebirth, the synagogue comes across as too sacramental." At the same time, the pre-Holocaust divisions relating to liturgical and covenantal interpretations that generated into Orthodox, Conservative, and Reform denominations contradict the unity called for today. According to Greenberg, synagogue leadership has reacted defensively to this shift, insisting that the synagogue must remain the center of Jewish life. Often these Third-era institutions are opposed by the synagogue leadership.

The danger for Greenberg is that the synagogue leadership might become like the B'nai Bateyra of ancient times. The B'nai Bateyra were members of a group that opposed Rabbi Yohanan ben Zakkai's decision to transfer the legal and religious authority of the Temple to the court and academy of Yavneh, the place where new institutions were emerging after the destruction of the Temple. Then the reliance on the familiar led to an opposition that was essentially obstructionist. Over time the synagogue and academy won out and those who hoped to rebuild the Temple died out. For Greenberg, our time is different, in that the danger is compounded: "The Temple was visibly destroyed, encouraging the search for alternative ways of religious expression, whereas the synagogue remains physically intact although its theological and cultural substrata have been fundamentally transformed."[12]

Finally, the Third era of Jewish history represents an age of renewed revelation, where the covenantal way is undergoing a major reorientation and a new sacred literature is being written. Rather than a discontinuity, the Third era represents a continuation of a people who for over 5,000 years have found themselves in the throes of history and have sought out meaning and value within history.

While the Bible, shaped by the Exodus and the message of redemption, represents the first era of Jewish history, and the Talmud, affected by the exile and a new understanding of the human-divine partnership, represents the second era, the third era is providing its own way of revelation and its own scriptures, albeit in a hidden manner.

> The Scriptures of the new era are hidden. They do not present themselves as Scripture but as history, fact, and, sometimes, as anti-

Scripture. Revelation has been successfully obscured thanks to the deep hiddenness of the events and the continuing grip of modern ideas which seemingly cut off human culture from revelation channels. The inherited traditions in Judaism and Christianity that [say] there will be no further revelation, which are defensive and designed to protect them from supersession, also serve to block consciousness of revelation by dismissing it in advance. Yet the Scriptures are being written. They are the accounts that tell and retell the event, draw its conclusions and orient the living. In the Warsaw Ghetto, Chaim Kaplan wrote in his journal: "I will write a scroll of agony in order to remember the past in the future."[13]

Greenberg's analysis elucidates the dialectic of community and empire in the Jewish community today, yet often obfuscates it in religious language. His working principle, that after the Holocaust "No statement theological or otherwise should be made that would not be credible in the presence of the burning children," is a profound call away from empire to community. While he continually calls for models of restraint—telling us to reject unimpeded power—his drift is unmistakable. Pragmatism, alliances, and power are the new watchwords for an ancient community in a hostile world.

Greenberg argues that the prophetic was nurtured by the coalescence of Jewish values and powerlessness, and that with the exercise of power the prophetic should be deemphasized, for it may at certain moments endanger the community. What Greenberg fails to discern about the prophets is that they were not simply speaking in vague generalities or posing ideals impossible to implement in society; they were speaking, sometimes in poetic, figurative language, at other times in realistic detail, about faults in the community that could not be ignored.

The prophets, in their explication of transgressions, pointed to the potentially disastrous course the community was taking. They spoke about survival in no uncertain terms. However, more than the prophetic seems to be losing ground in Greenberg's argument. The ability to understand another's story and hear another's pain, to recognize the formation of other peoples and their struggle for freedom to be as important as our own and as a legitimate demand upon us—this seems to be nonexistent in Greenberg's analysis.

There is no doubt that Greenberg upholds the right to discuss and criticize within certain parameters. His warnings, though, of excommunication from the Jewish community, along with his analysis of prophecy and power, contribute to a fear already deeply imbedded in the Jewish community. The insights and sympathies of our people, even the teachings of our tradition, no matter how much in need of modification, are repressed in order to maintain our recently acquired empowerment and must, therefore, either exist underground or disappear altogether. If it is true that a totally ethical people cannot survive, it is also true that we may be in danger of becoming a people void of ethics.

Though Greenberg's understandings do not explicitly support a neoconservative political policy, and though he himself may be progressive on social issues, the tendency of his theology is to provide a theological foundation for the neoconservative movement within the Jewish community. And Greenberg is not alone here: the political statements of other Holocaust theologians, including Wiesel, Fackenheim, and Rubenstein, display the same tendency.

The dynamic balance between Holocaust and empowerment, found within their analyses of the Holocaust, is lost when they enter the realities of the post-Holocaust world. Empowerment, almost without restraint, becomes the watchword. Greenberg's analysis of the state of Israel as *the* answer to the Holocaust, as *the* sign of deliverance, as *the* redemption out of nothingness, threatens to destroy the balance.

The Jewish people recently liberated from the hell of Nazi Germany can become, in some minds, reluctant heroic warriors charting the historic course of redemption in a hostile world. Though the forms of oppression vary, the world remains essentially the same—hostile to Jewish interests and survival.

The New Anti-Semitism

For Nathan and Ruth Ann Perlmutter the post-Holocaust world can be explored by examining the shifting nature of anti-Semitism. In their book, *The Real Anti-Semitism in America*, the Perlmutters agree that a significant number of Americans still accept the stereotypes of shrewd Jewish business persons and the conspiratorial theories about Jewish bankers, but the financial status of American Jews and the strength of Israel mitigate the effects of this more traditional form of anti-Semitism. The important anti-Semitism of the moment is found in the political arena among those who advance policies inimical to the Jewish community in the United States and in the state of Israel. Their book, written in the 1980s, provoked a series of books by a number of authors on the same theme.

The United Nations is one such example, especially when it equated Zionism with racism in 1975, which the Perlmutters label as "our time's Big Lie." According to the Perlmutters, the United Nations is a hotbed of anti-Semitism in language and activity. They cite a speech delivered by a Jordanian delegate in the 1980s which, among other things, invoked the infamous "protocols of the Elders of Zion," a forged document that speaks of a Jewish international conspiracy to rule the world. At its con-

clusion there was silence. "The delegate from France, birthplace of lib-
erty, fraternity and equality, said nothing. The delegate from West
Germany, a nation which has labored mightily to distance itself from its
unspeakable past, sat silently. President Carter's delegate, himself no
stranger to racism, deepened the silence with his silence. Not a murmur
of protest . . . from anyone . . . save the Israeli ambassador."

For the Perlmutters the surprise was not the anti-Semitic tirade but
the lack of response from other delegates. The reason for the silence was
the national interest of maintaining friendly relations with the Arab
OPEC nations. It was as if the expedient silence of the diplomats was a
message to Jews saying, "You have been abused, and while our silence is
our complicity, really, it's nothing personal."[14]

The Perlmutters's thesis is that Jewish interests are beset by realpolitik as much as by the more familiar anti-Semitic diatribes. Revolutionary
governments and movements supported by left-leaning Jewish and non-
Jewish intellectuals often provide the model of this realpolitik, which is
essentially anti-Jewish. According to the Perlmutters, the major revolutionary causes since the 1960s—Cuba, Nicaragua, El Salvador, Vietnam,
and Iran—produced new forms of tyranny that the political Left originally opposed. As important to the Perlmutters is a fundamental shift:
many of these revolutionary movements were allied with the "colonialist
Soviet Union or at least with the Jew-hating Yasser Arafat." The
Perlmutters conclude that today's revolutionary governments all too
often align themselves against the United States, alongside the Soviet
Union, or with Arab powers. In the United Nations they contribute to
the voting margins of victory for enemies of Israel.

This is also true on the American scene where traditional liberal
allies, such as African-Americans, argue for a quota system that is, in the
Perlmutters's mind, harmful to Jewish interests and increasingly show
pro-Palestinian sentiments harmful to Israel. Though the Perlmutters
wrote their book before the 1984 presidential campaign, where Jesse
Jackson emerged as a national African-American leader and his
"Hymietown" remarks became national headlines, Jackson is mentioned
as a part of the Black leadership that is increasingly anti-Jewish in its attitudes and pronouncements.

Beyond the specific movements and political figures, the
Perlmutters's understanding that old friends slip away and new alliances
are formed. For example, in the past, liberal Protestantism showed more
tolerance toward Jews than did other groups, but increasingly its political stances, especially in the National Council of Churches, have dam-
aged Israel. The intolerance of fundamentalists, who are traditional
enemies of the Jews, is currently "not so baneful as its friendship for
Israel is helpful," and, thus, a new alliance is possible.

The Perlmutters's description of the National Council of Churches, like their analysis of the United Nations, finds a wide resonance among Jewish neoconservatives. Citing the silence of the National Council during the 1967 war and its immediate condemnation of Israel for its occupation of the West Bank soon after, and the selection of the "anti-Semite" Imamu Baraka, formerly LeRoy Jones, to be their principal speaker at the Triennial General Assembly in 1972, the Perlmutters cite a pattern of betrayal. Two other incidents confirm their understanding. According to the Perlmutters, the National Council of Churches did little better during the Yom Kippur War and the United Nations resolution equating Zionism with racism.

For the Perlmutters, fundamentalist Christian groups that have long held anti-Semitic views are now in the vanguard of pro-Israel sentiment and, thus, need to be courted. This means a reversal of long-held Jewish views toward fundamentalist Protestants, or at least a tolerance toward disparate views on the bottom-line support of the state of Israel. Fundamentalist views on abortion, the Equal Rights Amendment, prayer in the public schools, and pornography need to be overlooked or fought in a different arena. Jews, like all groups, have different convictions on many issues and will continue to express those views even when differing with allies who agree on the subject of Israel. But for the Perlmutters, not all the issues are of equal importance. The security of Israel is far more crucial than the issues on which fundamentalists and Jews differ. "The conservative fundamentalists today are friends indeed, because unlike the National Council of Churches' liberal Protestants, they have been friends in need."[15]

In many ways the Perlmutters's analysis was prophetic. At the turn of the century, it is increasingly held by American Jews and is the one most available through media and from Jewish institutions such as the Anti-Defamation League, for whom Nathan Perlmutter worked. It is in a sense a logical extension of Greenberg's theological work—one way of looking at the post-Holocaust world.

However, there also exists an articulate and active minority that is critical of such views and seeks to reestablish the prophetic and ethical dimensions of the Jewish community. These views were also articulated in the 1980s and in some ways are even more relevant today.

Jews Without Mercy

As Greenberg and the Perlmutters argued for the need of Jews to reconsider their foundational worldview, they were engaged by two important books: *Jews Without Mercy: A Lament*, by Earl Shorris, a novelist and commentator, and *The Fate of the Jews: A People Torn Between Israeli Power and Jewish Ethics,* by Roberta Strauss Feuerlicht, a long-time political activist. Both reflect on Jewish history and ethics as a means to criticize the present.

For Earl Shorris, Jewish history is one of woes and contribution: "Suffering and philosophy, poverty and poetry, exile and community, tears and mercy are all intertwined in Jewish history." Though Jews are diverse in time periods, interests, and definitions—whether ghetto Jews or early Zionists, universalists or assimilationists—historically a commonality can be found in the ethical and historical basis of Judaism: "Whatever the subtle differences in interpretation of the yoke of the Law, the ethical basis of the Law remained. Judaism was the first ethical religion, the first ethical civilization, and so it remains, even to the assimilationists, who are willing to give up everything but the ethics of their fathers."[16]

However, to Shorris, the new definition of Jewish interests put forward by the Jewish neoconservative movement differs from previous definitions. He begins by outlining their fundamental analysis.

> Blacks betrayed the Jews, the very people who helped them up out of racism and poverty into their current situation. Blacks are anti-semitic. Jews should not help Blacks anymore, nor should they help other minorities, such as Hispanics, because they will only turn on the Jews as the Blacks did. . . .
>
> The state of Israel can do no wrong.
>
> The Palestinian people have no right to exist as a state, nor do Palestinian territorial claims have any validity.
>
> The killing of an Israeli civilian by a Palestinian is an act of terrorism.
>
> The killing of a Palestinian civilian by an Israeli is a justifiable act of self-defense.
>
> Occupation and colonization of foreign territory by Israel is not imperialism.
>
> Any political position taken by an American Jew is justified if it can be associated with the survival of Israel. . . .
>
> The poor of America are wretches without dignity. They constitute an underclass that it is best to neglect, for only through the rigors of necessity can they achieve dignity in the last decades of the twentieth century as the Jews did in the first decades of this century.[17]

This leads Shorris to a series of questions which are, at the same time, a lament:

> The new definition of Jewish interests belongs to an arrogant people. How can it belong to a small and humble people? The new definition belongs to a selfish people. How can it belong to a people who have been instructed to be "a light to the nations"? The new definition belongs to a people of unlimited power and no history. How can it belong to a people who remember that they were "sojourners in Egypt"? One can understand how Jews could fear the outside world or wish for a homeland or wish to disappear safely into another culture or seek the good life for all so that they might enjoy it as well. The new definition has the chill of loneliness about it. The expressions of it are sometimes grasping, sometimes combative, sometimes vengeful.[18]

Shorris's descriptions lead to important questions he does not shirk: Are not those who take these neoconservative positions fundamentally changing the definition of what it means to be Jewish? Are those who adhere to these positions on social issues really justified in claiming to be Jewish? Or are they searching out a new religion that is something other than Judaism?

Roberta Strauss Feuerlicht also addresses the drift in the Jewish community, but from an even more critical angle. Like Shorris, Feuerlicht sees the essential heritage of the Jewish people as bound up with the ethical imperative. For Feuerlicht, the heritage of the Jews is not power but ethics: "Whether Jews are a religion, a people, a civilization, a historical process, or an anomaly, whether they are Hasidim or heretics, what binds all Jews from antiquity to the present is not statehood but the burden they placed upon themselves and posterity when they internalized morality and gave the world the ethical imperative."

Yet, more often than not, Jews have violated that imperative. For example, Jews were slave owners and slave traders. The golden age of Jewry in Spain owed some of its wealth to an international network of Jewish slave traders where Bohemian Jews purchased Slavonians and sold them to Spanish Jews for resale to the Moors. In the American South before the Civil War, a disproportionate number of Jews were slave owners, slave traders and slave auctioneers. When the line was drawn between the races, by and large, Jews were on the white side.[19]

Though many Jews worked in the Civil Rights movement of the 1950s and 1960s, more recent Black-Jewish relations have been characterized by a Jewish posturing that borders on arrogance. For Feuerlicht, the Andrew Young affair, which began with a meeting with representatives of the PLO and ended in Young's dismissal as the U.S. representative to the United Nations in August 1979, illustrates the problem.

According to Feuerlicht the Jewish establishment never liked Young because of his gift for the controversial and his pronounced bias toward the Third World, which, in neoconservative Jewish terms, meant that he was an enemy of Israel. Jewish leaders believed that Young was one of the Jimmy Carter insiders who tilted him toward the Arab world. And yet, Young was the only powerful African-American in government and, thus, a symbol of progress and hope for the Black community.

Young's resignation thus introduced a new phase in Black-Jewish relations. African-American leaders were angered by the statements of Jewish leaders suggesting that they had no right to comment on Mideast affairs. Within a week of Young's resignation, African-American leaders met with PLO representatives at the United Nations. As a result, Southern Christian Leadership Conference president Reverend Joseph Lowery endorsed the "human rights of all Palestinians, including the right to self-determination in regard to their own homeland."

Yehuda Blum, then Israel's chief UN delegate, criticized African-American leaders for supporting a Palestinian homeland, commenting, "Understandably, they are less knowledgeable about the Middle East conflict than other parties." Lowry replied, "We make no apologies for our support of human rights for Palestinians." Afterward they went to the American Jewish Congress and met with Jewish leaders who said it was "a grave error" for the African-Americans to meet with the Palestinian leadership. After the meeting an African-American minister said, "There will be no peace in the Middle East until justice comes to the Palestinians. All you have to do is visit a refugee camp one time and you will know that the Palestinians are the niggers of the Middle East."[20]

Feuerlicht, like Shorris, confronts the most controversial issue, the state of Israel. Though she admits historical reasons for the state and supports its continued existence because of the now-resident Jewish population, Feuerlicht believes that no further movement toward justice can take place without an honest look at its development.

For Feuerlicht, the Zionists chose to create a state by imposing on an indigenous population and culture, descendants of Jews from all over the world who had not lived there in any significant number for thousands of years and who shared little except their Jewish identification. Because Israel was imposed upon the indigenous population by a nonresident people, Feuerlicht sees the state as a form of colonialism, not of liberation. She quotes Professor Israel Shahak, then chairman of the Israeli League for Human and Civil Rights, who said of Israeli development that almost 400 Arab villages "were completely destroyed, with their houses, garden-walls, and even cemeteries and tombstones, so that literally a stone does not remain standing, and visitors are passing and being told that it was all the desert." She also quotes Moshe Dayan, who once said, "We came to this country which was already populated by Arabs, and we are establishing a Hebrew, that is a Jewish state here. Jewish villages were built in the place of Arab villages. There is not one place built in this country that did not have a former Arab population."[21]

More than two decades later this policy of expropriation and denial of Palestinian rights continues, especially in the occupied territories. Palestinians have been forced into a dependency upon Israeli corporations and government through expropriation of their land and a conscious policy of underdeveloping the Palestinian economic infrastructure. Palestinians are discriminated against in employment, education, and land use. Resisting these injustices can result in blacklisting and arrest, often without legal remedy. Once Palestinians are imprisoned, brutality and torture are commonplace. Feuerlicht cites Felicia Langer, then an Israeli attorney and human rights activist, who reported on West Bank prisons. Describing crowded prison conditions, bad food, and inadequate medical care, Langer wrote that prisoners are also beaten and tortured. Like Langer, B'tselem, the Israeli human rights organization, has documented such abuses over the years.[22]

Through these and other policies, Israel fosters an internal colonialism that, in Feuerlicht's view, creates an interesting, though tragic, twist to Jewish history. For centuries Jews lived as an exiled people. Denied rights and privileges, they were forced into certain occupations by discriminatory laws. When certain rights were granted Jews in the eighteenth and nineteenth centuries, they were granted to individuals, not to the Jewish people. As the French philosopher Clermont-Tonnerre wrote, "Everything should be denied to the Jews as a nation; everything should be granted to them as individuals." The continuing policy that Israel will give Arabs rights as individuals but not as a nation strikes Feuerlicht as ironic. The editorial in *Ha'aretz*, an Israeli newspaper, which states that, though this "is not optimal from a national point of view," it is the "maximum they can expect as a minority," saddens Feuerlicht, for to her mind the Israelis have made the Arabs the Jews of Israel.[23]

In some ways, the Israeli invasion of Lebanon in June 1982 was an extension of this internal colonialism. The atrocities committed by the Israeli military are well documented, and Feuerlicht cites the July 18, 1981 bombing of Beirut, almost a year before the official invasion began, as a reflection of the brutality with which Arabs within Israel and the Palestinian territories are treated.

Though the bombing was ostensibly conducted to strike terrorists' targets, most of the buildings demolished in that bombing were apartment houses. More than three hundred civilians were killed. To a *Washington Post* query, the Israeli chief of military intelligence responded that the motive of Israel's bombing raids in Beirut was to generate Lebanese civilian resentment against the presence of Palestinian militias. A few days later, Israeli bombers again struck Lebanon. Feuerlicht cites

The New York Times, which reported that witnesses, including Western reporters caught in the attacks, said that nearly all the casualties were civilians, some of them burned alive in their cars, trapped in clogged traffic.

In spite of her analysis, Feuerlicht concludes that Israel must continue to exist because the alternative would mean another holocaust. However, if Israel continues on its present course, it will be morally bankrupt and the ethical imperative, the foundation of Jewish life, will be smashed. In a startling and controversial conclusion that directly confronts Greenberg and the Perlmutters, Feuerlicht writes: "Judaism as an ideal is infinite; Judaism as a state is finite. Judasim survived centuries of persecution without a state; it must now learn how to survive despite a state."[24]

And yet, for Feuerlicht, as for Shorris, Jews carry forth the often defeated ethical ideal, an ethical imperative derived from Moses and the prophets, and from our history of fidelity and martyrdom. Often this has placed Jews in a position of exile within the nations of the world; today it increasingly demands an exilic posture within the Jewish community itself. This is a difficult and unexpected place for a Jew, especially after the Holocaust. Such an awakening, however, might provide the physical and psychological space to develop critical insights and activities that call the Jewish people to pursue ethical, rather than oppressive, power.

Thus, the critical questions of Shorris and Feuerlicht, posed to Greenberg and the Perlmutters decades ago, remain relevant today. If it is true that the new scriptures, the scrolls of agony written with bitterness and hope, come from the ghettos of eastern Europe, have not similar scrolls been written today by Lebanese and South African women and men and their "burning children"?

The global economic system, in which the United States is the most powerful and from which many Jews benefit, reinforces a form of triage that translates into millions of malnourished and starving children. Can we continue to mourn our dead, and at the same time refuse to act as if these are not "burning children"? In the eyes of the Palestinians, expansionist Israel, linked to American military and economic support, is the empire against which it struggles. If heard at all, their story is secondary. It is difficult to expect Guatemalan and Salvadoran peasants to understand the Jewish struggle for empowerment when Israeli arms sales and military training support the ever-growing landscape of death littered with orphaned children.

Can we honestly say that critiquing Israel's participation in the equipping of Somoza's forces before the Nicaraguan revolution in 1979, or Israel's contributions to the scientific, military, and economic interests of South Africa under the apartheid regime, or the wholesale expropriation of Palestinian land on the West Bank and Gaza since 1967, is the role of the prophet in the Jewish community? And further, do such questions need to be silenced in the Third era of Jewish history?

For Shorris and Feuerlicht, the Third-era sacred institutions, Yad VaShem and Beit Hatefutsot, may relate our scroll of agony, but increasingly neglect the scrolls scripted today. This other side of our history is today being recorded. One day it will become part of the scripture we are forced by conscience to recite to our children. From this critical posture, Feuerlicht and Shorris believe that we can begin to name the new forms of idolatry the Jewish community has embraced: unbridled capitalism; expansionist nationalism; survival at any cost. Their critique of the Jewish community lifts us beyond the dialectic of Holocaust and empowerment to a reasoned understanding of the dilemmas of Jewish life and the choices before us as a community. It may also open a path of generosity toward other struggling communities and decrease our new found arrogance and our consequent isolation from liberation movements around the globe.

We have inherited a history of anguish and possibility. What history shall we bequeath to our children?

CHAPTER 3

Memory as Burden
and Possibility

There is little question that the Holocaust and the birth of the state of Israel represent the two formative events of the Jewish people in the twentieth century. But how Jews understand these events today, and how Jews understood these events as they were occurring, is more diverse than most commentators on Jewish life acknowledge.

What is crucial for the future of the Jewish people is to recover this diversity of opinion and interpretation, past and present, so that we are not overwhelmed by grief or by power. If Jews are overwhelmed by their history, is it not too easy to use Jewish suffering and power as a blunt instrument rather than as a humble path of justice and compassion?

The need for total agreement is less than the need for airing of different views: the plurality of Jewish life may represent the breakthrough to deeper reflection on the crisis that Jewish thinkers have outlined so vividly.

Holocaust as Burden

In an important essay, Phillip Lopate, a Jewish essayist and novelist, reopens the extremely emotional subject of the Holocaust. He begins with a most provocative title: "Resistance to the Holocaust." Lopate's intention is less to speak of the atrocities of the Nazi era, which are to his mind "enormous and unforgivable," than to address the cultural, political, and religious uses to which the disaster has since been put.

Born after World War II, but before the term Holocaust had become commonplace, Lopate, as a child, heard "concentration camp; gas chambers; six million Jews; what the Nazis did." Some might see it as an improvement to use a single designation for the event. Yet, for Lopate, placing a label on such suffering serves to tame the experience.

As use of the term Holocaust became more common in the 1960s and beyond, Lopate found it to have a self-important, almost vulgar, tone: "Then, too, one instantly saw that the term was part of a polemic and that it sounded more comfortable in certain speakers' mouths than in others; the Holocaustians used it like a club to smash back their opponents. . . . In my own mind I continue to distinguish, ever so slightly, between the disaster visited on the Jews and the 'Holocaust.' Sometimes it almost seems that the Holocaust is a corporation headed by Elie Wiesel, who defends his patents with articles in the Arts and Leisure section of the Sunday *Times*."[1]

Taken in a certain context, Lopate's words seem almost too easy. Yet, it is clear throughout that he is participating in the most ancient of Jewish practices: refusing idolatry insofar as the Holocaust, or the use of it, becomes crystallized, untouchable, almost a God. What suffers, of course, when everything is reduced to the Holocaust or analogous to the Holocaust, is the ability to think through the issues that confront the Jewish people. As Lopate notes: "The Hitler/Holocaust analogy dead-ends all intelligent discourse by intruding a stridently shrill note that forces the mind to withdraw. To challenge the demagogic minefield of pure self-righteousness from an ironic distance almost ensures being misunderstood. The image of the Holocaust is too overbearing, too hot to tolerate distinctions. In its life as a rhetorical figure, the Holocaust is a bully."[2]

The Holocaust as a bully can also become Holocaust as kitsch. The Israeli philosopher Avishai Margalit explores this theme in an essay titled "The Kitsch of Israel." According to Margalit, kitsch is based on an easy identification of the represented object; the emotion evoked in the spectator comes simply from a reference to the object. Although genuine art always maintains a distance from the represented object, thus involving the spectator in interpretation and allowing a variety of perspectives to merge, the idea of kitsch is to arouse a strong emotion from the spectator's relation to the original object. Thus, in the Jewish context "a glimpse of Masada, or the Wall, or the Temple Mount is enough to move the Jewish heart," and the marketing of Israel takes full advantage of these adages.

Kitsch can also be politicized and become, in Margalit's terms, part of a state ideology whose "emblem is total innocence." The image of the Israeli soldier and the Wailing Wall are two such items of kitsch, evoking easy emotional identification with the important secondary understanding of a beleaguered nation. Of course, as Margalit points out, the opposite of total innocence is total evil: "The innocent and pure with whom we sympathize have to be relentlessly protected from those plotting their destruction.³

For Margalit, however, the place that should be furthest from such easy emotion, Yad VaShem, the Holocaust memorial in Israel, has, paradoxically, become an element of state kitsch. He cites the Children's Room, pitch dark with tape-recorded voices of children crying out for their mothers in Yiddish. Margalit believes that the real significance of the Children's Room is not its "commemoration of the single most horrible event in the history of mankind—the systematic murder of two million children, Jewish and Gypsies, for being what they were and not for anything they had done. The Children's Room, rather, is meant to deliver a message to the visiting foreign statesman, who is rushed to Yad VaShem even before he has had time to leave off his luggage at his hotel, that all of us here in Israel are these children and that Hitler-Arafat is after us." This is the message for internal consumption as well. For Margalit, talking of the Palestinians in the same tone as one talks of Auschwitz is an important element in "turning the Holocaust into kitsch."⁴

Increasingly in Israel, the Holocaust is seen in a similar light, as an event that is consciously manipulated by the state and its leadership. This is the theme of Boas Evron, an Israeli writer and commentator, in his essay "The Holocaust: Learning the Wrong Lessons." For Evron, two terrible things happened to the Jewish people over the last half-century: the Holocaust and the lessons learned from it.

The ahistorical interpretations of the Holocaust made deliberately or out of ignorance have become, in Evron's mind, a danger both to the Jewish people and to the state of Israel for the following reasons: The term Holocaust is rhetorical and ambiguous; it exists almost as a myth, without historical reference and becomes indefinite and movable, almost exempting one from understanding it. "The murder of the Jews in Europe," though not as galvanizing, more accurately reflects and locates a historical event in which there were murderers and those who were murdered. Such an event becomes worthy of historical investigation and is lifted from the mystical and pseudo-religious.

By analyzing the historical context, Evron finds different lessons to be drawn from the event than Holocaust theologians do. For example, Evron points to the basic assumption that the Nazi policy of mass murder was directed almost exclusively against Jews. The facts speak differently: Gypsies and three million non-Jewish Poles were murdered, and millions of Russian prisoners of war and forced laborers were murdered as well. The enslavement and extermination of the Slavic people was also a possibility for the Nazis. For Evron, anti-Semitism served as a "catalyst, as the focal point of the extermination system" that was destined to become a central and permanent institution of the Third Reich.

Thus, in Evron's understanding, the Nazi murder of the Jews was unique only in preparing the world for the institutionalization of extermination. The argument presented as a corollary, that the Jews of Palestine were saved by Zionism is also false; they were saved by the defeat of the Nazis at El Alamein and Stalingrad, which prevented the Nazis from conquering Palestine and exterminating the Jewish population.

The lesson of the Holocaust is, therefore, different: "The true guarantee against ideologically-based extermination is not military power and sovereignty but the eradication of ideologies which remove any human group from the family of humanity." For Evron, the solution lies in a common struggle aimed at overcoming national differences and barriers, rather than increasing and heightening them, as strong trends within Israel and the Zionist movement demand.[5]

There were many reasons why the historical presentation of the murder of the Jews in Europe was rejected for an ahistorical view summarized in the word Holocaust. According to Evron, the Germans were interested in this because it limited, in a sense, their liability. Instead of focusing on the systemic and expanding possibilities of a system of extermination, a focus that might have kept alive the feelings of fear and suspicion, after the war, in Germany's neighbors, limiting the memory to the Jews and the Holocaust enabled Germany to more easily reintegrate itself into the world of nations. The Western powers were also interested in this insofar as it allowed them to wipe the slate clean and begin to rebuild Germany as a barrier to Soviet expansion.

The "Jewish monopolization" of the Nazi experience was also welcomed by Jewish leadership in Israel and in the Diaspora, as a way of strengthening German guilt consciousness, thus continuing and increasing the amount of compensation payments for survivors, and as a way of mobilizing world support, moral, political, military, and financial, for the Jewish state. For Evron, this new and creative policy of inducing moral guilt shifted the policy of Germany, as well as that of other countries; it lifted the tragedy out of the past and made it a basis for future preferential relationships. And as importantly, this policy became a blueprint for relations with most Western Christian states, especially the United States; they were to support Israel on the basis of guilt rather than self-interest.

Evron sees the ramifications of this policy to be enormous. In the first place, it contravenes an aim of the Zionist movement to normalize the status of the Jewish people, by reducing Israel to the "level of an eternal beggar." Henceforth, Israel survives on the "six million credit" instead of, like any other country, on developing and marketing its energy and skills. Living off its past, Israel exists, like the Holocaust, in an ahistorical context, thus avoiding economic and political confrontation in the real world. Paradoxically, a renewed feeling of isolation grows as the adulation of the survivor Israel increases. The policy also generates what Evron considers a moral blindness: because the world is out to get Israel in the present and in the future, any links with oppressive governments and any oppression of non-Jews within and around Israel can be justified.

The Holocaust can also be used as a powerful tool by Israeli and Jewish leadership in the United States to organize and police the Jewish community. Diaspora Jews, for example, are made to feel guilty for not having done enough to prevent the Holocaust; at the same time, the message is conveyed that Israel is threatened with annihilation. The message is clear: unequivocal support for Israel to prevent a second holocaust. Evron sees the image of Holocaust past as Holocaust future as so important to Israel and American Jewry that the reality of Israel's strength is submerged in myth:

> When you try to explain to American Jews that we are not, in fact, in danger of annihilation, that for many years to come we will be stronger than any possible combination, that Israel has not, in fact, been in danger of physical annihilation since the first cease-fire of the War of Independence in 1948, and that the average human and cultural level of Israeli society, even in its current deteriorated state, is still much higher than that of the surrounding Arab societies, and that this level rather than the quantity and sophistication of our arms constitutes our military advantage—you face resistance and outrage. And then you realize another fact: this image is needed by many American Jews in order for them to free themselves of their guilt regarding the Holocaust. Moreover, supporting Israel is necessary because of the loss of any other focal point to their Jewish identity. Thus, many of them resist the suggestion that the appropriate aim for Israel is to liberate itself from any dependency on outside elements, even Jewish ones. They need to feel needed. They also need the "Israeli hero" as a social and emotional compensation in a society in which the Jew is not usually perceived as embodying the characteristics of the tough, manly fighter. Thus, the Israeli provides the American Jew with a double, contradictory image—the virile superman, and the potential Holocaust victim—both of whose components are far from reality.[6]

The equation of Arab hatred of Israel with the Nazi hatred of Jews, for Evron, arises logically out of the ahistorical quality of the Holocaust. The Nazis, who created an irrational hatred of the Jews so as to justify their system of mass extermination, are likened to the Arabs, who, according to Evron, have a quite rational reason for opposing Israel as a powerful enemy that has expelled and displaced over a million of their compatriots. The difference between an illiterate Palestinian refugee and a highly trained SS trooper is blurred beyond distinction, and the defense of the country, in the 1967 war and in the Yom Kippur war in 1973, becomes less an integral part of sovereign political existence than a stage on which the destiny of the Jewish people is played out. Identifying Palestinians with Nazis, as the continuous reminder of the Holocaust does, leads to hysterical responses rather than reasoned policy.

These parallels have serious moral consequences as well. Because the choices presented to Israel are not realistic—only holocaust or victory—Israel becomes free of any moral restrictions, because any nation that is in danger of annihilation feels exempted from moral considerations that might restrict its efforts to save itself. For Evron, this is the rationale of people who argue that everything is permitted because the world wants Israel's destruction.

Evron concludes that Israeli and Jewish leadership, caught up in an ahistorical world, threaten to become victims of their own propaganda. They draw on a bank account continuously reduced by withdrawals. As the world moves on, there are fewer who remember the Holocaust, and those who do, including the Jews, become tired of it as a nuisance and as a reflection of a reality that does not exist: "Thus the leadership, too, operates in the world of myths and monsters created by its own hands. It has created this world in order to maintain and perpetuate its rule. It is, however, no longer able to understand what is happening in the real world, and what are the historical processes in which the state is caught. Such a leadership, in the unstable political and economic situation of Israel today, itself constitutes a danger to the very existence of the state."[7]

As Lopate, Margalit and Evron challenge the orthodoxy surrounding the discussions of the Holocaust, it is important to understand that such challenges are not without penalty. Richard Rubenstein, for example, who helped initiate the discussion of the Holocaust in 1966 with the publication of his book *After Auschwitz: Radical Theology and Contemporary Judaism*, was for years ostracized from the Jewish community, in part for his probing of Jewish suffering in the Holocaust as a failure of internal Jewish leadership, for his understanding of the attempted annihilation of the Jews as partly an example of economic displacement and surplus population reduction, and finally for his envisioning of the Jewish experience of Holocaust as both unique and paradigmatic for other sufferings in the twentieth century. In fact, his book, *The Cunning of History: Mass Death and the American Future*, published in 1975, was written partially in response to the unwillingness of the organizers of the Holocaust convocation at Saint John the Divine Cathedral in New York City to extend an invitation for him to speak. This was the convocation, later published under the title *Auschwitz: Beginning of a New Era?*, that represented the height of the influence of Holocaust theology and included, among many others, Elie Wiesel, Emil Fackenheim, and Irving Greenberg.

In *The Cunning of History*, Rubenstein approaches the most difficult of questions: Did Jews, in effect, no matter how involuntarily, cooperate in their own undoing? For Rubenstein the charge of desecrating the memory of the dead or even excusing their murderers cannot replace the objectivity of political reflection. "Regrettably, those who avoid objective reflection on the Jewish response add to the confusion concerning what took place. Every assault requires at least two actors.... Even the most innocent victim is part of the process of his own undoing by virtue of the fact that he did not or could not take protective measures."[8]

For Rubenstein, two factors were initially critical for the Nazis to carry out the mass murder of Jews: the cultural conditioning of two thousand years of Rabbinic Judaism, which counseled Jews to submit and endure rather than resist and the Germans' ability to utilize the existing leadership and organizations of the Jewish community wherever the extermination process was implemented.

Rubenstein boldly asserts that the process of transforming Jewish communal bureaucracies into components of the extermination was one of the organizational triumphs of the Nazis. Most Jews instinctively relied on their own communal organizations to defend their interests wherever possible. Yet, according to Rubenstein, these organizations of self-governance were transformed into subsidiaries of the German police and state democracies. "Thus, the official agency of German Jews led by the most distinguished German rabbi of the twentieth century, a man in whose memory an important rabbinical seminary has been named (London's Leo Baeck College), undertook such tasks as selecting those who were to be deported, notifying the families and, finally, of sending the Jewish police to round up the victims."

In the Warsaw Ghetto and in Lodz, Poland, the Jewish council, or *Judenrat*, did not resist German directives even when the Germans demanded the "selection" of 10,000 Jews a day for deportation. Jewish bureaucrats made the selection, Jewish police rounded up the victims. In a provocative conclusion, Rubenstein states that Germany "demonstrated that a modern state can successfully organize an entire people for its own extermination."[9]

Still the fate of the Jews was sealed earlier than the Nazi period, with the active promulgation of Christian anti-Jewishness, as well as by economic and demographic changes relating to the capitalist revolution in Europe. For Rubenstein, from the moment of the Christian triumph in Europe, Jews were in an inherently dangerous position, and here, Rubenstein simply reiterates the sense of other religious writers on the anti-Jewish aspects of the Holocaust.

But Rubenstein raises a further question: Why, with almost two millennia of hatred, did Jews survive Christendom? Why did the activities of

Christendom toward Jews, conversion, and isolation become, in the twentieth century, the pursuit of the final solution?

According to Rubenstein, the reason for the survival of Jews and Judaism in the harsh Christian ethos was that in premodern times the consequences of religious conflict were moderated by Europe's precapitalist economy, in which Jews played a necessary, though often despised, role. Like the ethnic Chinese of Southeast Asia, the Ibos of Nigeria, and the Armenians of the Ottoman Empire, Jews functioned as an elite minority filling certain commercial and professional roles that were not being filled by the dominant majority.

As the urbanized middle class arose within the capitalist revolution, Jews ceased to play a complementary role and became highly visible competitors of a more powerful and rooted group, the rising Christian bourgeoisie. Thus, already in the sixteenth century, European Jews were being forced out of these elite though dangerous positions and entered marginal roles as peddlers of second-hand goods and pawnbrokers. Eventually the majority of the Jews were closed out of viable economic activity and were forced to migrate from western to eastern Europe, precisely because the latter remained feudal and agrarian.

In the nineteenth century, this process of capitalist development took place in eastern Europe, which reversed migration back to the west. In a great, though tragic, irony, Jews in these various migrations became identified with the general trends of disorientation and displacement of the native populations of East and West, and as competing with them for scarce resources, and, therefore, with the triumph of a capitalist, anonymous, uprooting society.

For Rubenstein, Jews, in religious terms but also now in economic and social reality, became pariahs in the ultimate sense, unwanted and unneeded, thus superfluous. From that moment on, segregation into ghettos and the policy of extermination were policies that only awaited a certain configuration of events.[10]

Though the complexities of Rubenstein's argument for bureaucratic self-destruction and transformation of Europe's economic order are many and controversial, they point to his major contribution: broadening the understanding of the Holocaust. Rubenstein affirms that the Jewish experience of suffering is unique and tied to a long history of anti-Jewishness, but something happened in the capitalist revolution, culminating in the twentieth century, that allowed the transformation of contempt into mass death.

Yet, the mass death of Jews involves and moves beyond the experience of the Jewish people, in effect binding Jewish suffering with others, past and present. In fact, Jewish suffering must take its place alongside other examples of mass death that help define the twentieth century. For

Rubenstein, the mass death that took place in the West during World War I was only a prelude to the carnage that took place in Russia at the time of the revolution. Here civil war, demographic violence, and large-scale famine came together in an ominous way. An estimated two to three million died as a result of hard violence and six to eight million as a result of long-term privation. Rubenstein uses British historian Gil Eliot as a guide to assert that the foundations of twentieth-century military slaughter on a mass scale were laid during World War I; mass civilian slaughter followed immediately thereafter, especially in Central and Eastern Europe, the very geographic area in which Jews were to perish during the Second World War. By the millions. The Turkish massacre of about one million Armenians during World War I is of interest here, an event that Rubenstein believes to be the first successful attempt by a modern state to practice disciplined, methodically organized genocide. The victims of twentieth-century mass slaughter also include the following: "those who perished in the Sino-Japanese War and the Spanish Civil War; the millions who were killed in the various Stalinist purges, as well as those who died in the man-made famines which resulted from Stalin's slaughter of peasants who resisted collectivization between 1929 and 1933; the Russian and Polish prisoners of war exterminated by the Germans; the Russian prisoners of war who escaped death at the hands of the Germans only to be murdered when they returned home; those who perished at Hiroshima and Nagasaki, and the victims of the wars and revolutions of Southeast Asia."[11]

For Rubenstein, rather than an exception or a unique event, the Jewish Holocaust becomes a paradigm, "an expression of some of the most significant political, moral, religious and demographic tendencies of Western civilization in the twentieth century." Rubenstein concludes his analysis with a prophetic warning:

> Perhaps it was no accident that the most highly urbanized people in the Western world, the Jews, were the first to perish in the ultimate city of Western civilization, Necropolis, the new city of the dead that the Germans built and maintained at Auschwitz. Auschwitz was perhaps the terminal expression of an urban culture that first arose when an ancient proto-bourgeoisie liberated its work life from the haphazard, unpredictable, and seasonable character of agriculture and sustained itself by work which was, in the words of Max Weber, "continuous and rational." In the beginning, removed from immediate involvement in 'the vital realities of nature,' the city was the habitat of the potter, the weaver, the carpenter, and the scribe; in the end, it houses the police bureaucrat and his corporate counterpart coldly and methodically presiding over the city of the dead.[12]

There are, of course, many other ways of looking at the Holocaust, but the themes surfaced by Lopate, Margalit, Evron, and Rubenstein—the Holocaust as block to creative and emphatic thought, as kitsch, as open to political, economic, and sociological interpretation, as paradigmatic rather than unique—forces Jews to be open continually to history rather than be determined by it.

Dissenters in Zion

All this suggests further questioning of still another almost sacred assumption, that of the relationship of the Holocaust to the state of Israel. So often is the connection presumed without a second thought that one may be startled by such a question. Yet historically, the Zionist movement predated the Nazi period by at least four decades and the death camps by five.

The assumed link between Holocaust and Israel and the way the two are discussed, especially since the 1967 war, in a sense cuts off much of the most principled and interesting dissent that Jews have provided over the last century, and thus makes it more difficult to gauge the limits of dissent in the present. It is as if Zionism, and thus the state of Israel, has no history. Of course, without history, there is no accountability.

How many Jews, for instance, know that many of the most interesting and important Jews at the formative period of Zionism actually opposed the creation of Israel as a state? And know that, despite its existence, there always has been and still remains systematic and sustained opposition to many of Israel's most fundamental policies and outlooks? What does the suppression of this knowledge mean for the future? In fact, there is now a tradition of dissent vis-à-vis Israel that is largely unmentioned by Holocaust theologians and commentators, and unspoken—perhaps unknown—within the Jewish community at large.

There is little question that Zionism represented a revolutionary force in Jewish life at the end of the nineteenth century. Although we often think of Zionism almost exclusively in relation to anti-Jewishness, it is important to see it, as well, within the framework of the forces unleashed by the Enlightenment and the French Revolution.

This is the point made by Shlomo Avineri in his book *The Making of Modern Zionism: The Intellectual Origins of the Jewish State*. For Avineri, those Jews who were seeking mere survival and economic security, those who were suffering pogroms and pauperization, tended to emigrate to America. Those who went to Palestine, then within the Ottoman Empire, where living conditions were similar or worse, went seeking a liberation announced within post-1789 European culture—self-determination, identity, the fulfillment of a newly awakened self-consciousness.

Hence, early Zionism was less a response to anti-Jewishness (or even religious sentiment, though both were surely present) than to the challenge of liberalism and nationalism. This is why the anti-Jewishness of the previous millennium occasioned only sporadic and individual returns to the land—and almost always within the framework of religious orthodoxy.

According to Avineri, Zionism was the fundamental revolution in Jewish life (possible only in the post-1789 European culture) precisely because it substituted a secular self-identity of the Jews as a nation for the traditional and orthodox self-identity in religious terms, and because it changed a passive, quietistic, and pious hope of the return to Zion into an effective social force, moving millions of people to Israel. Finally, it transformed Hebrew from a language of mostly liturgical use into the modern, secular language of a nation. Clearly, as Avineri sees it, the rise of Zionism and ultimately the state of Israel is a completely modern phenomenon—in fact, a response to the challenge of modernity.

Of course, this journey of a dispersed people to a modern state was fraught with puzzling dilemmas and contradictions. If Zionism was a modern secular phenomenon, how did it relate to Jewish tradition? If Zionism was a revolution in Jewish consciousness and activity, how did it transform a minority movement among Jews into a majority? What was a Jewish nation, and what would it represent? Was the task of Zionism to normalize the Jewish condition, that is, to form a nation like all others? Or was the gathering of Jews in Palestine to represent a rebirth of a special calling to be a light among the nations?[13]

From the beginning of the Zionist movement, there were fundamental divisions relating to these questions and many others. What is of interest here is the initial division between political Zionism and cultural Zionism. Political Zionism, represented by Theodore Herzl, an assimilated Austrian Jew who became the founding leader of the Zionist movement, saw the main task of Zionism as founding and creating a functioning Jewish state. Cultural Zionism was championed by Asher Ginsburg (1852–1927), who wrote under the pseudonym of Ahad Ha'am "one of the people"; it saw the gathering of Jews in Palestine as critical to the cultural and spiritual renewal of Judaism and the Jewish people, and, thus, the essential task of the Zionist movement.

For Ahad Ha'am, who was born into a Russian Hasidic family but, like many Jews of his generation, participated in the secular, emancipatory atmosphere of Odessa, Zionism needed to address the two faces of Jewry: those in Western Europe faced with the failure of nineteenth century Europe to provide an adequate answer to the individual quest for Jewish identity in the modern world, and those in Eastern Europe who found themselves faced with the collective difficulty of finding a place in emerging national cultures. For Western European Jews, a Jewish state would mean an ideal and an opportunity:

> If a Jewish state were re-established in Palestine, a state arranged and organized exactly after the pattern of other states, then the western European Jew could live a full, complete life among his own people, and find at home all that he now sees outside, dangled before his eyes, but out of reach. Of course, not all the Jews will be able to take wing and go to their state, but the very existence of the Jewish state will raise the prestige of those who remain in exile, and their fellow citizens will no more despise them and keep them at arm's length as though they were ignoble slaves, dependent entirely on the hospitality of others. As the western European Jew contemplates this fascinating vision, it suddenly dawns on his inner consciousness that even now, before the Jewish state is established, the mere idea of it gives him almost complete relief. He has an opportunity for organized work, for political excitement, he finds a suitable field of activity without having to become subservient to non-Jews, and he feels that thanks to this ideal he stands once more spiritually erect, and has regained human dignity, without overmuch trouble and without external aid. So he devotes himself to the ideal with all the ardor of which he is capable, he gives rein to his fancy, and he lets it soar as it will, up above reality and the limitations of human power. For it is not the attainment of the ideal that he needs: its pursuit alone is sufficient to cure him of his moral sickness, which is the consciousness of inferiority; and the higher and more distant the ideal, the greater its power of exaltation.[14]

For Eastern European Jews, a Jewish state would forge a new focus of identity:

> So Judaism seeks to return to its historic center, in order to live there a life of natural development, to bring its powers into play in every department of human culture, to develop and perfect those national possessions which it has acquired up to now, and thus to contribute to the common stock of humanity, in the future as in the past, a great national culture, the fruit of the unhampered activity of a people living according to its own spirit. For this purpose Judaism needs at present but little. It needs not an independent state, but only the creation in its native land of conditions favorable to its development: a good-sized settlement of Jews working without hindrance in every branch of culture, from agriculture and handicrafts to science and literature. This Jewish settlement, which will be a gradual growth, will become in course of time the center of the nation, wherein its spirit will find pure expression and develop in all its aspects up to the highest degree

of perfection of which it is capable. Then from this center the spirit of Judaism will go forth to the great circumference, to all the communities of the Diaspora, and will breathe new life into them and preserve their unity, and when our national culture in Palestine has attained that level, we may be confident that it will produce men in the country who will be able, on a favorable opportunity, to establish a state which will be truly a Jewish state, and not merely a state of Jews.[15]

The challenge of bringing culture and spirit together is primary for Ahad Ha'am and hardly new to Jewish history. He uses the conflict of the Sadducees, who saw the very existence of the Jewish state as the essence of national life, and the Pharisees, who saw the spiritual context as the mainstay of Jewish existence, as the dialectical tension worthy of consideration in the contemporary Zionist discussion.

For Ahad Ha'am, the Pharisees represent the true synthesis of the spiritual and the material, holding a dialectical defense of political power that views power as a tool rather than an end in itself. Thus, they were faced with a twofold battle: "On the one hand, they opposed the political materialists from within, for then the state was only a body without an essential spirit; and, on the other side, they fought together with these opponents against the enemy without, in order to save the state from destruction." When Rome defeated and destroyed the Jewish nation, the Pharisees held out the possibility for the continuation of the people.

> The political materialists, for whom the existence of the state was everything, had nothing to live for after the political catastrophe [the destruction of the Temple by the Romans]; and so they fought desperately, and did not budge until they fell dead among the ruins that they loved. But the Pharisees remembered, even in that awful moment, that the political body had a claim on their affections only because of the national spirit which found expression in it, and needed its help. Hence they never entertained the strange idea that the destruction of the state involved the death of the people, and that life was no longer worth living. On the contrary, now they felt it absolutely necessary to find some temporary means of preserving the nation and its spirit even without a state, until such time as God should have mercy on His people and restore it to its land and freedom. So the bond was broken: the political Zealots remained sword in hand on the walls of Jerusalem, while the Pharisees took the scroll of the Law and went to Jabneh.[16]

For Ahad Ha'am, the work of the Pharisees bore fruit in preserving the Hebrew national spirit, in organizing a cultural and spiritual life for a scattered and despised people, and in preparing Diaspora communities for a "single aim and perfect union in the future."

Ahad Ha'am's initial visit to Jewish settlements in Palestine in 1890 occasioned an essay, "Thoughts from the Land of Israel," in which he recognized the complexities of realizing the Zionist vision. He dealt with the myths of Palestine as a relatively empty place and the Arabs as a backward people. "We tend to believe abroad that Palestine is nowadays almost completely deserted, a non-cultivated wilderness, and anyone can come there and buy as much land as his heart desires. But in reality this is not the case. It is difficult to find anywhere in the country Arab land which lies fallow; the only areas which are not cultivated are sand dunes or stony mountains, which can be only planted with trees, and even this only after much labor and capital would be invested in clearance and preparation." Ahad Ha'am also warns against use of violence and humiliation toward the Arab population:

> One thing we certainly should have learned from our past and present history, and that is not to create anger among the local population against us. . . . We have to treat the local population with love and respect, justly and rightly. And what do our brethren in the Land of Israel do? Exactly the opposite! Slaves they were in their country of exile, and suddenly they find themselves in a boundless and anarchic freedom, as is always the case with a slave that has become king, and they behave toward the Arabs with hostility and cruelty, infringe upon their boundaries, hit them shamefully without reason, and even brag about it. Our brethren are right when they say that the Arab honours only those who show valour and fortitude, but this is the case only when he feels that the other side has justice on his side. It is very different in a case when [the Arab] thinks that his opponent's actions are iniquitous and unlawful, in that case he may keep his anger to himself for a long time, but it will dwell in his heart and in the long run he will prove himself to be vengeful and full of retribution.[17]

By 1912 he wrote, protesting the boycott of Arab labor as a strategy to conquer the land: "Apart from the political danger, I can't put up with the idea that our brethren are morally capable of behaving in such a way to humans of another people, and unwittingly the thought comes to my mind: if it is so now, what will be our relation to the others if in truth we shall achieve at the end of times power in Eretz Israel? And if this be the 'Messiah': I do not wish to see his coming."[18]

At his death in 1927 in Tel Aviv, Ahad Ha'am was brokenhearted, outraged by what he considered to be a cycle of violence almost impossible to break. "My God is this the end? . . . Is this the dream of our return to Zion, that we come to Zion and stain its soil with innocent blood? It has been an axiom in my eyes that the people will sacrifice its money for the sake of a state, but never its prophets."[19]

Prophetic Warnings

Another early critical Zionist was Judah Magnes (1877–1948), a Reform rabbi born in America, who emigrated to Palestine in 1923, where he became chancellor of Hebrew University. As chancellor, Magnes became a symbol of hope for Zionists who believed in the progressive endeavors of the Jewish return to the land. He became closely tied to such luminaries as Martin Buber and Hans Kohn. He also challenged some of the most important and powerful Jewish leaders of his time, Louis D. Brandeis, Stephen S. Wise, Chaim Weizmann, and David BenGurion. In Magnes we find American pragmatism and Jewish faith, a crusader's zeal and a deep commitment to the renewal of his people. And, like Ahad Ha'am, Magnes realized both the possiblities of Zionism for renewal of Jewish culture and spirit and the limitations of a Zionism that ignored the Arab/Palestinian population or, worse, sought to subjugate them in or outside a Jewish state.

In a 1924 journal entry, written just after his arrival in Jerusalem, Magnes outlined one of his basic themes in relation to Zionism, the possibility that through Jewish nationalism, nationalism itself would be transcended by an internationalism worthy of the Jewish spirit. For Magnes, it is only after being rooted in a nation that nationalism can be overcome. Being rooted in a nation allows one to transcend the nation without fear of assimilation and the loss of self that results. A freedom ensues that Magnes compares to the technique of a musician that is so perfect it ceases to be of concern. What concerns the musician is the higher things, those of the spirit.[20]

This is not easy for a Jew. Though many things predispose Jews to universalism—including the historical experience of wandering and the prophets—Magnes believes Jews have a much harder job overcoming their nationalism. Only Jews who feel themselves firmly rooted in the Jewish nation, for whom there is not the slightest possibility of being anything other than a Jew, can overcome this difficulty.

This is precisely where, for Magnes, the universalist doctrine of Reform Judaism—of the merging of nations, races, and peoples into a spiritual synthesis of prophetic human solidarity—fails. By uprooting themselves from their nationality, Jews lack roots in "Jewish earth." While preaching the doctrine of universalism, they are trying to escape from Judaism and their Jewish selves, only through the care of which a true internationalism can grow. In essence, for Magnes, two kinds of Jews can become universalists: "The Jew who knows and thinks so little of himself as a Jew that he can in very truth say he is no Jew but an internationalist, universalist (e.g., Trotsky) and the Jew who has so thoroughly grounded himself in his Judaism that his universalism becomes the development and crown of his Judaism." For Magnes, the latter type of Jew is predisposed to a higher attitude, but fears that Jews are not strong enough nationally to bear this development. Magnes sees this question as fundamental, and his response is clear. "Jews are a strong, vital people and not a weak one," Magnes writes, "and this despite pogroms and wanderings. They are mighty and vital physically. They seem incapable of being annihilated, and give Jewish children a chance in fresh air and with good food and see how they blossom. His spiritual forces are equally great." Magnes notes how contemporary Jews are maintaining themselves and growing in the Diaspora. At the same time, the Jewish community is growing in Palestine. "This very experiment must give every one of us courage. It shows that the Jew can and will live apart and at the same time render homage to the highest of human ideals—witness his communistic settlements."[21] Thus, for Magnes—and this is often forgotten today—Zionism was a movement that emerged from the strength rather than from the weakness of the Jewish people. The renewal of the Jewish community in Palestine needed and was possible only within the context of a strong and vibrant Diaspora. Magnes concludes his journal entry with a general rule, to act from Jewish strength, as if Zion were already rebuilt: "Therefore let us seek our brethren of all peoples. Fear for the Jews or fear of others cannot be our guiding force, only confidence in Jewish strength and belief in great human ideals."[22]

By 1929, Magnes's sense of nationalism and universalism was undergoing a rigorous refinement in the context of new agitation over the possibility of the establishment of a Jewish state in Palestine. In a letter to Chaim Weizmann, a leading advocate of such a development, Magnes outlined the two possibilities before the Jewish people and the consequences of those choices: statehood, which would base Jewish life in Palestine on militarism and imperialism or a "pacific" policy that focused less on a Jewish state than on the development of a Jewish educational, moral, and religious center in Palestine.

For Magnes, the first policy would involve politics, governments, and armaments and deal only secondarily with Jews and lastly with Arabs. The pacific policy would deal first of all with the Jews, then the Arabs, and only incidentally with all the rest. "The imperialist, military and political policy is based upon mass immigration of Jews and the creation (forcible if necessary) of a Jewish majority, no matter how much this oppresses the Arabs meanwhile, or deprives them of their rights. In this kind of policy the end always justifies the means. The policy, on the other hand, of developing a Jewish spiritual center does not depend upon mass immigration, a Jewish majority, a Jewish state, or upon depriving the Arabs (or the Jews) of their political rights for a generation or a day but on the contrary, is desirous of having Palestine become a country of two nations and three religions, all of them having equal rights and none of them having special privileges; a country where nationalism is but the basis of internationalism, where the population is pacifistic and disarmed—in short, the Holy Land."[23]

Magnes posed the critical question to Weizmann, of whether Jews would genuinely desire to conquer Palestine, as in the time of Joshua, or would take into account the religious developments of Judaism since Joshua—the prophets, psalmists, and rabbis—and, thus, be in harmony with the words "not by right, and not by violence, but by my spirit, saith the Lord." Just five years after Magnes's entry into Palestine, that question was as much addressed to himself as to Weizmann. Was it possible to enter any country—no less the Holy Land—and build it up pacifistically? "If we cannot (and I do not say that we can rise to these heights), I for my part have lost half my interest in the enterprise. If we cannot even attempt this, I should much rather see this eternal people without such a 'National Home,' with the wanderer's staff in hand and forming new ghettos among the peoples of the world." One week later, in a letter to Felix Warburg, a New York financier and philanthropist, Magnes wrote even more directly:

> Palestine does not belong to the Jews and it does not belong to the Arabs, nor to Judaism or Christianity or Islam. It belongs to all of them together; it is the Holy Land. If the Arabs want an Arab national state in Palestine, it is as much or as little to be defended as if the Jews want a Jewish national state there. We must once and for all give up the idea of a "Jewish Palestine" in the sense that a Jewish Palestine is to exclude and do away with an Arab Palestine. This is the historic fact, and Palestine is nothing if it is not history. If a Jewish national home in Palestine is compatible with an Arab national home there, well and good, but if it is not, the name makes very little difference. The fact is that nothing there is possible unless Jews and Arabs work together in peace for the benefit of their common Holy Land. It must be our endeavor first to convince ourselves and then to convince others that Jews and Arabs, Moslems, Christians and Jews have each as much right there, no more and no less, than the other: equal rights and equal privileges and equal duties. That is practically quite sufficient for all purposes of the Jewish religion, and it is the sole ethical basis for our claims there. Judaism did not begin with Zionism, and if Zionism is ethically not in accord with Judaism, so much the worse for Zionism.[24]

In 1930, Magnes published a pamphlet with the provocative title "Like All the Nations?" and prefaced with the biblical quotation "a unique nation" (2 Sam 7:23). Here, Magnes begins with the startling admission that if the evolving definition of Zionism takes hold—that is, creating a Jewish state by force, if necessary, including the subjugation of the Palestinian Arabs and the massive immigration of the Jews in the

Diaspora—then, though living in Zion, Magnes defines himself no longer as a Zionist, but rather, as the traditional *hibbat Zion*, the lover of Zion.

For Magnes, it is increasingly clear that despite the central emerging theme of Zionist ideology, Palestine cannot solve the so-called Jewish problem of the Jewish people. The Diaspora will neither disappear nor be subsumed by Jewish life in Palestine. On the contrary, Magnes feels the Jewish people to be growing stronger, as they should, for Palestine without communities in the Diaspora would lose much of its significance as a spiritual center for Judaism.

Because of this confusion in Zionist ideology, Magnes felt it necessary to redefine the three chief elements of Jewish life in order of their importance: the living Jewish people around the world; the Torah, seen in its broadest sense of the documents, history, and ethical ideals of the Jewish people; and the land of Israel, where the people and the Torah "can exist and be creative as they have existed and have been creative without the Land." The importance of the land for Magnes was that it was one of the chief means of "deepening the People and the Torah." Because the living Jewish people is primary, as the carrier and vessel of Judaism and the Jewish spirit, the Diaspora has spread light and learning throughout the world. "Palestine can help this people to understand itself, to give an account of itself, to an intensification of its culture, a deepening of its philosophy, a renewal of its religion."

But it is also a testing ground, a dangerous frontier land for the lovers of peace in Judaism. For Magnes, much of the theory of Zionism had been concerned with making the Jews into a "normal" nation in Palestine, like the Gentiles of the lands and the families of the earth. "The desire for power and conquest seems to be normal to many human beings and groups, and we being the ruled everywhere must here rule; being the minority everywhere, we must here be in the majority. There is the State, the army, the frontiers. We have been in Exile; now we are to be master in our own Home. We are to have a Fatherland, and we are to encourage the feelings of pride, honour, glory that are part of the paraphernalia of the ordinary nationalistic patriotism. In the face of such danger one thinks of the dignity and originality of that passage in the liturgy which praises the Lord of all things that our portion is not like theirs and our lot not like all their multitude."[25]

In 1943, in the midst of the Holocaust, Magnes continued his argument for a Jewish presence in Palestine, alongside of and in harmony with the Palestinian Arabs, with an essay "Toward Peace in Palestine," published in *Foreign Affairs*. To those who sought the accommodation of millions of persecuted Jews in Palestine and the establishment of a Jewish state, Magnes welcomed the idea, if only Palestine were large and empty.

The fact of the matter was that Palestine was neither; another people had been in possession of the land for centuries. The concept of a Jewish state in Palestine would quite properly be regarded by the Palestinian Arabs as "equivalent to a declaration of war against them." Thus, in the first place, there was a need to distinguish between messianic expectation and hard reality. The growth of Palestinian Arab nationalism also created a new problem: the desire for a Palestinian Arab state at the price of Jewish subjugation.

Though each side's argument for statehood assured the others of full and equal rights, there was already ominous discussion of transferring populations. Magnes cites a Jewish commentator who assured the Palestinian Arabs of Jewish support for independence, if they recognized Palestine as a Jewish state. As for the transferring Arabs, the commentator added, "The question of the exchange of populations is likely to become pressing in our days. I believe this question to be essential for us and also for them." At the same time, a spokesperson for the Arabs sought the establishment of a Palestinian Arab state: "No other solution seems practicable, except possibly at the cost of an unpredictable holocaust of Arab, Jewish and British lives. . . . No code of morals can justify the persecution of one people in an attempt to relieve the persecution of another. The cure for the eviction of Jews from Germany is not to be sought in the eviction of the Arabs from their homeland; and the relief of Jewish distress may not be accomplished at the cost of inflicting a corresponding distress upon an innocent and peaceful population."

Magnes instead offered a compromise he called "Union for Palestine," which included a union between Jews and Arabs within a binational Palestine, a union of Palestine, Transjordan, Syria, and Lebanon in an economic and political federation, and finally a union of this federation with an Anglo-American union that would work together in a post-World War II reconstruction. In Magnes's plan, Palestine as a binational state would provide for equal political rights and duties for both the Jewish and Arab nations, regardless of which was the majority and which the minority, and the larger federation would allow increased immigration of homeless Jews without altering the balance of power in the union. Jerusalem might become the federal headquarters or capital and thus would flourish again as a center of spiritual and intellectual exchange.[26]

Magnes spent the years until his death in 1948 arguing for his understanding of a binational state. He spent the last months of his life in Washington, lobbying the State Department against the United Nations resolution of 1947, partitioning Palestine into Jewish and Arab states, which he understood intuitively, and correctly, would lead to imminent war and a cycle of violence continuing for generations.

In the last few months of his life, Magnes met and worked with the, as yet, relatively unknown Hannah Arendt, who continued Magnes's work after his death. Arendt, who became known for her monumental study on European anti-Semitism and the rise of fascism, *The Origins of Totalitarianism* (1951), was a German philosopher who emigrated to France after Hitler's rise to power in 1933, and then emigrated to the United States in 1941. By the 1940s, she was, like Magnes, actively and perceptively engaged in a Zionism that supported a renewed Jewish presence in Palestine but opposed the establishment of a Jewish state.

After Magnes' death, just months after the partition of Palestine and the establishment of a Jewish state in 1948, Arendt wrote a perceptive and troubling essay "To Save the Jewish Homeland: There Is Still Time." According to Arendt, the declaration of statehood had polarized positions on both sides, as non-Zionist Jews were now diehard enthusiasts and moderate Palestinian Arabs were being forced to choose sides. Palestinian Jews and American Jews were essentially in agreement on the following propositions, propositions that Arendt felt were detrimental to the possibility of peace:

> The moment has now come to get everything or nothing, victory or death; Arab and Jewish claims are irreconcilable and only a military decision can settle the issue; the Arabs—all Arabs—are our enemies and we accept this fact; only outmoded liberals believe in compromises, only philistines believe in justice, and only schlemiels prefer truth and negotiation to propaganda and machine guns; Jewish experience in the last decades—or over the last centuries, or over the last two thousand years—has finally awakened us and taught us to look out for ourselves; this alone is reality, everything else is stupid sentimentality; everybody is against us, Great Britain is anti-Semitic, the United States is imperialist—but Russia might be our ally for a certain period because her interests happen to coincide with ours; yet in the final analysis we count upon nobody except ourselves; in sum—we are ready to go down fighting, and we will consider anybody who stands in our way a traitor and anything done to hinder us a stab in the back.[27]

Arendt saw this unanimity of opinion as ominous, though characteristic of our modern mass age. It tended to limit discussion and reduce social relationships to those of an "ant heap": "A unanimous public opinion tends to eliminate bodily those who differ, for mass unanimity is not the result of agreement, but an expression of fanaticism and hysteria. In contrast to agreement, unanimity does not stop at certain well-defined objects, but spreads like an infection into every related issue."[28]

The loyal opposition, so important to critical thought and politics, was in the process of being eliminated. For Arendt, the two great contributions of Jewish settlement, the kibbutz movement and Hebrew University, as well as the great precedent of cooperation between a European and a colonized people, were in danger of collapse. The advantage of the Jewish people in having no imperialist past to live down was also threatened; thus, their ability to act as a vanguard in international relations on a "small but valid scale" was being lost. Even if the Jews won the war and affirmed their claim to statehood, the unique possibilities and achievements of Zionism in Palestine would be destroyed. For Arendt, the society that would come into being would be something quite other than the dream of world Jewry. Jews would be victorious Jews, but they would also live surrounded by a resentful and combative Arab population, "secluded inside ever-threatened borders, absorbed with hysterical self-defense to a degree that would submerge all other interests and activities." The growth of a Jewish culture would cease to be the foremost concern, and the social experiments would ultimately be seen as utopian fantasies and be jettisoned. "Political thought would center around military strategy; economic development would be determined exclusively by the needs of war. And all this would be the fate of a nation that—no matter how many immigrants it could still absorb and how far it extended its boundaries." Jews would still remain a numerically small people, outnumbered by hostile neighbors.[29]

The ends of such an endeavor were clear to Arendt: degeneration into a warrior state with the political initiative in terrorist hands. The Jewish state could only be erected at the price of a Jewish homeland. Arendt closed her essay with the following propositions and hopes:

1. The real goal of the Jews in Palestine is the building up of a Jewish homeland. This goal must never be sacrificed to the pseudo-sovereignty of a Jewish state.

2. The independence of Palestine can be achieved only on a solid basis of Jewish-Arab cooperation. As long as Jewish and Arab leaders both claim that there is "no bridge" between Jews and Arabs the territory cannot be left to the political wisdom of its own inhabitants.

3. Elimination of all terrorist groups (and not agreements with them) and swift punishment of all terrorist deeds (and not merely protests against them) will be the only valid proof that the Jewish people in Palestine has recovered its sense of political reality and that Zionist leadership is again responsible enough to be trusted with the destinies of the Yishuv.

4. Immigration to Palestine, limited in numbers and in time, is the only "irreducible minimum" in Jewish politics.

5. Local self-government and mixed Jewish-Arab municipal
   and rural councils, on a small scale and as numerous as possible, are the only realistic political measures that can eventually lead to the political emancipation of Palestine. It is
   still not too late.[30]

Two years later, Arendt wrote of the non-nationalist tradition in
Zionism and of the danger of nationalism for small nations as lying in
military and economic dependency. To continue support from abroad,
Israel might find itself in the "unenviable position of being forced to create emergencies, that is, forced into a policy of aggressiveness and expansion." Arendt concluded, "The birth of a nation in the midst of our
century may be a great event; it certainly is a dangerous event."[31]

In Ahad Ha'am, Magnes, and Arendt, we have an analysis of the situation in Palestine that is both committed and generous. The desire of a
minority of the Jewish people for return to the land is bound more to culture and education and less to nationality and statehood. The Nazi years,
which Magnes observed from Palestine, and Arendt from within Europe,
intensified rather than diminished their desire to be connected with
international politics, culture, and religion, with the Palestinian Arabs,
and, indeed, with the Arab world. From their perspective, Jews were not
usurping the land or colonizing, if equality with Palestinian Arabs was
offered, struggled for, and achieved. They feared, a fear to some extent
realized today, that the achievement of a Jewish state would isolate the
Jews of Palestine in a ghettoized reality and mentality and, thus, lead to
a fortress Israel. If this happened, the hopes and dreams of the Jewish
return would dissipate into endless violence. Instead of a final break with
the ghetto, Israel would become a ghetto in continuity with the ghettos
of Europe.

What relevance does this have today, especially to the Holocaust
under whose influence Jews interpret much of contemporary reality?
That these ideas of a cultural and spiritual Zionism, of honest equality
with Palestinian Arabs, of a Jewish presence as part and parcel of the
Middle East—and the names identified with these ideas—are rarely
invoked by those who support or demur from Israeli policy shows how
narrow the contemporary discussion has become.

We might say that Israeli policy, since the foundation of the state, has
perforce narrowed the limits of discussion and dissent, lest a contemporary disaster overtake it, which is precisely what the early dissenters in
Zion predicted. Thus, Jewish spokespersons like Wiesel, Fackenheim,
and Greenberg have lost the vocabulary of such ideas, at least publicly.
These ideas are, in their truest sense, unmentionable.

But what if it is precisely this vocabulary from the past that can open Jews to a future beyond isolation and war, and, thus, beyond policies and understandings that are difficult, if not impossible, to defend? Could it be that once again Jews can reclaim clear reasoning on the issues that constrain them—clarity often exhibited by Ahad Ha'am, Magnes, and Arendt—rather than the labored, sometimes tortuous connections and justifications offered today in the name of the Holocaust and the state of Israel? Is there any possibility of committed thought beyond the categories of innocence and redemption?

The idea that Jews must at this point begin clarifying the issues of Holocaust and Israel is daunting. Fortunately, it need not be. In fact, a framework already exists for linking the early dissenters within the Zionist movement with those who oppose certain Israeli policies in the present; it only needs to be rediscovered.

As we shall see, dissent hardly ended with the creation of Israel, and the lessons of the Holocaust were intimately related to that dissent. If it is true that Jews have inherited the formative events of Holocaust and Israel, it is also true that a difficult and often painful dissent has accompanied these events and awaits a renewed hearing.

CHAPTER 4

A Tradition of Dissent

The idea of a Jewish homeland seems today, when considered at all, a faded memory of a distant utopian vision, given the reality of a Jewish state. Yet, as a symbol of dissent, as a cornerstone of a tradition of disparate voices, its power is formidable. In the twenty-first century it may become relevant again.

The non-nationalistic tradition of the Jewish people, as Hannah Arendt wrote of it in 1948, remains alive today, though transformed in language and outlook in response to more than five decades of Israeli statehood. The very titles of Arendt's essay, "To Save the Jewish Homeland: There Is Still Time," and of Roberta Strauss Feuerlicht's book, *The Fate of the Jews: A People Torn Between Israeli Power and Jewish Ethics*, are themselves testimony to a continuity that remains in the twenty-first century.

Many of those who have spoken of Israel's reversal from beacon to burden, over the years of statehood, have been ostracized from the Jewish community, excommunicated, as it were, as heretics. Non-Zionist and even anti-Zionist Jews, who were certainly a majority of the Jewish people earlier in the twentieth century and who may have a significant, albeit inarticulate, following today, have been stricken from Jewish history, erased from our inheritance.

Yet, many of their ideas are now found without attribution in contemporary Jewish dissent. To recall the vision of those ostracized and excommunicated, as well as their limitations, provides a line of continuity for dissent and, perhaps, a depth lacking in the discussion today.

The Internal Conflict over Zionism, 1937–1967

One of the major struggles over the adoption of Zionism as normative for the Jewish people can be found in the divisive debate within the Reform movement that took place in the 1940s and continued after the war with the development of the American Council for Judaism. In his book *Turning Point: Zionism and Reform Judaism*, Howard Greenstein traces the historical struggle for the acceptance of Zionism and a Jewish state within a movement that was founded in the nineteenth century as explicitly universalist in orientation.

Formed in the post-French Revolution era of liberalism and universalism, as was Zionism, the Reform movement took a different path: it sought to divest Judaism of its parochial features and to emphasize the moral principles around which all people could unite. As Greenstein portrays them, the early leaders of Reform Judaism in Germany, and later in America, were not only liberals intellectually, they boldly proclaimed the brotherhood and sisterhood of all men and women. "They joined their political liberalism to their spiritual liberalism and declared that Reform Judaism was not only a religion for the liberated mind of the new day, but it was now and forever anti-nationalist. Whereas traditional Judaism had temporarily suspended all laws depending upon residence in Israel for their fulfillment, Reform Judaism completely abrogated them. It rejected all laws pertaining to the priests and Levites and declared instead that all Jews were a 'kingdom of priests and a holy people' and that the obligations for moral purity applied to every Jew with equal responsibility."[1]

To accomplish this goal, Reform leaders eliminated all references to the exilic condition of the Jewish people or to a messiah who would restore world Jewry to the land of Israel. The nationalist period of Jewish life was regarded as a stage in the evolutionary development of Judaism, preparatory for the more universalistic mission among all peoples. Thus, the essence of Reform Judaism was that Jews constituted a religious community seeking to advance, with others, universal understanding and goodwill. Reform Jews were to be at home among the nations, wherever they lived.

In tracing the conflict between Zionism and Reform Judaism, it is important to recognize the degrees and kinds of opposition and support within the debate. For example, few Reform Jews objected to Jews going to Palestine to live as a creative embrace of Jewish language and culture. The overwhelming opposition was related to the establishment of an independent political Jewish state in Palestine. In the main, Reform Jews saw no need to create a Jewish home, as they were at home in America, a home fueled with the promise of democracy and prosperity.

As Greenstein articulates it, the clash was substantial. To the majority of early Reformers, Zionism was the antithesis of every principle they affirmed. The Pittsburgh Platform of 1885 looked toward a world where Jews would enjoy equal rights and privileges with other citizens in whatever nation they lived. On the one hand, Zionism held that Jews would be estranged wherever they lived until they had their own homeland. Reform Judaism, on the other hand, regarded nationalism as the cause of Jewish suffering. For Zionists, the essence of Jewish existence was the concept of peoplehood; for Reform Jews the essence of Jewish existence was faith and the conviction of a universal "mission" through which Jews would labor to achieve ideals of justice, brotherhood and peace. "Zionism emphasized the ethnic bonds that united all Jews and did not require any specific spiritual commitments;" Greenstein writes, "but in Reform Judaism the priorities were exactly the reverse: the spiritual ties transcended whatever other differences existed among Jews, and ethnic distinctions were among the least important or meaningful of all those differences. All Jews, in their view, were primarily "Americans of Mosaic persuasion."[2]

The ideological antithesis issued into a sustained political controversy, perhaps the most significant in the history of the Reform movement. It caused a crisis in the three major bodies of the movement—its seminary, the Hebrew Union College; its lay organization, the Union of American Hebrew Congregations; and its rabbinic arm, the Central Conference of American Rabbis (CCAR). The controversy threatened to split and undermine the movement itself. But, more than that, Zionism challenged Reform Judaism to reexamine its most basic suppositions: its optimism about the world in the face of two world wars and in relation to the Jewish people and the rise of Nazi Germany.[3]

What brought the controversy to a head was the passing of a platform, in an afternoon session with many rabbis absent, at the 1937 annual convention of the Central Conference of American Rabbis in Columbus, Ohio. Henceforth, it was known as the Columbus Platform and included the following:

> Judaism is the soul of which Israel is the body. Living in all parts of the world, Israel has been held together by the ties of a common history, and above all, by the heritage of faith. Though we recognize in the group loyalty of Jews who have become estranged from our religious tradition, a bond which still unites them with us, we maintain that it is by its religion and for its religion that the Jewish people has lived.

> In all lands where our people live, they assume and seek to share loyally the full duties and responsibilities of citizenship and to create seats of Jewish knowledge and religion. In the rehabilitation of Palestine, the land hallowed by memories and hopes, we behold the promise of renewed life for many of our brethren. We affirm the obligation of all Jewry to aid in its up-building as a Jewish homeland by endeavoring to

make it not only a haven of refuge for the oppressed but also a center of Jewish culture and spiritual life.[4]

Though by today's standards innocuous, this platform statement touched off bitter invective and political maneuvering. Coupled with the platform adopted in the 1942 convention of the CCAR in Cincinnati supporting the creation of a Jewish army in Palestine, this act was the turning point in the Reform movement and led to a particularly interesting confrontation when Congregation Beth Israel of Houston, Texas, passed a restatement of its own principles relating to membership the following year. In what is perhaps the last statement of classical Reform Judaism, Congregation Beth Israel promulgated in 1943 the following as principles for membership in their synagogue:

> We believe in the mission of Israel which is to witness to the Unity of God throughout the world and to pray and work for the establishment of the kingdom of truth, justice and peace among all men. Our watchword is "Hear, O Israel, The Lord Our God, the Lord is One." We accept it as our sacred duty to worship and to serve Him through prayer, righteous conduct and the study of our Holy Scriptures and glorious history.

> We are Jews by virtue of our acceptance of Judaism. We consider ourselves no longer a nation. We are a religious community, and neither pray for nor anticipate a return to Palestine nor a restoration of any of the laws concerning the Jewish state. We stand unequivocally for the separation of Church and State. Our religion is Judaism. Our nation is the United States of America. Our nationality is American.

> We believe in the coming of a Messianic Age and not in a personal Messiah. We recognize that it is our hallowed duty to speed the coming of the Brotherhood of Man under the Fatherhood of God, which is the Messianic ideal for which the righteous of all people work and pray.[5]

By the 1950s, the voices of Jewish dissent were quieted. The Reform movement made its peace with the fledgling state of Israel. The postwar reconstruction of Europe and the emerging Cold War diverted much of the intellectual and ideological energy of the community. Holocaust consciousness, at least as articulated publicly, lay in the future.

Yet, dissent continued with the *Jewish Newsletter*, which began publication in 1948 and was guided by William Zukerman (1885–1961), who was born in Russia and emigrated to the United States in 1909. His editorial board included, among others, distinguished Jews and non-Jews such as Roger Baldwin, Abraham Cronbach, Erich Fromm, Norman Thomas, Dwight MacDonald, and David Riesman.

In October 1949, Zukerman, in an essay entitled "Jews as Conquerors," began a series of editorials relating to the new Jewish condition of statehood and its effects on Jews in Israel and around the world. Zukerman refers to an essay by the Yiddish-American dramatist and story writer, David Pinsky. Living in Israel, surrounded by Jewish settlers who had taken over Palestinian Arab villages, homes, gardens, orchards, and fields, Pinsky asks the question of how Jews, after two thousand years of wandering and subjugation, comport themselves as victors and conquerors. According to Pinsky, most of the Jewish refugees occupy former Arab homes and villages "with the laughter of victors," regretting only the condition in which many of the former occupants left their homes.

Yet some, especially former refugees from Nazi Europe, felt uncomfortable, remembering their own experience of homelessness. Pinsky relates the story of one such refugee who occupied a home of a formerly well-to-do Arab family. When, one day, the children discovered a closet full of toys and began to play with them, the mother was suddenly struck by the thought that the children, whose toys these were now, were themselves exiled and homeless. Ordering the children to put the toys back in the closet, she began to brood. "What right had she and her family to occupy a house which does not belong to her? To use a garden and field which were taken by force from other people who ran away in a panic of war and are not permitted to return? Are she and her family not living on goods robbed from others? Is she not doing to the Arabs what the Nazis did to her and her family?"[6]

Two years later, Zukerman describes the visit of Joseph Shlossberg, a veteran American Jewish labor leader, to a Palestinian town recently occupied by the Israelis. Finding the Arabs confined to a "ghetto," Shlossberg writes that it is difficult to believe and make peace with this reality. "Jews who are now in Israel were just now in a ghetto themselves. In Eastern countries they are still segregated in ghettos. How can these ghetto people of yesterday introduce ghettos themselves?" Zukerman also records the words of the Jewish Israeli Nathan Chofshi on the tragedy of the Arab refugees. For Chofshi, whatever the political and other causes which have brought about this tragedy, the fact is that hundreds of thousands of people are suffering hunger, cold and disease. Among them are "small, innocent children who live in tents, in cold and heat, and do not even know why they are suffering," and grandfathers and grandmothers and "simple folk in general who never participated in the war on Israel and want only to be permitted to return to work their fields and workshops." "How can one remain indifferent in the face of such an awful tragedy?" Chofsi writes. "Have we no conscience? What did we use to say to non-Jews who remained indifferent to similar tragedies of the Jews?"[7]

Contemplating a call among some in Israel to transfer the Palestinian Arabs remaining in Israel to other Arab countries, Zukerman is outraged:

> For nothing could be more outrageous morally and more disastrous politically for Israel and for the Jewish people outside it, than such a shabby attempt on the part of Israel to get rid of its small Arab minority by a maneuver of "exchange" after having eliminated the majority through a common accident of war. Can any sane person reasonably believe that Israel could ever have real peace with her Arab neighbors after such an "exchange"? And what would be the position of Jewish minorities all over the world after an act of this kind? For two thousand years the Jewish people have lived among others as a minority, and by their very existence repudiated the lie that a country must consist only of one people. Now that they have established a state of their own, are they to create their own minority not only as second-class citizens but attempt to eliminate it altogether? Would not that be an open invitation to other states which, for one reason or another, do not want Jews in their midst, to follow the example set by Israel? And what about the morality of it all? In what way does an "Arab-rein" state differ from a "Juden-rein" state? It is terrible to contemplate the depths of moral degradation to which nationalism can lead even liberal-minded people in our age.[8]

In 1953, Zukerman wrote two essays concerning a recent Israeli reprisal attack in the Jordanian town of Quibya, which took the lives of more than sixty Arabs. Zukerman compared the massacre to the one in Deir Yassin in 1948, in which more than 100 Arabs were massacred in the early phase of the Israel's War of Independence; the fear of such events led in large part to the Arab exodus. Clearly there was a line of continuity, both in forcing the Arabs to flee and in keeping them from returning.

But there was also a great difference. The Deir Yassin massacre was carried out by Irgunist extremists, and a "cry of protest and pain arose from every Jewish heart in Israel." The government at that time dissociated itself from the crime and denounced it. Five years later, a similar crime was committed by the Israeli army. This time, the government took "semiofficial" responsibility for it, rather than repudiate or express moral outrage against it.

For Zukerman, the horror of the incident was the "alarming moral deterioration" in Israel; it showed how far Israel "had advanced on the road to militarization and reaction." What Israel needed now was humility, not a false moral superiority; repentance not self-righteousness. The massacre at Quibya reenforced Zuckerman's understanding of the changes in Jewish character brought on by deliberately avoiding facing the consequences of the rise of nationalism and its effects on Jews, as on most other people of our age. "Together with the normal emotions of love for wronged and persecuted people, it has awakened also the feeling of group selfishness and chauvinism and has unleashed the latent forces of cruelty from which the Jews are not exempt," Zukerman writes. "It has transformed the entire character of the people." But this is not a new manifestation. It began with the upsurge of nationalistic Zionism in the 1930s and increased dramatically during the Holocaust, when the "Irgunist terrorist movement sprang up in Palestine and was glorified and supported by American Jews."[9]

Five years later, in 1958, in an editorial titled "The Arab Refugees: Summary of a Tragedy," Zukerman wrote, in angry tones, of the ability of modern propaganda to "control minds, sway emotions and brutalize people" as demonstrated by the effect of "Zionist propaganda on the Arab refugees during the last decade." For Zukerman, black was turned into white, a "blatant lie into a truth, a grave social injustice into an act of justice glorified by thousands." It effectively turned "clever people with more than average intelligence into starry-eyed fools, believing everything they are told, and has converted kindly and gentle men and women with a strong sense of mercy into fanatics, insensible to the suffering of any people except their own." Zukerman was beside himself: "In no other way can this writer explain the many paradoxes which the Arab refugee problem has created in Jewish life."[10]

Victory and Occupation, 1967–1987

With the Israeli victory in the 1967 war, the possibilities and limitations of dissent shifted radically. The euphoria with which many Jews greeted the defeat of the Arab countries and the reunification of Jerusalem helped to create a consensus surrounding Israeli power and initiative, at the same time birthing a Holocaust theology that saw empowerment as the response to Jewish suffering. For many who were indifferent to the state, or even opposed it, the 1967 war represented a conversion experience.

At the same time, institutions that had arisen in the 1940s and 1950s to support Israel assumed a new power and authority. Dissenters in the previous decades (for example, those who argued for a binational state and the spiritual elements of education and culture), though often attacked by political Zionists, had a constituency from which to operate. In the aftermath of the war, that constituency diminished.

The debate also took place among public intellectuals, in print and at organizational conventions. After the 1967 war, however, the concept of Jewish statehood achieved a significance for Jewish leaders and the mass of Jews hitherto unknown. The institutional framework for promoting Israel began to operate with a power, an almost irrational power, that raised the cost of dissent to its highest level.

Though chastened, dissent continued. Just days after the conclusion of the 1967 war, I. F. Stone, social critic and political activist, wrote of the dangers of the complacency of military victory. In 1970, Michael Selzer, educator and political scientist, edited a book of essays titled *Zionism Reconsidered: The Rejection of Jewish Normalcy*, which included a historical survey of dissent relating to the state of Israel and had it published by a major publishing house. One year earlier, Noam Chomsky, professor of linguistics at MIT, who was to become a much-vilified Jewish intellectual, published what in retrospect can be seen as a highly balanced account of the tension and possibilities existing in the Middle East after the 1967 war.[11]

Chomsky argued that both Palestinians and Jews can make their case with a high degree of plausibility and persuasiveness. The Palestinian case is based on the premise that the "great powers imposed a European migration, a national home for the Jews, and finally a Jewish state, in cynical disregard of the wishes of the overwhelming majority of the population, innocent of any charge." The result: hundreds of thousands of Palestinian refugees in exile, while the "law of return" of the Jewish state confers citizenship, automatically, on any Jew who chooses to settle in their former homes. The Zionist case relies on the "aspirations of a people who suffered two millennia of exile and savage persecution culminating in the most fantastic outburst of collective insanity in human history, on the natural belief that a normal human existence will be possible only in a national home in the land to which they had never lost their ties, and on the extraordinary creativity and courage of those who made the desert bloom."

For Chomsky, the conflict between these claims is obvious, especially when raised to the level of a demand for survival, in that sense becoming an absolute demand. Each side sees itself as a genuine national liberation movement. To the Israelis, the 1948 war is the war of liberation. To the Palestinians, it is the war of conquest. This formulation leads to an unresolvable conflict.

And more, the exilic condition of the Palestinians is likely to take on the characteristics of the Zionist movement itself. For Chomsky, each Israeli victory, especially the victory in the 1967 war, is likely to strengthen Palestinian nationalism. Both Jews and Palestinians are locked into a "suicidal policy" with the ante constantly being pushed higher.

In Chomsky's view, the only way out is to create a democratic Palestine that preserves, for Jew and Palestinian, some degree of communal autonomy and national self-government, and where each people will have the right to participate in self-governing national institutions. Individuals will be free to live where they want, free from religious control, and free to define themselves as Jews, Palestinians, or something else, and to live accordingly. "People will be united by bonds other than their identification as Jews or Arabs (or lack of any such identification). This society in former Palestine should permit all Palestinians the right to return, along with Jews who wish to find their place in the national homeland. All oppressive or discriminatory practices should be condemned rather than reinforced. The society will not be a Jewish state or an Arab state, but rather a democratic multinational state."[12]

By 1983, in the second decade of Israeli occupation of the West Bank and Gaza, Chomsky was less optimistic than he had been in 1969. His book *The Fateful Triangle: The United States, Israel and the Palestinians*, written just after Israel's invasion of Lebanon, details the policies of occupation and the war in Lebanon in vivid and exhaustive detail. As in his earlier work, Chomsky begins with the framework "that Israeli Jews and Palestinian Arabs are human beings with human rights, equal rights; more specifically, they have essentially equal rights within the territory of former Palestine. Each group has a valid right to national self-determination in this territory. Furthermore, I will assume that the state of Israel within its pre-June 1967 borders had, and retains, whatever one regards as the valid rights of any state within the existing international system."

For Chomsky, those parties who accept these principles seek accommodation; those who do not accept these principles should be labeled rejectionists. The standard use of the term rejectionism—for the position of those who deny the right of the state of Israel to exist and as the term is applied to Palestinians, the Arab states, and critics (Jewish and non-Jewish) on the political left—needs now to be broadened. In Chomsky's words, "Unless we adopt the racist assumption that Jews have certain intrinsic rights that Arabs lack, the term 'rejectionism' should be extended beyond its standard usage to include also the position of those who deny the right of national self-determination to Palestinian Arabs, the community that constituted nine-tenths of the population at the time of the First World War, when Great Britain committed itself to the establishment of a 'national home for the Jewish people.'"

For Chomsky, the international consensus that emerged after the 1967 war seeks accommodation; the main barriers are not, as Israeli supporters suppose, the Palestinians and the Arab states, but Israel itself, backed by the United States. In Chomsky's view, U.S.-Israeli rejectionism has blocked the achievement of a viable and comprehensive settlement. With the occupation then in its second decade and the development of settlements in the West Bank and Gaza expanding, the discussion was urgent.

As it turns out, Chomsky was prophetic in his predictions. Already in 1983, Chomsky saw that if accommodationist policies did not replace the rejectionist policies of Israel and the United States, the struggle would move to a new phase, to forestall the "expulsion of a substantial part of the Arab population on some pretext, and conversion of Israel into a society on the South Africa model with some form of Bantustans."[13]

In the case of Israel, Chomsky finds the two major political parties in Israel, Labor and Likud, to be in fundamental agreement regarding the occupied territories: both are rejectionist as to any expression of Palestinian national rights west of the Jordan. The problem stated by both Labor and Likud is one of security, though, as Chomsky points out, the Palestinians have already "suffered the catastrophe that Israelis justly fear," that is, denial of the legitimacy of national rights and displacement.

But, for Chomsky, the motives of Israeli rejectionism are much deeper: the occupation of the West Bank and Gaza provides Israel with a substantial unorganized, cheap labor force, a controlled market for Israeli goods, and badly needed water. This accounts for the so-called Allon plan adopted in 1970, a plan that envisions the annexation of 30–40 percent of the West Bank, with the centers of dense Arab settlement to be excluded. Those areas are to remain either under Jordanian control or stateless, to avoid the "demographic problem" of absorbing too many non-Jews into a Jewish state.

For Chomsky, the Allon plan is designed to "enable Israel to maintain the advantages of the occupation while avoiding the problem of dealing with the domestic population." However, the Allon plan, submitted by the Labor minister Yigal Allon, is complemented by the Likud policy of extending sovereignty into the occupied territories as "a more subtle device, which allows Israel to take what it wants while containing the Arab population to even narrow ghettoes, seeking ways to remove at least the leadership and possibly much of the population, apart from those needed as the beasts of burden for Israeli society. Outright annexation would raise the problem of citizenship for the Arabs, while extension of sovereignty, while achieving the purposes of annexation, will not, as long as liberal opinion in the West is willing to tolerate the fraud."[14]

As described by Chomsky, the war in Lebanon was also a part of this rejectionism; its purpose was to continue the Israeli policy of dispersing Palestinian refugees and destroying Palestinian nationalism. Destruction of the Palestinian leadership and organizational structure would help suppress meaningful forms of Palestinian self-expression in the occupied territories and end Palestinian opposition to Israel's power in the international arena. This action was in accordance with Ariel Sharon's assumption that peace on the West Bank requires the destruction of the Palestinian presence in Lebanon, and it would also further Israel's policy of rejecting accommodation, a position that was becoming more and more difficult to uphold in the international arena.

The propaganda for and casualties of the Lebanese war were enormous. After the first months, it became increasingly clear that no matter what interpretation one gave to past Israeli-Arab wars, this one was less a defensive war than a bold act of aggression. Chomsky systematically debunks the myths of Israel's hesitant invasion and desire to avoid civilian casualties. Israel's "Peace for Galilee" was a war of precision bombing organized against an unarmed civilian population. The official Lebanese government casualty figures of nineteen thousand dead and over thirty thousand injured were, to Chomsky's mind, both horrific and too low.[15]

The most horrible symbol of the Lebanese war was the September 1982 massacre in the Palestinian refugee camps of Sabra and Shatila. Though actually carried out by Christian Phalange troops, it became clear that they operated under the close supervision and with the permission of the Israel Defense Forces (IDF). From Chomsky's point of view, Israel was culpable in the massacre, which may have left as many as two thousand dead. He analyzed the massacre in continuity with Deir Yassin and Quibya, the former atrocity involving Menachem Begin, the latter led by Ariel Sharon, the two architects and leading proponents of the Lebanese war.

Chomsky cites the Kahan Commission Report as it details that the "higher political and military echelons, in their entirety, expected that Phalangists would carry out massacres if they were admitted into Palestinian camps. Furthermore, they knew that these camps were undefended." Within a few hours after the Phalangists had entered the camp, clear evidence reached the command post several hundred meters away that massacres were taking place. Chomsky continues: "At the command post, the IDF and Phalange commanders and their staffs, including intelligence and liaison, were present and in constant contact. The IDF then provided illumination, and the next day, after receiving further corroboratory evidence that massacres were in process and that there was no resistance, sent the Phalange back into the camps, with tractors, which the IDF knew were being used to bury bodies in the mass grave."[16]

By 1983, Chomsky, as a prime carrier of the tradition of dissent between the miracle of 1967 and the horror of Sabra and Shatila and beyond, is joined by others who are both outraged by Israeli violence in Lebanon and surprised by it. This includes Roberta Strauss Feuerlicht and Earl Shorris and soon Jacobo Timerman, whose book-long essay on the Lebanon war discusses themes that Chomsky emphasizes and for which he, in the past, was so vilified: Jews are no longer innocent. Timerman also voices the intuitive linkage of Nazi Germany and Israeli power, found earlier in the 1950 editorials of William Zukerman.

Timerman, who was the victim of anti-Jewishness in Argentina and who, upon his release from prison, left for Israel, writes in regard to the Lebanese war, "In these past months I have left behind many illusions, some fantasies, several obsessions. But none of my convictions. Among all these things, there is one that shatters me beyond consolation. I have discovered in Jews a capacity for cruelty that I never believed possible. . . . A man walks among those ruins, carrying in his arms a child of ten. A group of men, women and children with their arms raised are under guard, and the expression on their faces, what their eyes say, is easily understood by almost any Jew. Yet we are forbidden to equate today's victims with yesterday's, for if this were permitted, the almost unavoidable conclusion would be that yesterday's crimes are today's."[17]

The arrest and conviction of the American Jew Jonathan Pollard in 1987 for spying for the Israeli government rekindled a discussion that Holocaust theologians had almost buried: the question of dual loyalty and the possibility that U.S. and Israeli foreign policy interests might at some points diverge or even be in opposition. Like the Bitburg affair to be discussed in chapter 5, the Pollard spy scandal tended to focus the energy of Jews in the United States, and indeed around the world, and crystallized trends in Jewish dissent.

At the time of the Pollard affair, Jacob Neusner, then professor of Judaic studies at Brown University, perhaps the best known non-Zionist in America, wrote a startling series of commentaries titled "The Real Promised Land Is America" and "It Isn't Light to the Gentiles or Even Bright for Most Jews." Originally published in the *Washington Post*, the pieces were also republished in the *International Herald Tribune*.

In these articles Neusner analyzed the achieved promise of America compared with the unrealized goals of Zionism. He begins his article with a provocative statement: "It is time to say that America is a better place to be a Jew than Jerusalem. If ever there was a Promised Land, Jewish Americans are living in it. In the United States, Jews have flourished, not alone in politics and the economy but in matters of art, culture and learning. Jews feel safe and secure in ways that they do not and cannot in the state of Israel. And they have found an authentically Jewish voice—their own voice—for their vision of themselves."

The warnings of Israelis, that Jews will disappear in the Diaspora through assimilation or have to leave for Israel because of anti-Jewishness, are for Neusner contradicted by the experience of Jews in America. On the contrary, Jewish commitment in America is flourishing, and anti-Jewishness is on the wane.

But what is behind the fears that Israelis express is even more problematic than the sociological mistake: that a free and open environment is destructive to Jewish culture and that Jews can maintain themselves only in segregated circumstances. "What I hear in the odd turning of ideology is that Jews cannot live in a free and open society, that Judaism requires the ghetto, and that freedom—an absolute good for everyone else—is bad for the Jews. What a remarkable judgment upon the human meaning of Judaism!"[18]

Neusner then reverses the question to inquire about the quality of Jewish life in Israel. If America has kept its promise to the Jews in America, has Israel kept its promises to Jews in Israel and around the world?

The answer, for Neusner, is clearly that it has not, either as a spiritual and educational center or even in the matter of Jewish independence and security. As to the former, Neusner exposes the "poorly kept secret" that Israeli scholarship is dull and boring and that, in the time since Martin Buber and Gershom Scholem (both born outside of Israel), Israel has not produced a single scholar in theology, philosophy, or history who is important outside of Israel.

Further, Israel is a client state dependent economically and militarily on the United States. Neusner concludes: "So much for being a Jew in the state of Israel. Here in the Diaspora we can be what we want, when we want—from nothing to everything, all the time or once in a while. Freedom is nice, too. And the United States really has become a free country for us Jews. For American Jews—Jewish Americans—the American dream has come true. I wonder how many Israelis think the Zionist one has come true, too."[19]

With this statement, we have come full circle in reviewing the activity and literature of dissent and have discerned what might be termed a tradition of dissent, the themes of which are important to identify.

First, from the beginning of this tradition, the question of Jewish interest has been foremost. Even the pioneers of a Jewish homeland were to some degree paternalistic toward Palestinian Arabs, an attitude perhaps inherent in what was at least partially a Western and colonialist adventure. And in fact, it was precisely within this framework that people like Ahad Ha'am, Magnes, Arendt, and others understood the challenge of cultural and spiritual Zionism, that is, to spark a rebirth of Jewish culture and creativity without consciously participating in the history of Western colonialism and imperialism or even appearing to do so. Though this could not be avoided completely, from the Jewish perspective, the intention was crucial to the project involved. The early critics of Zionism understood that a repetition of Western history vis-à-vis the Palestinian Arabs would place the Jews in that framework as well, either again as victims, or this time as conquerors. Power and nationality for its own sake was a blind alley that Jews had suffered within and sought to escape.

Second, if the early dissenters were idealists whose vision was overcome by Palestinian Arab intransigence and violence, as many claim today, they saw themselves as practical observers trying to implement that vision. In their collective wisdom, the Jewish people could not sustain or, over the long run, sponsor a revival of Jewish culture and spirituality built on the oppression of others. They recognized Palestinian rights (within a strategic framework, as some do today), and, beyond that recognition, they saw the possibility of peace with justice in the land. Though their main concern rested with the Jewish enterprise, they saw little possibility of or reason for separation of Jews and Arabs. To be sure, a measure of autonomy was crucial for both—and realizable within a framework of integration. The last thing that the early dissenters in Zion longed for was a re-ghettoization, with or without power to Jews.

Third, the non-Zionist and anti-Zionist Jews belong to the dissenting tradition as well and contribute what is, even in today's climate, the unmentionable: that most Jews were not and are not Zionists. As it turns out, the major discussion in Reform Judaism revolved less around Zionization, the issue of whether it was vital for Jewish people to live in Palestine (even the Columbus Platform upheld the legitimacy of Jews living in the Diaspora); rather, it concerns whether or not the Jewish people in the Diaspora will lend their hearts, religious belief, political strength, and financial resources to the growing Jewish community in Palestine.

Fourth, although the decision cost the Reformers little—few then went or since have gone to Israel itself—the battle is seen as a significant turning point in Jewish consciousness and commitment. Those who supported and those who opposed Zionism in this struggle understood, at some level, the stakes involved, for it meant the reorientation of Jewish self-consciousness and spirituality, and ultimately, the birth of a theology that undermined the essential tenets of Reform Judaism.

This was also true in the Zionist struggle within Orthodox Judaism, a movement founded, like Reform Judaism, in the nineteenth century, but that harkened to the witness and learning of the rabbis after the destruction of the Temple and loss of nationhood. Here again, the triumph of Zionism shifted the fundamental basis of Orthodox Judaism, which, like Reform Judaism, was non or even anti-nationalistic.[20]

Though the stakes were high, the argument in the early 1940s and, to some extent, in the 1950s revolved around potentialities rather than established history. The rise of Nazi Germany, the refugee problem that it generated, and the discovery, after the war, of the extent of mass death in the Holocaust provided the Zionist argument, however its objectives and methods are interpreted, with a fuel difficult to suppress. Thus, the level of naiveté about the actual events in Palestine, and later the state of Israel, was almost equal to the genuine horror of the atrocities that preceded it in Europe. Still, as shown by our following of Zukerman's editorials and the literature he uses to sustain his commentary, this naiveté was less widely shared or even accepted than one might expect. However, at this stage already, the level of argument is sinking and charges of anti-Jewishness and Jewish self-hatred are increasing. Invective rather than critical thought is triumphing.

With the trial of Adolf Eichmann in 1961 in Jerusalem and the Israeli victory of 1967, the consensus was formed and a new orthodoxy promulgated. Israel leaves its position on the periphery and moves to the center as the defining point of Jewish identification and faith. The innocence of Israel, Israel as redemptive, concepts that previously existed on the periphery of Jewish consciousness, are now beyond contention.

Or so it seems. In the assertiveness of Holocaust theology and in the anger vented on those who dissent, one sees more and more a defensive posture, as if to preempt the inevitable questions and suspicion. And here the question of Israel, which up until the 1967 war, to some extent, remained an internal discussion within the Jewish community, becomes a prominent public discussion involving the call for unqualified American support of Israel, a complete accounting for the theological components of Christian anti-Jewishness, and a projection of Jewish suffering as unique unto itself in scope and quality. Thus, dissent comes to be treated in the public arena as having consequences that go to the heart of the evolving American-Israeli alliance, the evolving ecumenical dialogue between Christians and Jews, and the interpretation (and the lesson) of the history of the twentieth century.

Nevertheless, it is inevitable that dissent also finds a public voice. As the public arena for Holocaust commentary expanded, so, too, did the arena of public dissent. In a sense, the triumph of Holocaust theology, which was articulated in theological language (albeit leaving unmentioned these two most disturbing qualities of occupation and unlimited power), establishes a new orthodoxy whose foundations lie in innocence and redemption.

Yet, Holocaust memory carries within itself the seeds of its own demise, as it becomes less and less possible to leave unmentioned or to defend the soon-to-be-challenged triumphant power of Israel. In retrospect, the heyday of Israel's power and the power of Holocaust theology is in the years 1967–82.

The dissent that emerged at the time of the Lebanese war brings many themes of the pre-1967 critique forward, even as it reaches a new level of strength and outrage. It is as if the dream of an empowered Israel has been fulfilled and turned into a nightmare. If Israel's other wars could be justified in terms of national defense, Lebanon could not. At the same time, it had become clear that the occupation of the West Bank and Gaza was hardly a temporary reality, but more and more an integral part of the daily ideological substance of Israeli life.

By the early 1980s, it could be stated unequivocally by dissenters that Israel, far from being innocent and beleaguered, was now an aggressor and a conqueror. The dire predictions of the early dissenters in Zion had been realized.

Jewish Responses to the First Palestinian Uprising, 1987–93

On January 23, 1988, a little more than a month after the Palestinian uprising had begun, Alexander Schindler, president of the Union of American Hebrew Congregations, sent a telegram to Chaim Herzog, president of the state of Israel. The telegram protested the policy of force, might, and beatings announced by Defense Minister Yitzhak Rabin just weeks before. His message read in part, "I am deeply troubled and pained in sending you this message, but I cannot be silent. The indiscriminate beating of Arabs, enunciated and implemented as Israel's new policy to quell the riots in Judea, Samaria and Gaza, is an offense to the Jewish spirit. It violates every principle of human decency. And it betrays the Zionist dream."

Two weeks before Schindler's telegram, Albert Vorspan, senior vice-president of the Union, recorded these thoughts in his diary: "Beyond any issue in recent years, American Jews are traumatized by events in Israel. This is the downside of the euphoric mood after the Six-Day War, when we felt ten feet tall. Now, suffering under the shame and stress of pictures of Israeli brutality televised nightly, we want to crawl into a hole. This is the price we pay for having made of Israel an icon—a surrogate faith, surrogate synagogue, surrogate God. Israel could not withstand our romantic idealization. Israel never asked us to turn it into a kidney machine to pump some Jewish blood into our moribund lives."[21]

Over the next months, *The New York Times* was inundated with messages of Jewish concern and anger published as op-ed pieces and paid for on that paper's advertising scale. In February 1988, four well-known Israeli writers—Yehuda Amichai, Amos Elon, Amos Oz, and A. B. Yehoshua—implored Jewish Americans to speak up against Israel's policy of occupation and its subsequent attempt to use military force to end an uprising whose only solution was political compromise. In March a half-page advertisement appeared, a statement signed by Jewish Israeli and American Jewish teachers, writers, and intellectuals under the heading "Israel Must End the Occupation." The statement reads:

> Out of deep concern for the character, the security and the future of the State of Israel, we, the undersigned, demand a reassessment of Israeli policy so that it may become possible to treat the fundamental causes of the recent violent unrest. It is impossible to ignore or deny

the connection between the latest escalation in the expression of hostility between Arabs and Jews and the political stalemate that has existed for twenty years. There can be no solution to the problem in which Israel finds herself so long as rule by force is exercised by Israel over the Arab populations of the occupied territories. To present the problem as merely a matter of the necessary use of force to restore order is an evasion of the core of the issue, as is the placing of responsibility for finding a solution upon the shoulders of the army, diverted from its proper task of national defense in order to quell the disturbances. We cannot and must not tolerate situations in which our young soldiers find themselves forced to open fire upon demonstrations of civilians, many of them mere youths. The refusal of the government of Israel to face up to the root causes is both immoral and futile. We call upon the government of Israel to take immediate steps towards political negotiation before the rapidly changing situation gets completely out of hand.[22]

At the same time, Arthur Hertzberg, former president of the American Jewish Congress and then professor of religion at Dartmouth College, began writing a series of articles for the *New York Review of Books*, beginning with "The Uprising" and ending with "An Open Letter to Elie Wiesel." A main theme of these essays is the seemingly intractable quality of the Israel-Palestine conflict, the futility of Israel's military reaction to the uprising, the coming end of American Jewish innocence regarding Israel, and finally, the illusion of Jewish unity regarding Israel.

In his first essay, written in January 1988, Hertzberg concludes on a somber note: "Everyone with whom I have talked in the past few years about the Middle East—and, at various times, I have met with leaders of all the different camps—agrees that stalemate leads to disaster, but no one seems to have summoned up the political will to say that a settlement can no longer be postponed. After each visit to the Middle East, I return more pessimistic. Prophets of gloom rarely like the words they utter: they feel compelled to describe a despairing vision in the hope that someone will act to prove them wrong."

Nine months later, in September, Hertzberg ends his essay with pleas for both sides to finally accept partition and, in furtherance thereof, the need for forgiveness:

The time is now past for pragmatic politics. The majority in Israel cannot even persuade itself that it is in its pragmatic interest to do business with the P.L.O. even as a way of curbing the intifada and avoiding the Palestinian ultra-nationalists and Muslim fundamentalists—as it once did business with Abdullah to avoid the Palestinian question. The leaders of the P.L.O. will probably look for ways of adopting a position that will not drive their extremists out, and thus the P.L.O. may avoid the issue of Israel's legitimacy. The turning point that came with Hussein's speech of July 31, leaving the Palestinians and the Israelis to work out their relationship directly with each other, demands nothing less than confronting fundamental issues between Israelis and Palestinians. It is an old Middle Eastern tradition that enemies do not end their quarrels with lawyers' negotiations; they have a Sulha, a publicly staged act of forgiveness in which they wipe out past angers and begin anew in mutual acceptance. Such a Sulha must precede the negotiation for the final enactment of partition, for without it there will not be passion enough among the moderates of both camps to create the necessary majorities for such a settlement, and the result will be ceaseless conflict between two nations fought with more and more dangerous weapons.[23]

In June, after months of virtual silence, Elie Wiesel wrote an op-ed piece for the *The New York Times*. Several months earlier, he had written a short note commemorating the Warsaw Ghetto uprising. The following paragraph from that earlier piece contains a veiled reference to the current situation: "Little did we know that in our own lifetime, pseudo-scholars would write books to deny that the greatest of Jewish tragedies ever took place. And that the Jewishness of the Jewish victims would be watered down and cheapened. And that the uniqueness of the Holocaust would be questioned. And that anti-Semitism would be clothed in anti-Zionism. And that vicious minds would dare to compare the state of Israel to Nazi Germany." However, his article "A Mideast Peace—Is It Impossible?" had a different tone. It was his first official statement on the uprising and told the story of his first trip to Israel since the uprising had begun.[24]

Wiesel records the Israeli military presence in Gaza and the "implacable plight of the tens of thousands of refugees who dwell in inhuman conditions nearby. Their suffering could be sensed everywhere, as if it had a life of its own." He spoke to Palestinians, whose aspirations were for a Palestinian state, and he spoke to Jewish Israeli soldiers about the possibility of reconciling the needs of security with Judaism's concept of humanism. Within the soldiers, Wiesel finds determination and sadness, hatred and sorrow. The televised images of the beating of prisoners, breaking of bones, and demolition of houses have taken their toll, and, in the world's eyes, Israel is taking the place of "America during Vietnam, France during Algeria and the Soviet Union during the Gulag."

Unfortunately, from Wiesel's perspective, many of these critics are being outdone by "some Jewish intellectuals who had never done anything for Israel but now shamelessly used their Jewishness to justify their attacks against Israel." Wiesel feels criticism is justified, but it often goes beyond the boundaries of the acceptable: "Israel is being presented as mostly blood-thirsty—and that is simply not true. In certain pro-Arab circles, the argument is even more vicious and ugly: Israel is being compared to Hitler's Germany, its policy to Nazism and the Palestinians of today to the Jews of yesterday. How are we to convince Israel's political adversaries that the Holocaust is beyond politics and beyond analogies?"

Wiesel understands the anger of Palestinians who have been denied self-determination and laments the fact that the territories had been "imposed on Israel in war." Contrary to opinions expressed by others, Wiesel feels that Israel has not lost its soul and that its soldiers are not sadists, but a realistic solution—Israeli security and Palestinian self-determination—escapes him. Right-wing fanatics who speak of transferring Palestinians to Jordan are, to Wiesel's mind, a disgrace, but the liberals ready to give up all the territories immediately—to whom are they going to give them? "As long as the P.L.O. remains a terrorist organization, as long as it has not given up on its goal of destroying Israel, why should Israel negotiate with its leaders? But then, if the P.L.O. is not an interlocutor, who could be? There must be, and are, moderate Palestinians. But many have been assassinated—not by Israelis." Wiesel concludes with a hope that harkens back to his visit to Jerusalem after the 1967 war, a six-day war that now has entered its third decade: "And yet, one must not lose hope. Somehow there must be a solution, acceptable to both sides, that would end a tragedy that generates such hatred. If extremists in both camps gain ground, all will suffer. I think of the Arab children whom I watched walking to school—and of the young Jewish soldiers with their tormented gaze. How long will joy be denied to all of them? More than ever, I would like to believe in miracles."[25]

Hertzberg's response to Wiesel's essay begins by recalling their initial meeting in the 1950s, after the publication of their first books, Wiesel's *Night* and his own *The Zionist Idea*. They spoke Yiddish together, reminiscing about their respective childhoods in Eastern Europe and their loss of family during the Holocaust. It is their common background that poses the first question: "We are, both of us, part of what is left of the Hasidic communities of your birthplace in Vishnitz and of mine in Lubaczow. What have we learned from the murder of our families? How must we live with their memory? You and I read and reread the Bible and Talmud: What do the sacred texts command us to think, to feel, and to do?"

Hertzberg finds Wiesel, like many others, deeply troubled by the cycle of violence between Israelis and Palestinians, at the same time being sympathetic to Palestinian aspirations of self-determination. Hertzberg agrees with Wiesel's appeal to Palestinians to halt the throwing of stones and start negotiations.

Yet, Hertzberg is astonished that Wiesel does not accompany such an assertion with an appeal to the Israelis to do anything at all—in particular to move away from the policy of repression and toward negotiation. In the statements that Hertzberg has seen, Wiesel seems to have avoided saying anything about the content of Israel's policies:

> In a speech in Washington on March 13, after saying that American Jews behave "appropriately" when they question actions by Israel, you quickly added that "I am afraid of splitting the Jewish community with regard to Israel." How appropriate are the questioners, in your view, if their questions "split" the community and thus, so you clearly imply, do harm to Israel? You have reduced the political questions before Israel to all-or-nothing choices. You condemn the "right-wing Israeli fanatics" for the "disgraceful suggestion" of transferring all the Palestinians immediately to Jordan; you are equally critical of "some liberals who are ready to give up all the territories immediately," for there is, in your view, no one to whom to give them. Thus you are able to throw up your hands, as you have done repeatedly in interviews and statements since January, and say, "What are we to do?"[26]

For Hertzberg, the effect of what Wiesel is saying is to support the conservative Likud Party line, that there are no options other than the present course. The discussion of Palestinian extremists, for example, so often cited by Likud and by Wiesel, ignores Jewish extremists who feel commanded to expel Muslims and Christians from Israel. "That a former chief of staff, Rafael Eitan, called the Palestinians 'drugged cockroaches' has, surely, not escaped your attention. I wonder whether you, and I, would have been silent if a Russian general had uttered a comparable slur about Jews demonstrating in Red Square. You know that the prime minister of Israel, Yitzhak Shamir, has been saying that he will not return a single inch of the West Bank to Arab sovereignty; he has thus stalled even the beginnings of negotiation."

Jewish dissidents, as well, are placed within the dangerous category of disloyal Jews betraying their people and endangering their survival. Wiesel's predilection is to accuse Jewish dissenters of endangering Jewish support of Israel, of using their Jewishness to defame Israel:

> You have found no place, so far, in any of your writings or statements that I have seen to suggest that there are Jews in the world who have been devoted to Israel for many years and who have expressed outrage at such actions as dynamiting houses in the Arab village of Beta. Some of these villagers had tried to protect a group of Jewish teenagers who were on a hike against stone throwers. In the melee a girl was shot by accident by one of the group's Jewish guards. The army then blew up

fourteen houses in the village. According to accounts in the Israeli press, this was done not to punish anyone who was guilty but to appease the angry hard-line settlers in the West Bank. You were not among those who said anything in public after this and all too many other incidents. Are such figures in the Diaspora as Sir Isaiah Berlin, Philip Klutznick, Henry Rosovsky, and the president of Yeshiva University, Rabbi Norman Lamm, and hundreds of others like them, who have spoken up in criticism of actions that they could not countenance, simply to be written off as people whose public statements endanger Jewish unity?[27]

To Wiesel's question of what Israel and the Jewish people are to do, Hertzberg's response is clear: accept the principle of partition and agree that Palestinians have a right to a territorial base for their national life. But to accept this principle and act upon it, Wiesel has to make a choice that represents an unequivocal break with the Likud party line and to accept the command to act justly, especially when "actions seem imprudent and embarrassing, and never to be silent, even to protect Jewish unity."

In short, Hertzberg calls on Wiesel to re-embrace the prophetic tradition with regard to Israel as he has so eloquently done with the Holocaust. To give aid to the "armed Zealots" in Israel today, even through silence, is to lead to disaster, as it has done in the past in Jewish history. Hertzberg concludes his letter with a plea to move beyond the illusion of Jewish unity and to speak prophetically. He recalls the early days of their relationship when they used to discuss Menachem Mendel of Kotsk, the tormented Hasid of the last century, who "once said that when the Evil One wants to destroy us, he tempts us not through our wicked desires but through our most virtuous inclinations; we do good deeds at the wrong time, with the wrong intensity, and in a setting in which they do devastating harm." Hertzberg concludes: "I fear that for all your love of Israel, you, in what you say, sometimes risk falling into the moral trap that Menachem Mendel described. You belong among those who speak the truth, even to Jewish power, and who do not look away because of real or invented Jewish weakness. We show the truest love of Israel and the Jewish people when we remind ourselves that, in strength or in weakness, we survive not by prudence and not by power, but through justice."[28]

As the Jewish debate heated up in the *The New York Times* and *The New York Review of Books*, two established and respected venues of public opinion, a major new voice arose that claimed to represent the rebirth of progressive Jewish concern in America. This voice took the form of the journal *Tikkun*—from the Hebrew phrase *tikkun olam*, meaning "to repair or mend the world"—with its editor, Michael Lerner, as its driving editorial force. Though publication began in 1986, with the uprising, *Tikkun* clarified its position and found its place in the public debate.

In the March/April 1988 issue, just four months after the beginning of the uprising, Michael Lerner wrote a lengthy editorial titled "The Occupation: Immoral and Stupid." Lerner begins the editorial with a passionate statement invoking Jewish memory of suffering as a command to halt the violence:

> The pain and sorrow many American Jews feel about Israel's policies on the West Bank and Gaza are rooted deep in our collective memory as a people. Israel's attempt to regain control of the refugee camps by denying food to hundreds of thousands of men, women and children, by raiding homes and dragging out their occupants in the middle of the night to stand for hours in the cold, by savagely beating a civilian population and breaking its bones—these activities are deplorable to any civilized human being. That they are done by a Jewish state is both tragic and inexcusable. We did not survive the gas chambers and crematoria so that we could become the oppressors of Gaza. The Israeli politicians who have led us into this morass are desecrating the legacy of Jewish history. If Jewish tradition has stood for anything, it has stood for the principle that justice must triumph over violence. For that reason, we typically have sided with the oppressed and have questioned the indiscriminate use of force. We, who love Israel, who remain proud Zionists, are outraged at the betrayal of this sacred legacy by small-minded Israeli politicians who feel more comfortable with the politics of repression than with the search for peace.[29]

The time for silence is over. Of the Israeli government Lerner demands: "Stop the beatings, stop the breaking of bones, stop the late-night raids on people's homes, stop the use of food as a weapon of war, stop pretending that you can respond to an entire people's agony with guns and blows and power. Publicly acknowledge that the Palestinians have the same right to national self-determination that we Jews have, and negotiate a solution with representatives of the Palestinians!"[30]

Though Lerner expressed his anger in moral terms, he was also willing to discuss the end of the occupation in terms of Israel's survival and the survival of the Jewish people. In Lerner's understanding, the occupation is immoral and, at the same time, self-defeating for the following reasons.

First, the longer the occupation continues, the angrier and more radical Palestinians become. As time goes on, Palestinians will be less inclined to negotiate a two-state solution, as they will come to regard a state on the West Bank and Gaza as a sellout of a fully liberated Palestine.

P.L.O. leadership, at this point willing to settle for such a state, will, as time goes on, be seen as "betrayers of the struggle." A more radical option relating to Islamic fundamentalism, which "makes it a sin to live in peace in Israel," may then be embraced.

Second, Palestinians within the pre-1967 borders are being drawn into the struggle for the first time since the creation of the state of Israel. Through participation in general strikes and protest demonstrations, the situation within Israel may come to resemble that in Beirut or Northern Ireland.

Third, a logic of domination will take hold, and, as the occupation continues, Israelis will necessarily become increasingly insensitive toward those they have so long dominated. Thus, Israeli politics will continue to move to the right, and dissenters in Israel will swell the already large emigration rate. Increasingly, the people who leave—scientific, technical, and professional personnel so important to the defense technology, economic strength, and intellectual creativity of the country—will do so because they find the political and moral situation of Israel unjustifiable.

Fourth, because of the silence of much of American Jewish leadership, the only voices articulating clear moral criticism have been those of "Israel's enemies."

According to Lerner, anti-Semites and anti-Zionists now have a clear field of attack because Israel's current policies give "credibility to the worst lies about Judaism." And the Jewish people also face criticism from those who are neither anti-Jewish nor anti-Zionist, but who are justifiably indignant toward a Jewish state that embodies a "viciousness and moral callousness" that they find abhorrent in other places of the world. Additionally, Lerner finds that the occupation threatens popular support for the state of Israel in the United States, within the American governmental and corporate structure, as well as among individual citizens. As the United States is Israel's lifeline, politically, militarily, and financially, loss of support would be a disaster. The images of Israelis "beating, teargassing, shooting and starving a civilian population" erode U.S. support for Israel.

Finally, the occupation threatens the survival of Judaism and the Jewish people in the Diaspora. Lerner cites the revival of interest in Judaism over the past two decades among Jewish Americans who find the values of American society lacking in depth and morally questionable. These Jews have turned to Judaism because of Judaism's emphasis on morality and transcendence, which stands in opposition to the logic of domination and empire that permeates American life. However, the occupation may reverse this trend as Jews dismiss this vision as pious moralizing without substance: "A Judaism that has lost its moral teeth and becomes an apologist for every Israeli policy, no matter what its moral context, is a Judaism that not only betrays the prophetic tradition, but also risks the adherence of the Jewish people."[31]

For Lerner, the moral and practical reasons for ending the occupation complement the religious reasons. The continuing occupation puts Jewish supporters of Israel in an agonizing dilemma: either reject its policy of occupation or reject the central teachings of Judaism. Here, Lerner refers to the Exodus tradition, the commands relating to treatment of the stranger, and the wisdom of the Torah, which asks Jews to resist the pattern of oppressing others as Jews were once oppressed.

Hence, the period of wandering in the desert—to let the mentality of slavery die off and the acceptance of God's command of moral responsibility enter the land. According to Lerner, God's voice here is demanding: "There is no right to the Land of Israel if Jews oppress the ger (stranger), the widow, the orphan, or any other group that is powerless." The liberating message of Passover insists that the logic of domination can be broken, and therefore, in the present, we must resist the tendency to justify Israeli policy in relation to past Jewish suffering.

Though Lerner cannot justify the Israeli occupation and the attendant violence, he also cannot ignore the aspects of Jewish history that may lead to the brutality of Israeli soldiers in the face of the Palestinian uprising:

> The rage that these soldiers exhibit when they beat civilians they suspect have been involved in rock-throwing may be understood, in part, as a response to the two thousand years during which the world systematically denied their right to exist as a people, a denial that culminated with extermination in gas chambers and crematoria. This oppression occurred not only in Europe; many Jews also had to flee Arab lands after hundreds of years of oppression and de-legitimation. This same process of de-legitimation has been further perpetuated by the Arab states in their refusal to relocate Palestinian refugees in 1948, in their insistence that these refugees stay in camps in Gaza and the West Bank, and in their failure to follow the lead of other countries that resettled much larger refugee populations, such as Pakistan's resettlement of nearly ten million Moslems after the struggle for Indian independence. This conduct by the Arab states was a loud proclamation: "You Jews don't really exist for us. Your presence here is temporary. We don't have to resettle the Palestinians or deal with this problem because you will soon be gone."

Thus, Lerner has strong words for Palestinians as well: "So we say to the Palestinians: stop the rock-throwing, stop the talk of violently overthrowing Israel, reject the rejectionists, and publicly proclaim your willingness to live in peace with Israel. Begin to talk publicly about peaceful coexistence. You will not be granted genuine self-determination until you allay the legitimate fears of many Israelis that you are still committed to destroying Israel."[32]

What is the solution to the crisis of Israel and the Palestinians? For Lerner, it is a demilitarized and politically neutral Palestinian state in the West Bank and Gaza, guaranteed by the United States and the Soviet Union and coupled with Israel's right to intervene to prevent the introduction of tanks, heavy artillery, or airplanes. A unified force comprising the United States, the Soviet Union, and Israel will be established to protect the new Palestinian state from attack by foreign powers, be they Arab or others, and the United States and Israel will join in a collective security pact guaranteeing American support if Israel is attacked. Palestinians will police their own factions who seek to continue the struggle against Israel and renounce all claims to the rest of Palestine. After an agreed-upon period of peaceful coexistence, Israel and Palestine will enter into an economic confederation.

Lerner ends with a call to action, for the crisis in Israel is a "moment of truth for all of us. It should be considered with the deepest seriousness and with the full understanding that the choices we make now may have consequences that reverberate for centuries to come."[33]

Beyond the writings of Diaspora Jews, Israel was experiencing its own new level of dissent. Simple demonstrations begun to protest the Lebanon war seemed less and less effective. In January 1988, a group calling itself the Twenty-first Year was established in Tel Aviv as an umbrella group of activists, working in different sections of Israel "to confront the various elements of Israeli society and consciousness which allowed the continuation of the occupation." Its founding document, "Covenant for the Struggle Against Occupation," was signed by over one thousand Israelis, including writers Yoram Keriuk and David Schutz, poets Yosef Sharon and Harold Shimel, and academics Amos Funkenstein, Ruth Garrison, and Paul Mendes-Flohr.

The covenant called for moving beyond protest to resistance and refusing any longer to "collaborate with the occupation." The occupation, existing for more than half of Israel's existence as a state, has infiltrated cultural and individual life and, thus, has to be rooted out bit by bit. If the presence of the occupation is total, the struggle against occupation had to be total as well:

> The occupation has become an insidious fact of our lives; its presence has not been confined to the occupied territories; it is, alas, among and within us and its destructive effects are in evidence in every aspect of our lives:

The Israel Defense Forces and the conception of our national security are subordinated to the dictates of the occupation.

The Israeli economy benefits from the blatant exploitation of Palestinian labor; it has developed a distorted colonialist structure.

The educational system is based on a double message: while promoting "democratic values," it condones a repressive regime which controls the lives of disenfranchised subjects.

The Hebrew language has undergone a process of contamination. It has been harnessed to the imperatives of the occupation. It has been called upon to provide a misleadingly benign vocabulary to anesthetize the repression and flagrant violations of human rights.

Because the occupation encompasses all aspects of Israeli life, resistance has to take the form of practical steps:

We shall not abandon our national symbols to the distorting interpretation of the occupation. We shall not participate in any celebration, ceremony, or symbolic occasion held in the territories under occupation or in one which lends it legitimation in any way whatsoever.

We shall not collaborate with the exploitation of Palestinian labor taking place under the sponsorship of the occupation. We shall publicize and boycott institutions, places of entertainment and the products of companies whose Palestinian employees are denied human dignity and decent working conditions.

We shall not tolerate the willful ill-treatment of Palestinians which has become rampant within Israel proper. We shall act to stop such conduct; we shall expose each incident of this sort and take all legal measures to eradicate it.

We shall not stand by while the Palestinians in the occupied territories are subjected to coercion, humiliation, and physical maltreatment through measures such as collective punishment, banishment, arrest without trial, torture, beatings and daily harassment.

We shall not obey any military command ordering us to take part in acts of repression or policing in the occupied territories.[34]

Oslo, the Assassination of Yitzhak Rabin and Beyond, 1993–98

The ongoing struggle in Israel/Palestine has a series of benchmarks, sometimes forgotten in ensuing years. One such benchmark was the assassination of Yitzhak Rabin in 1995 and the electoral defeat of Shimon Peres in June 1996. After the initial euphoria accompanying the signing of the Oslo Accords in 1993, Rabin's assassination forced the crisis in Israel and Palestine to reemerge in the consciousness of the world community.

In fact, the situation had a paradoxical quality over the Oslo years, for as the climate for peace improved dramatically, the economic and political situation of the Palestinians progressively deteriorated. The original idea of the accords was to begin with Palestinian self-government in Jericho and Gaza. Yet, the peace process, so heralded in the world press and welcomed by political and religious leaders, had been one of Palestinian surrender to a victorious Israel.

Certainly the Palestinians recognized the Oslo agreements as a surrender—the ultimate renunciation of vast areas of land that made up a pre-1948 unified Palestine—but with the hope that over time the agreements would be expanded. The hope was for a peace dividend, which would come as the two peoples came to know and appreciate one another. Feeling more secure and benefitting economically and politically from the improved situation, the Israelis would understand that new compromises are essential to a shared future between Jews and Palestinians. These new understandings included sharing Jerusalem, dismantling many of the Jewish settlements, and the recognition and empowerment of a Palestinian state.

The Palestinian surrender was a "negotiated surrender," one that saw the negotiations as a process necessary within the context of the Israeli-Palestinian conflict of the past century. A negotiated surrender is a political decision and a tool; it is a way of working within a situation of unequal power.

Sometimes, a negotiated surrender is the only viable way of preserving the possibility of a renewed struggle for equality and justice. If the very presence of a people on the land is threatened, if the economic and political situation deteriorates to the point where it is impossible to continue to preserve, reproduce, and recreate the culture of a people, then the refusal to surrender may represent a principle which will have no redress. In this situation, a negotiated surrender is itself a form of resistance, a strategy that places survival before pride, possibility before the difficulty of compromise.

At the same time, a negotiated surrender places faith in the power which has brought a people to the brink of disaster. It is a strange combination and a precarious one at that; Palestinians could only surrender on a negotiated basis, and the basis for their ability to surrender was a political decision that a moral appeal could be made to the political leadership of Israel, to acknowledge their victory and begin a process of reconciliation.

With the power configuration so unequal, the negotiated surrender could only be made within the understanding that there is something in Jewish history and culture that recognizes the Palestinians as a people with their own dignity and aspirations. The Jewish recognition of the dignity of the Palestinian "other" would affect the political calculations of the Israeli state vis-à-vis the aspirations of the Palestinian people. Hence, a new relationship would evolve over time.

The bitter arguments within the Palestinian community over this negotiated surrender illustrated the risk that Yassir Arafat and his advisors took in signing the Oslo agreements. For what could justify confidence in Israel, a state which forced the Palestinian people into exile, refused their return, humiliated them in their various uprisings, and even denied their essential claim to peoplehood and nationality?

Indeed, some Palestinian intellectuals, like Edward Said, saw ignorance, stupidity and corruption—even betrayal—in a leadership that signed such a surrender. How could a leadership which had witnessed a disciplined and relentless Israeli power believe that such a surrender would be seen as anything but a weakness to be exploited to its fullest? Would this surrender provide cover for the completion of the plan to permanently displace and conquer the Palestinian people?

To add insult to injury for the Palestinians, the agreement was signed with Yitzhak Rabin, one of the architects of Israel and who, in various decades since the founding of the state, was instrumental in the displacement and humiliation of the Palestinian people. Had the Palestinian leadership living outside the land lost touch with reality by believing somehow that this very same state and political leadership would change their minds and hearts and translate that change into political realities? Would Israel, after decades of creating facts on the ground, change those facts, that is, move from a position of exclusion to inclusion, exclusivity to mutuality, a singular ownership of the land to a sharing of the land between two peoples?

Clearly, Rabin's policy of strength and peace did not change the facts on the ground, which Rabin had helped establish earlier in his career. The redeployment and withdrawal of troops in parts of Gaza and parts of the West Bank simply affirmed a long-standing Labor party policy of seeking maximum land for Jews while leaving Palestinian population centers outside of Jewish control, or, to put it more accurately, outside Jewish life. Rabin, as with the Labor party in general, always favored a strict separation of Jew and Palestinian, and the Oslo accords ratified that understanding.

For Rabin, the possibility of more land for Israel came up against the hard reality of Palestinian demographics; to incorporate Palestinian population centers alters the fundamental Zionist enterprise of which he was a primary architect. Incorporating millions of Palestinians into Israel effectively makes the state of Israel into the state of Israel/Palestine.

As we have seen, there were those within the Jewish community who affirmed Zionism and the Diaspora, and among them some who affirmed an empowered Jewish community in Palestine alongside an empowered Arab community. In general terms, these Jewish intellectuals, rabbis, and activists supported a "home" for Jews, that is an enhanced and structured Jewish community in Palestine, rather than an exclusive, religiously defined state.

When Rabin spoke on the White House lawn in September 1993, he invoked the ethical ideals of Jewish history as communicated by the prophets, the Jewish liturgy of destruction as it comes down through the ages, with special reference to the Holocaust, the ancient Jewish messianic yearnings found in the Hebrew Bible, and the liturgical prayers developed in an exile of over two thousand years. What else merits the attention paid to Israel, and why do Jewish leaders think themselves so important to merit such attention, if not this broader vision of importance beyond politics and time?

From Rabin's perspective, that the Jews warrant such attention is obvious, in light of the role played by Jews throughout history. Even the desire for normality is couched in the messianic language of Judaism—of Deuteronomy and Ecclesiastes—as when Rabin asserted the desire of Jews and Palestinians to build homes, to bequeath those homes to their children, to affirm the proper seasons when it is proper to make war and to make peace, a time to kill and a time to love.[35]

To recall these sensibilities—the Diaspora vision of the traditional Orthodox, the homeland vision of Magnes, Buber, and Arendt, and what might be termed the "secular-religious" sensibility of the founders of the state, including Rabin—is to help understand the present configuration of Jewish discourse regarding the future of Israel. For if Rabin is seen as battling and losing to the right-wing vision of the religiously devout, they should be seen as involved in their own enterprise of religious history and the struggle to embrace, balance, deflect, and even bury aspects of their own inheritance.

Rabin battled the transformed Diaspora Orthodox position, which often appears today as a militant settler Judaism, but he also struggled against a homeland and secularized Diaspora mentality, which has resurfaced, albeit in different forms and on the periphery of contemporary Jewish thought. In this sense, Rabin is one of the last of the founders to hold the highest office in the land; he is also one of the last to have lived within the internal struggle of Jewish culture and intellect over the formation of the state and its relation to Jewish history.

Rabin left an ambivalent legacy. From the perspective of Jewish history, Rabin will be remembered by some as having laid the foundation of independence, strength, and an energetic secular social democracy. Other Jews will remember him as a secular Jew who fought for the state, but erred in his vision of Jewish faith and history. For these Jews, lacking this ultimate commitment, Rabin faltered at the end, attempting to cede areas of the Land of Israel to the enemy. In his denial of the religious nature of Jewish life, Rabin was willing to settle for a political empowerment that violated God's will and law. In doing this, he became a traitor to the Jewish people. Still other Jews will see Rabin as upholding rhetorical aspects of the Jewish tradition of justice and peace, while violating that tradition in his use of power.

Rabin spoke of the biblical notions of justice *and* also ordered the breaking of Palestinian bones during the Palestinian uprising; Peres, as Rabin's successor, spoke even more eloquently of a new Middle East *and* did not hesitate to bomb villages and civilians in a pre-election show of strength in 1996, seeking to insure his election as prime minister. From the Palestinian perspective, both men were as flawed as the enterprise of state building itself. Though they spoke from the heights of Jewish history, and in eloquent language, Palestinians experienced the reigns of both Rabin and Peres as reigns of destruction and death. In fact, the rhetoric of Rabin and Peres are part of the Palestinian predicament, as it covers over the policies of expropriation and death which define the Palestinian experience of Jewish ethics in the past century.

Yet, at the same time, both Rabin and Peres crossed boundaries, which has changed the relationship between Jew and Palestinian forever. Much of this change is seen in the realm of the symbolic: the reluctant handshake of Rabin and Arafat and then, in their subsequent meetings, the evolution of a more cordial, even respectful relationship. It was also realistic, as Rabin came to understand Arafat's role within the context of the Palestinian struggle. When negotiations were brought to a standstill by the assassination of Rabin, Arafat, with the permission of Peres, journeyed to Tel Aviv to console Leah Rabin. Arafat's presence in Israel and in the home of the slain prime minister—with photographs published around the world—was even more powerful a symbolic gesture than their initial handshake.

It was as if the cycle of dislocation and destruction, so identified with these two men, had come to an end, or, at least, the potential was there for an ending. The assassination of Rabin and the perilous quality of

Arafat's own survival brought a profoundly human touch to a conflict rife with ideological posturing. In the end, both Rabin and Arafat recognized each other as adversaries and as representatives of their peoples, for decades involved in war and now seeking to resolve the dispute that many on both sides saw as intractable. The opening of Leah Rabin's home to Arafat and Arafat's offer of praise and sympathy for the slain prime minister raised the possibility of a mutual recognition well beyond the details of the accords themselves.

In this evolving relationship and recognition, nurtured and carried on by Shimon Peres, a hope was born that the negotiated surrender would bear fruit in the future, even as the immediate situation of the Palestinians deteriorated. The symbolism of the evolving relationship among Rabin, Peres, and Arafat touched off heated debates in both communities about motives, substance, and hope for a future beyond the present.

In the Jewish world, anxieties and hope co-mingled. The militaristic strain of Jewish life, which seeks the complete defeat of the Palestinians and the expansion of Israel, intensified, as did the liberal strain, which hopes for a resolution of the conflict by way of Israeli security and some sense of justice for the Palestinians.

The militaristic and liberal camps are both diverse and centered; the Likud and Labor parties represent these camps in a politics fraught with an intensive, almost obsessive, concern. Both camps recognized that decisions could set the course for Israel over the next decades, if not forever. One path sees Israel as perpetually embattled, on the defense, expanding, and with an historic and religious mandate. The other path sees Israel as a limited state, secure within the framework of peace, a Jewish state fulfilling its destiny by providing a place for Jews to live in harmony with their neighbors.

Yet, there are other strains of thought and commitment that haunt both camps, even without their verbal articulation or recognized and structured following. The question of the mission of Israel with regard to the Jewish people and Jewish history, and the question of the meaning of Palestinians to that history in their displacement and empowerment, infused the debate with a passion which ultimately led to the assassination of Rabin and the defeat of Peres. The militaristic and the liberal strains recognized this foundational debate, even as the party platforms and the policies motivating Labor and Likud actions denied these differences. The initial dislocation of Palestinians was carried out by Labor, not Likud, as were the settlement policies that provided the foundation of Israel. Rabin fought in the 1948 war, commanded the Israeli military in its sweeping victory in the 1967 war, and sought to crush the Palestinian uprising in 1987. Could the difference between Labor and Likud be so great as to justify this emotion and anger?

On election day, when Peres's lead shifted to Benjamin Netanyahu, Leah Rabin threatened to pack her bags and leave Israel for good. An Israel led by Netanyahu was unrecognizable to her as the Israel her husband lived and died for. Was there such a profound difference in thought and policy between Peres and Netanyahu, or for that matter between her slain husband and the new prime minister? How could the welcome of Arafat into her home be seen in light of her refusal to accept any form of condolence from Netanyahu? Was all of this simply a personal animus toward the man she blamed for helping create the climate for her husband's assassination?

Leah Rabin's meeting with Arafat has a double significance. Perhaps she came to understand Arafat's insistence on Palestinian rights and accepted Palestinians as a people intimately involved in a Jewish future of peace and prosperity. To her, Netanyahu represented the politics of a past, which no longer has an emergency situation—the birth and defense of the state—to justify it. For Leah Rabin, Netanyahu's politics of might and hate continued a cycle her husband had hoped to end.

What Rabin and Peres ultimately represent, and what is perhaps their ultimate contribution to Jewish history, is the realization that the mobilization and militarization of Jewish consciousness cannot be pursued forever and, while perhaps necessary at certain points in history, can cripple and distort Jewish culture and ethics if carried beyond the need for self-defense. Clearly they were guilty of this offence themselves, but ultimately, when faced with the "other" in a personal and secure setting, they recognized the limitations of these policies. In short, a current in Jewish history and tradition precluded the normalization of unlimited power against a defeated foe.

Both Rabin and Peres helped create a catastrophe for the Palestinian people, but something in Jewish culture and life prevented that victory from being celebrated without remorse and, ultimately, without some kind of reconciliation. At least with their leadership, the Palestinian surrender seemed to bode an outcome which generations later might celebrate as the decisive moment for sharing the land of Israel/Palestine.

Yitzhak Rabin's assassin, Yigail Amir, tried to forestall the movement toward the end of the era of Auschwitz. As it had for Baruch Goldstein, who, a year before Rabin's assassination murdered dozens of Palestinian Muslims as they were at prayer, the sense that a solidarity could be extended to Palestinians threatened the Holocaust worldview Amir embraced and in which he felt at home.

Even the first tentative steps toward a restoration of the ordinary were seen as fundamental betrayals of the commanding voice of Auschwitz. Political compromise violated the boundaries of Auschwitz, as both Goldstein and Amir felt Palestinians to be the new Nazis. The era of Auschwitz, in their view, had to continue, lest Jews fall into a lethargy that would allow the actual Auschwitz to be reconstructed. Continuing the era of Auschwitz is equated with following the will of God, whose renewed voice can be heard in the Jewish settlements that spearhead the reclamation of the greater land of Israel.

Still, if only for a moment, the facing of the "other"—the new "other" of Jewish history—was recognized as a rendezvous with Jewish history. Such a facing of the "other" should be seen, in the context of the Holocaust and the 1967 war, as the possibility of ending an era of history as well. The handshake on the White House lawn represented the possibility of ending a cycle of suffering and violence, which Jews have both endured and perpetrated. When Rabin spoke of ending that cycle, one felt an opening toward a responsibility grounded in history and hope.

Responses to the Second Palestinian Uprising— 2000 and Beyond

By 1999, when Ehud Barak became prime minister, the hopeful years of Oslo were behind us. Benjamin Netanyahu was always opposed to the Oslo accords; he refused to even implement the minimum requirements of the accord. Barak came to office with a sense of urgency as, in his mind, the time to settle the Israeli-Palestinian conflict finally had come. Yet, his understandings of that settlement betrayed a lack of understanding. Over the years, the very landscape of the West Bank had changed, perhaps irrevocably, through a sustained, almost omnipresent grid of settlements filled with hundreds of thousands of Jewish settlers. By 2000, Ariel Sharon had become prime minister with even more dire consequences. The second Palestinian uprising had begun.

If the positive response to the hope of Oslo had faded only to be replaced by the mourning of a slain prime minster, the Jewish responses to the failure of Barak and Sharon moved beyond hope and lament and concentrated instead on a detailed analysis of the settlement policies and the development of a new form of Judaism.

As has often been the case in Israeli history, security concerns that Israel was too small to defend itself were used to argue for expansion. The Old City of Jerusalem was, for most Israelis, non-negotiable from the moment Israeli forces entered the ancient walls. Could such a symbol of Jewish history ever be returned?

The forces of religious zeal were thus unleashed within a broader spectrum of war, occupation and state policies of consolidation and expansion. To see the subsequent decades of Israeli history only, or even primarily, within the context of Jewish fundamentalism is to miss the larger story. The combination of politics, ideology and religion that intersect in the expanded Israel require a broader conceptual understanding than Jewish fundamentalism.

It was at this time that Michael Lerner suggested "Settler Judaism" as this framework, precisely because it encompasses the diverse aspects of Israeli and American Jewish life that have led to the present impasse. Settler Judaism brings together the radical right, religious fundamentalism, and liberal politics into a coherent, if unexpected, framework of overt and covert sensibilities that increasingly define Israeli and American Jewry.[36]

To analyze Settler Judaism, four elements are important: 1) the settlements themselves, who formed them and who lives within them; 2) what Barak and others call the "generous offer" of "concessions to the Palestinians" at Camp David in the summer of 2000 as a way of demonstrating the continuing involvement of the Israeli government in the settlement process; 3) Sharon's proposal for the final settlement of the Israeli-Palestinian question; and 4) the campaign by major Jewish organizations to silence dissent with regard to these policies during the Palestinian uprising.

According to Avishai Margalit, the Schulman Professor of Philosophy at the Hebrew University in Jerusalem, with respect to the Jewish settlements, the West Bank is divided into three parts or three long strips of land. The first strip of settlements was established in the Jordan Valley. Comprised of fifteen settlements, these were set up after the 1967 war and just before the war of October 1973. These settlements were developed by traditional Labor Zionist settlement institutions—the Kibbutz and Moshav movements.

The second strip, further west in the Jordan Valley, was pioneered by Gush Emunim—Bloc of the Faithful. These settlements were a form of resistance to the 1967 Allon Plan, a plan that sought to avoid settlements near Palestinian population centers in the West Bank. For Gush Emunim, not settling near these centers meant conceding these areas in any future agreements. Interestingly, these religious settlements had many and diverse allies: those identified with the political right, including Menachem Begin, Yitzhak Shamir and Ariel Sharon—but also those identified with liberal politics, such as Shimon Peres and Moshe Dayan. Both conservative and liberal politicians wanted to destroy the Allon Plan and share joint control over the entire West Bank with Jordan.

Most settlers live in the third strip, closest to the pre-1967 border of Israel. Three types of settlers can be identified here: those seeking a better quality of life, the economically needy, and those who are both economically needy and ultra-Orthodox.

As Margalit points out: "What the Palestinians find most worrying is the increase of over fifty percent in the number of housing units as well as the settler population since the Oslo agreements of September 1993."

Indeed, since 1993, Israeli statistics show an increase of the settler population by about 8 percent per year, rising from 116,000 in the West Bank and Gaza to over 200,000 settlers at the beginning of the second intifada in September 2000. If you can add the number of Jews who live in areas of Jerusalem annexed after the 1967 war, then the number of settlers increases by another 210,000 Jewish Israelis.[37]

Barak's "generous offer" has been more often asserted than analyzed. It is instructive to see Barak's offer within a continuity of Israeli policy since 1967. In a paper delivered at the Center for International Studies at the University of Delaware, Sara Roy, Research Associate at the Center for Middle East Studies at Harvard University, offered the following analysis, which I paraphrase. By the time of the Camp David Summit in July 2000, there were several processes taking place simultaneously:

- The continuing confiscation of Arab lands in the West Bank and Gaza.

- The accelerated expansion of existing Israeli settlements and the construction of new settlements on recently confiscated lands.

- The near doubling of the settler population to 200,000 in ten years, a population that is hostile and armed, with freedom of movement and the privileges of Israeli citizenship.

- The division of the West Bank and Gaza Strip into enclaves disconnected from each other by territories under the control of Israel, a direct result of the terms of the Oslo agreements.

- The paving of 250 miles of bypass roads onto confiscated lands that run north-south and east-west. This created a grid that further bisects and encircles Palestinian areas, producing the 227 enclaves referred to by Amnesty International.

- The institutionalization of closure policy, which restricts and at times totally prohibits the movement of Arab people and goods. This closure policy locks Palestinians into the enclave structure created by the Oslo accords and makes difficult, if not impossible, a functioning Palestinian economy.

- The construction of hundreds of checkpoints and barricades throughout the West Bank designed to control and further restrict the movement of Palestinians.

Roy continues: "Barak's 2000 budget allocated $6.5 million for the construction of bypass roads, $30 million for settlement expansion, and $51 million for the confiscation of Palestinian lands among other categories. According to the Israeli group, Peace Now, the Barak administration issued permits for the construction of 3,575 new settlement homes, and earmarked $500 million for settlements in its 2001 budget. According to official data from Israel's housing ministry, Barak's government began construction of 1,943 housing units in the West Bank and Gaza in 2000, the largest number in any year since 1992. During the final quarter of 2000, as the Al-Aksa Intifada intensified, the Barak government began work on 954 housing units alone, up from 368 during the last quarter of 1999."[38]

As for the Camp David proposals of Barak in the summer of 2000, Roy concludes that they lacked the following crucial elements: contiguous territory, defined and functional borders, political and economic sovereignty and basic Palestinian national rights. Barak's offer was less than generous; it was a thinly disguised continuation and consolidation, in a permanent way, of the Israeli occupation of Jerusalem and the West Bank. For Roy, the problem began far before Barak, as occupation was the structural and policy cornerstone of the Oslo accords.

As devastating as Roy's political and economic analysis of the Barak record and proposal, is her eyewitness account of the devastation of the Palestinian territories in the middle of the uprising. She compared it with the celebratory mood she found in a previous visit, soon after the Oslo accords were signed in 1993: "The images are very different now. . . . During the six years of the previous uprising, 18,000 Palestinians were injured. In the first four months since the current uprising began, over 11,000 Palestinians have been injured. The Palestinian landscape has withered, wrenched of hope, suffused in rage, and devoid of childhood. During my visit to Gaza and the West Bank, I saw hundreds of acres of razed agricultural land—destroyed orchards and irrigation systems, and felled trees, some hundreds of years old—fertile land made desolate by army bulldozers. I saw residential apartment buildings, now charred and vacant, that had been attacked by Israeli tanks and Apache helicopters, parts of their sides ripped out, their inhabitants dead or displaced. I visited camp homes whose walls, ceilings and furniture were riddled with bullet holes."

As for the people, Roy saw a marked difference in their demeanor and their expectations: "Children no longer asked me for chocolate but for food, and they showed me their collection of bullets while their mothers brought out shopping bags filled with shrapnel they had collected in and around their homes. An elderly man in one of the camp shelters I visited broke down in tears, unable to breathe from the rage he felt as he described the attack on his family. His wife took me to their bedroom whose outer wall faces an Israeli settlement and Israeli outpost nearby. 'The only reason we are alive,' she told me, 'is that we were sleeping on the floor at the time they began shooting.' Their bedroom wall has twelve bullet holes in it and their closet has two."[39]

Rather than departing in a fundamental way, Sharon continued Barak's sensibility as prime minister. As reported in the *The New York Times*, Sharon's understanding of a settlement between Israel and the Palestinians conforms to his earlier sensibilities and the consensus of previous Israeli administrations. In fact, Sharon seeks to implement, as a final settlement with the Palestinians, the map of an expanded Israel that he, with others, helped to create.

That map is intriguing. According to the *Times*, Sharon wants to retain West Bank land in two security zones. These zones would comprise two north to south strips that would "bracket Palestinian areas like the sides of a ladder."

The western zone, whose width would be three to six miles, would parallel that edge of the West Bank, the same area where Sharon oversaw the building of settlements over twenty years ago. The second zone would run through the rift valley, just west of the Jordan River. This second zone, facing Jordan and, beyond it, Iraq, would be nine to twelve miles wide. Between the security zones would run Israeli roads that the *Times* article refers to as the "rungs of the ladder." According to the *Times*, the effect of the completed ladder would be the following: "This Israeli security system would not only consume swaths of land Mr. Arafat expects to govern, it would also wall off separate areas of the Palestinian state.[40]

Ron Pundak, an architect of the 1993 Oslo peace accords, voices the alarm of Palestinians: "The fear is that the idea behind an Israeli interim agreement is to create facts on the ground, and transform the interim into the permanent." Yet, Pundak's fear betrays a naiveté: these are the facts on the ground that have been built over the years through agreements, uprisings, and truces. Negotiating future agreements would have to roll back in a significant way Israel's "advance." What power is there to force such a roll back?[41]

The American Jewish establishment, with minor exceptions, seeks to protect Israel from the negative images resulting from the Palestinian resistance to these facts and from the Israeli repression of that resistance. With the beginning of the Palestinian uprising in 2000, American Jewish groups paid for full-page statements in major newspapers around the United States. These statements called for Jewish unity and unqualified support of the State of Israel.

An example of these statements appeared in the *Times*. The text read as follows: "Be heard. You could sit home and worry silently about 'the situation.' Or you could stand together with Israel and make your voice heard. Come to the SOLIDARITY RALLY FOR ISRAEL." With the slogan "ISRAEL NOW and Forever," the statement had the following co-sponsors: United Jewish Communities, Federations of North America, UJA–Federation of New York, Conference of Presidents of Major Jewish Organizations; Jewish Community Relations Council of New York, Jewish Council for Public Affairs, Central Conference of American Rabbis; Jewish Reconstruction Federation, Rabbinical Assembly, Rabbinical Council of America, Union of American Hebrew Congregations, Union of Orthodox Jewish Congregations of America and the United Synagogues of Conservative Judaism. Not surprisingly, the honorary chairman of the event was Elie Wiesel.[42]

At a similar rally in October 2000, more than a month into the uprising, Wiesel addressed his remarks to President Clinton. Stating that Jews stood by Israel in the present crisis "imposed on her" by the "intransigence" of Yassir Arafat, Wiesel identified himself as one who rejects "hatred and fanaticism." For Wiesel, those who consider peace as the "noblest of efforts" have no choice but to finally recognize that Arafat is "ignorant, devious and unworthy of trust." After all, Arafat has rejected the "unprecedented generous territorial concessions" offered by Barak. "I accuse him of being morally weak, politically shortsighted and an obstacle to peace," Wiesel said. "I accuse him of murdering the hopes of an entire generation. His and ours."

What is interesting in Wiesel's remarks is that which he does not say or that to which he makes no reference. He makes no reference to the map of Israel/Palestine. In Wiesel's narrative, settlements do not exist, nor do bypass roads or security zones that in Barak's plan continued to exist, and in fact, are consolidated in the final plan. Wiesel's narrative does mention the Jewish attachment to Jerusalem, except in a way that again mystifies its existence rather than explains its politicized nature. "Under Israel's sovereignty, Christians, Jews and Muslims alike could pray without fear in Jerusalem," Wiesel asserts. Jerusalem is "our capital," the center of Jewish history. Wiesel continued: "A Jew may be far from Jerusalem, but not without Jerusalem. Though a Jew may not live in Jerusalem, Jerusalem lives inside of him."[43]

Mention is made of neither the attempt to force Palestinians to leave Jerusalem, nor of the overall policies of remaking Jerusalem, especially the Old City, in Jewish and Israeli ways. The strong and equally claimed attachment of Palestinians and Islam to Jerusalem goes without mention. The possibility of Israel and Palestine claiming Jerusalem as a joint capital, a possibility envisioned by Palestinians and more than a few Jews, inside and outside of Israel, is similarly unmentioned.

During the uprising, the tradition of dissent continued, and when, in 2003, the Israel astronaut, Ilan Ramon, circled the earth in the ill-fated Colombia space shuttle, Gideon Levy, an Israeli journalist, wrote about the contradictions of the initial Israeli celebration of space flight and the daily travails of Palestinians, caused by Israel's occupation.

As the first Israeli astronaut took off into space, tens of thousands of Palestinians, among them sick people, children and elderly people, tried to get from their villages to a nearby city. As Ramon's satellite entered its orbit around the earth, they straggled through the mud and the rain, trying to break through the dirt barriers that seal off their villages, in an effort to get to work, to the doctor or to a shop. It is difficult to know what went through their minds when they heard about the soaring Israeli success. Perhaps someone among them recalled the bitter comfort of Said al Nahas al Mishtaal, the hero of Emile Habibi's novel "The Optimist:" "And now the moon is closer to us than the fig tree, whose fruit is late in ripening in our bereaved village." As the Israeli media were busy whipping to a frenzy the national carnival that accompanied the launch ("Fly, Ramon, cut through the skies," "A great step for Israel," "Touching the sky"), they made no mention, as usual, of the travails of those who only want to move around a bit here on earth. The festival surrounding the launch of Colonel Ilan Ramon into space only demonstrated acutely the gap that exists all the time between false enchantments and the cruel reality from which most Israelis turn their gaze. More than ever before, the Israelis' ignoring of the Palestinians' suffering is reaching dimensions that are difficult to comprehend. Here, their existence is remembered only when they come to spread death. The only Palestinian still talked about is the suicide bomber, the only children mentioned are "terrorist children." Not poverty-stricken children, not orphaned children, not children whose homes were demolished before their very eyes, and not children whose fathers were taken, humiliated, in the dead of night, to detention without trial, and did not return sometimes for months and years. In most newspapers and electronic media, there is no mention any more of the curfew, closure, poverty and suffering. The election campaign is not concerned with it. One hour's drive away from all this, many Israelis continue to go about their daily lives, which have hardly been disrupted in the last two years. Even those who suffer, and they are increasing, concentrate only on their own hardships. In Tel Aviv the restaurants and cafes are crowded while Jenin is dying.[44]

CHAPTER 5

Toward an Inclusive Liturgy of Destruction

During the years of the first Palestinian uprising, Israel Shahak, survivor of the Bergen-Belsen concentration camp and then professor of organic chemistry at the Hebrew University in Jerusalem, as well as chairman of the Israeli League for Human and Civil Rights, began to translate eyewitness testimony and articles in the Hebrew press, testifying to the brutality of the occupation. In his first collection, "Atrocities as a Method," Shahak compared the brutality of Israeli soldiers with that of the Nazis, whose butchery he himself experienced.

> It should be clear to everybody who reads this collection of testimonies, that the systematic use of the atrocities, which in their intensity and the special intention to humiliate are Nazi-like and should be compared to the analogous German Nazi methods, is intentional and in fact constitutes the Israeli method for ruling the Palestinians. There cannot be any doubt in my opinion that those Nazi-like methods, in whose effectiveness the stupid Israeli Army top command reposes a blind faith, have been devised by "experts," in this case by the Israeli "Arabists" together with the military psychologists. There should be also no doubt that those Nazi-like horrors can and probably will become worse, if not stopped from outside, and their use can lead to actual genocide, whether by a "transfer" or by an extermination. Indeed this is one of my reasons for assembling this collection: to show that the actual genocide of the Palestinians in the territories is now possible, since those Israeli soldiers and officers who have committed the outrages recorded here are capable of anything and everything, and will consider that they are only carrying out their orders.[1]

The stories of torture and humiliation were many and included bringing naked prisoners to open fields for "death parades," tying suspects to electricity poles for hours and harassing them with guard dogs, use of the "banana method," in which a person's hands are caught from behind and tied to their feet, so that a person's body is contorted into the form of a banana, and the "Jesus method" where prisoners are placed in the position of a cross, their hands tied up as to be stretched out to both sides, and finally, the almost standard practice of beating fathers in the presence of their children.

One soldier who testified at a hearing, on the methods of containing the uprising, said of a Palestinian they arrested and had beaten: "It was a beating for the hell of it. The man did not resist. We began to beat him at once. We hit his feet, his shoulders, and perhaps his head." The soldiers' commanding officer then spoke: "We were very nervous because of the incident. We found relief in beating him and in getting ecstatic about it. We kept beating him mindlessly."[2]

A victim of a second atrocity, a Palestinian who worked as a correspondent for the East Jerusalem-based daily, *Al Fajr*, related the following story. "The Givati brigade soldiers forced me to stand on all fours, to bray, and to behave as if I were a donkey. This lasted half an hour, during which time they beat me all over my body with clubs and electric wires. . . . When I told them I was a journalist cooperating with Israeli journalists, they laughed and replied, 'That's nice, because beating journalists is what we particularly like.' At one point, one of the soldiers took away my eyeglasses, saying 'From now on you will be a blind donkey,' whereupon he smashed the eyeglasses with his feet. I begged for his mercy but he kept hitting me saying 'You understand nothing but force.'"[3]

It is this theme of humiliation that permeates almost the entire corpus of writing regarding the Israeli reaction to the uprising, and the humiliation of the Palestinian people reminded some Jews at least of their own humiliation at the hands of others, including the Nazis. Thus, the Nazi analogy was being made by Jews intuitively, almost instinctively, and being made by those who, because of their own previous suffering, might be expected to avoid such comparisons. Coinciding with this theme of humiliation is the theme of refusal—the signatories to the Convenant, and the soldiers in Yesh Gvul who refused, out of conscience, to serve duty on the West Bank and Gaza.

Merged with the dissenting themes of humiliation and refusal is the theme of solidarity. Here, the destinies of Jews and Palestinians are seen as tied together, as if that solidarity might represent the mutual liberation of both peoples. This solidarity includes Jews working against the occupation inside Israel's 1967 borders, like the Women in Black, who every week gather in Jerusalem wearing mourners' clothes as a gesture of solidarity with the beaten and dead of the Palestinian community, and Jews working directly with Palestinians, sharing legal skills, medical supplies, and other intellectual and physical materials needed by the Palestinian movement.[4]

Where did these themes of humiliation, refusal and solidarity come from? Where were they leading? Could they be understood simply as a political response to power and suffering? Or did they respond to a deeper strain of compassion and justice within the Jewish tradition now in danger of being lost?

Important, here, is a fascinating and important book, *Against the Apocalypse: Responses to Catastrophe in Modern Jewish Culture*. In this book, David Roskies, a professor at Jewish Theological Seminary, examines the history of the Jewish people through its various responses to destruction.

What Roskies finds is a people with a remarkable ability to reclaim ancient Jewish archetypes and, therefore, to create meaning within suffering and death. "The greater the catastrophe, the more the Jews have recalled the ancient archetypes," Roskies writes.

This was true in the ghettos of Eastern Europe where the archetypes of destruction came alive in the minds of both the common people and the intellectual: the burning of the Temple (the sacred center), the death of the martyr (the sacred person), and the pogrom (the destruction of the holy community). The walls and barbed wire that separated Jews from the non-Jewish population paradoxically helped to bring some of the internal boundaries down. "The elite were brought closer to the masses, the assimilated closer to the committed, the secular closer to the religious, Yiddish closer to Hebrew. The modernists became, despite their long battles against it, part of the literature of consolation. With the ghetto's intellectuals moving closer to the people, the writers could use the polylingualism of Jewish eastern Europe to restore, conceptually and socially, the idea of a Jewish nation, which was the penultimate consolation for the ultimate destruction. And a literature that was for centuries retrospective (including prophecies 'after the fact') became increasingly prophetic—so that, in fact, "analogies could be used at last not for consolation but for action, including uprisings."[5]

The scribes of the ghetto wrote as an act of faith and, in fact, participated in and transformed the "liturgy of destruction" that the Jewish people had articulated over the millennia. Though overwhelmingly secular in background and outlook, the ghetto writings continually referred to religious themes. Yitzhak Katzenelson, a secular poet, organized a public reading of the Bible on the day the Warsaw Ghetto was sealed, though this was to demonstrate a continuity of history as a people rather than belief in God. However, when it came to the Psalms, Katzenelson rejected them as too placid a form of response to catastrophe. At the same time Hillel Zeitlin, for years a modern religious existentialist, began translating the Psalms into Yiddish, and, when his ghetto tenement was blockaded, Zeitlin arrived at the roundup point for deportation dressed in prayer shawl and *tefillin*.[6]

We have here, in its most difficult articulation, memory as a form of resistance: the refusal to cut oneself off from one's own people, while at the same time speaking to the world in cries of anguish. Roskies concludes that to understand the collective response of the Jewish people during the Holocaust, one must look to the writers, "who, because they shared the same fate and were intimately involved in all facets of the people's Armageddon, were able to transmute the screams into a new and terrible scripture."[7]

This power—the use of the archetypes of destruction in a time of crisis as a way of affirming Jewish commitment—continues after the Holocaust in the empowerment of the Jewish people. Some Jews relate directly to preserving the memory of the Holocaust as a day of liturgical remembrance, and to this end, Yom HaShoah has gained a place in the official liturgical cycle of the Jewish people.

In synagogues around the world, but also in special ceremonies of public and governmental remembrance in the United States and Israel, Yom HaShoah is the time to recall the untold sufferings of the Jewish people, as a sign both of respect for those who perished and of hope for the continuation of the people beyond the tragedy of the Holocaust.

In the United States, for example, the chairperson of the U.S. Holocaust Memorial Council and often the president of the United States deliver speeches on the Holocaust, and at the state level, governors and senators participate publicly as well. Ceremonies include survivors and clergy, both Jewish and non-Jewish, and the music of the ghettos and camps is often sung. In Israel, the president or prime minister participates in a nighttime ceremony at Yad VaShem as part of a national commemoration. During the day, all work, traffic, and broadcasts cease at 11:00 A.M., when a long whistle blast is heard throughout Israel, heralding a moment of national silence.

Bitburg and the Messianic

It is not surprising that two of the strongest and most articulate proponents of Yom HaShoah are Irving Greenberg and Elie Wiesel. As we have seen, for both, the path of destruction points to the path of redemption in Israel; therefore, Greenberg suggests contributions to the United Jewish Appeal, the central fundraiser for Israel, as an appropriate form of remembrance.

The announcement of Ronald Reagan's proposed visit to the military cemetery in Bitburg, Germany, in the spring of 1985, and the consequent furor surrounding the visit exemplifies the public quality of this liturgy of destruction.

Initially planned as a gesture of reconciliation between the American and German nations, whose armed forces opposed each other in World War II, and as a final act of normalization between countries who are now staunch allies, the event touched the nerves of American army veterans, U.S. political figures, and, of course, most specifically, the Jewish community.

The visit to Bitburg became even more controversial when it was discovered that along with ordinary German soldiers, members of the infamous Waffen SS were also buried there. This, coupled with Reagan's remarks, which seemed to equate the German soldiers and the victims of those soldiers, including the Jewish victims, as well as his initial decision not to visit the Dachau or Bergen-Belsen concentration camp sites, raised the gathering protest to a storm.

President Reagan and Chancellor Kohl's desire to, in a sense, close the chapter on World War II did just the opposite, opening old wounds and spurring new divisions. And it became the most prominent, widespread, and, paradoxically perhaps, one of the last public displays of the Jewish liturgy of destruction.

Prominent among the commentators on the event were Irving Greenberg and Elie Wiesel; Greenberg, because of his place in the ongoing development of Holocaust theology, and Wiesel, because of his national prominence and the coincidental timing of his acceptance of the Congressional Gold Medal of Achievement awarded by Reagan at the White House in a nationally televised ceremony. Greenberg's writings and Wiesel's acceptance speech demonstrate both their depth of feeling and some of the complexities involved in criticizing, in public, a president who, while betraying a deeply held trust in relation to the memory of the dead, fervently supported Israel.

In an essay titled "Some Lessons from Bitburg," Greenberg began by reflecting, sometimes angrily, on the reception of Holocaust memorials in the Jewish community itself. Some weeks before Bitburg, the *Baltimore Jewish Times* ran a story taking issue with the emphasis given to the Holocaust in contemporary Jewish life, with one person quoted as finding the hundred-million-dollar fund-raising campaign for a national Holocaust memorial to be an "obscenity."

Greenberg also cites the difficulties in the 1950s and 1960s, for thinkers like Wiesel and Fackenheim, in establishing the Holocaust as central to Jewish life. Often, they were attacked and vilified. For Greenberg, to criticize commemoration of the Holocaust today as excessive is to continue that denial and to accomplish what Reagan's visit to Bitburg did: equate German soldiers and their victims, make similar war and genocide. It also represents, in Greenberg's mind, confusion about

the reasons for a Holocaust memorial, "the fact that Holocaust commemoration is not a focus on death but a goad and entry into reaffirma-
tion of life and ethics."

For Greenberg, the primary message of the Holocaust commemora-
tions is that true reconciliation comes through repentance and remembrance and is necessary to prevent recurrence: "Repentance is the key to
overcoming the evils of the past. When people recognize injustice, they
can correct the wrongdoing and the conditions that lead to it. Memory
leads to higher levels of responsibility and morality and reduces the
anguish of the feeling that the dead may have died in vain. Repentance
has liberated many Christians from past stereotyping and hatred of Jews,
thus transforming Christianity into a true gospel of love—which it seeks
to be. Repentance has liberated many Germans from the sins of the Nazi
past. Those that resist are themselves implicated in the past, or give aid
and comfort to those who still identify with those days and those evil
forces in the German nation and soul."

Having disagreed vehemently with Reagan's decision to visit Bitburg,
and hoping that Holocaust commemoration would one day, through
affiliation with a United States agency, become part of the ebb and flow
of American public life, Greenberg cautions against too harsh a judgment
on Ronald Reagan. Citing Reagan's record in commemorating the
Holocaust in the White House, his service as honorary chair of the campaign to create a national Holocaust memorial, and his ongoing support
of Israel—"the single most powerful Jewish commitment that the
Holocaust shall not recur"—Greenberg pleads for American Jews not to
falsify the overall record of one who supports Jewish interests.[8]

In a nationally televised speech, with Reagan sitting by his side, Elie
Wiesel accepted his congressional award with a somber realism. Forty
years earlier, Wiesel, as a young man, had awakened "an orphan in an
orphaned world." The Jews were alone, and forty-two years before, on
the same date as the speech he was giving, the Warsaw Ghetto had risen
in arms to fight the Nazis—and they, too, were alone. "The leaders of the
free world, Mr. President, knew everything and did so little, or at least
nothing specifically, to save Jewish children from death. . . . One million
Jewish children perished. If I spent my entire life reciting their names, I
would die before finishing the task."

What had Wiesel learned over the past forty years? The perils of language and of silence; that neutrality, when human lives and dignity are at
stake, is a sin; that the Holocaust was a "unique and uniquely Jewish
event," albeit with universal implications, and that suffering confers no
privileges. "And this is why survivors, of whom you spoke, Mr. President,
have tried to teach their contemporaries how to build on ruins, how to
invent hope in a world that offers none, how to proclaim faith to a gen-

eration that has seen it shamed and mutilated. And I believe, we believe, that memory is the answer, perhaps the only answer."

Along with these lessons learned, Wiesel also expressed gratitude to America, whose army liberated the death camps, whose doors opened to survivors as haven and refuge, and whose support of Israel was ongoing. And Wiesel expressed gratitude for Israel: "We are eternally grateful to Israel for existing. We needed Israel in 1948 as we need it now." Then, he concluded with words that have a liturgical cadence:

> May I, Mr. President, if it's possible at all, implore you to do something else, to find a way, to find another way, another site? That place, Mr. President, is not your place. Your place is with the victims of the SS.
>
> Oh, we know there are political and strategic reasons, but this issue, as all issues related to that awesome event, transcends politics and diplomacy.
>
> The issue here is not politics, but good and evil. And we must never confuse them.
>
> For I have seen the SS at work. And I have seen their victims. They were my friends. They were my parents.
>
> Mr. President, there was a degree of suffering and loneliness in the concentration camps that defies imagination. Cut off from the world with no refuge anywhere, sons watched helplessly their fathers being beaten to death. Mothers watched their children die of hunger. And then there was Mengele and his selections. Terror, fear, isolation, torture, gas chambers, flames, flames rising to the heavens.[9]

For Greenberg and Wiesel, the liturgy of destruction is retrospective and future-oriented, representing the Holocaust and Israel. Here the ghetto pleas are placed before the public by affluent and honored men representing a community that has survived and now flourishes. But the memory, the internalized landscape of sufferings, remains, and Wiesel's words, especially, are meant to transport his listeners to another day and time.

In fact, we see both Wiesel and Greenberg living in two worlds, one vanished, the other, the present world, interpreted within that framework. The liturgy is a Jewish one, but with an invitation, almost a summons, for non-Jews to enter as well. However, beneath the rhetoric is a haunting lament that the true sense of suffering is slipping away and that the platform for such liturgies will one day be gone. The pledge of loyalty to the United States and to Reagan is a symbol of a liturgy that can be publicly enacted, and yet, ultimately is beholden to those who are distant in history and faith.

The return to the land of Israel has similarly brought to contemporary consciousness ancient Jewish themes, and this can be most clearly seen in the various forms of religious renewal now commonplace. Janet Aviad, in her book, *Return to Judaism: Religious Renewal in Israel*, documents the return of secular Jews to Orthodox or neoorthodox Judaism, people known as *ba'alei teshuvah*, or "those who return."

Many of these Jews are from upper- and middle-class neighborhoods in the United States. Their feelings of loss and alienation lead them to search for new foundations upon which to build a life. Many find their way to Israel, study in Jewish houses of learning, and make their lives in a new religious environment. Whether they remain in Israel or not, it is often the return to the ancient symbols and places of Judaism that lead to or help to solidify their new commitment. Clearly Yad VaShem and the yeshivas of Jerusalem are main centers of Jewish renewal, functioning as visible reminders of membership in an ancient suffering and now empowered people.[10]

One can also see the revival of Jewish religious fundamentalism in Israel as stimulated both by the crisis of the Jewish people and by the recovery of ancient myths and texts, as well as by renewed access to ancient Jewish sites. Thus, Ian Lustick, in his book *For the Land and the Lord: Jewish Fundamentalism in Israel*, emphasizes Israel's military triumph in 1967 as a crisis point in Israeli history that has polarized sentiment and opinion on the most profound questions facing Israeli society, at the same time serving as a catalyst for the formation of religious fundamentalist movements such as Gush Emunim (Bloc of the Faithful).

For Lustick, it is ironic that the transformation of Israel, known for its unity and intimacy, into a bitterly, perhaps irrevocably, divided society, can be traced to its lightning victory in the 1967 war. By opening questions of tremendous emotional and practical import, the war has divided rather than united. The "religious and emotional fervor surrounding the renewal of contact between Jews and the historic heartland of ancient Judea" has introduced religious language that allows little room for nuance and compromise.

As Lustick describes it, after more than eighteen centuries of dormancy, "the distinctive blend of messianic expectation, militant political action, intense parochialism, devotion to the land of Israel, and self-sacrifice that characterized the Jewish Zealots of Roman times caught the imagination of tens of thousands of young religious Israeli Jews and disillusioned but idealistic secular Zionists." Biblical references abound, exemplified in the following statement by a Jewish fundamentalist:

The commandment that pounded in the heart of Joshua and the generation who captured Canaan, in the heart of David and Solomon, and
their generation, the word of God in his Torah, is thus, as it was first
purely stated, what motivates us. The source of our authority will be
our volunteering for the holy because we only come to return Israel to
its true purpose and destiny of Torah and Holiness . . . we are looking
for the complete renewal of the true official authority—the Sanhedrin
and the anointed from the House of David—we are those who nurse
from the future, from which we gain our authority for the generations.[11]

As frightening is the conclusion of another fundamentalist:

Even if 100% of the Jewish inhabitants of Israel should vote for [the
West Bank and Gaza's] separation from the Land of Israel, that "hundred percent consensus" would not have any more validity than the
"hundred percent consensus" that prevailed within the people of Israel
when it danced around the golden calf. The fate of those dancers
around the golden calf, and they represented a massive "democratic"
majority, was branded as with a hot iron into the genetic code of the
Jewish people. The same is true of the fate of the spies [sent by Moses
into Canaan] who were ready to abandon the Land of Israel, ten of the
twelve of them at any rate, a solid "consensus," the fate of whom is also
deeply engraved on the historical consciousness of the people. The
history of Israel is the history of the minority, of Joshua son of Nun
and Caleb son of Yephunah, who said: "Let us arise and take it, we
shall succeed." In the end the consensualist majority turned on its
heels and died in the desert while these two did enter the Land.[12]

Lustick concludes that the influence of those movements on Israeli
society and government far outweighs their numbers, especially in their
willingness to challenge the legitimacy of any government that attempts
to withdraw from the West Bank and Gaza. By recalling the ancient glory
of the Jewish people and its attachment to the land, by looking forward
to the reconstruction of the Temple and the coming messianic age, and
by a willingness to seek these goals through violence and, if necessary, the
expulsion of the Palestinian Arabs, the Jewish fundamentalist movement
has become the greatest obstacle to a comprehensive Palestinian-Israeli
peace settlement.

Holocaust theologians, in their sorrow and in their commitment to
survival, and Jewish fundamentalists, in their certainty and violence, contribute in different ways to moving into the present Roskies's understanding of the liturgy of destruction. Yet, the liturgy of destruction,

which today spawns Holocaust memorials and Jewish settlements, is profoundly transformed in contemporary Jewish life because it takes place within the empowerment of the Jewish people and is intimately linked to it.

Within the context of empowerment, both the remembrance of the Holocaust and the messianic expectation take on an organized, conscious quality—one might say a strategic sense—that forms the basis of alliances and mutual interests. Clearly there is a difference between the secularist Hillel Zeitlin arriving for deportation dressed in religious garb and the speeches made by American political leaders on behalf of the United States Holocaust Memorial Council. So, too, is there a difference between Orthodox Jews in the death camps praying for the coming of the messiah, and Jewish Israeli underground terrorists attempting to blow up the Dome of the Rock mosque to make way for the messianic age through the reconstruction of the Jewish temple.

The liturgy of destruction, with its elements of remembrance and the messianic, is now in the service of power rather than of a precarious survival. Thus, it is met with an evident boredom; the need for constant rehearsal seems more and more to pervade the contemporary liturgy of destruction. For many, the liturgy of destruction rings hollow. It does not acknowledge those who have suffered, and are suffering today, because of that liturgy—the Palestinian people—and reveals a hollowness, almost a deceptive quality, that forces a reevaluation of the liturgy itself. A new inclusiveness in the landscape of the dead and dying is called for if the voices of the Holocaust are to be rescued from an artificial construct that threatens memory much more than the Bitburg affair did.

Thinking the Unthinkable

Though it goes unmentioned and is often repressed today, with the founding of the state of Israel, Jews, for the first time, began to see the suffering of another people, the Palestinian Arabs, in light of the suffering of the Jewish people. Here is the liturgy of destruction in its intuitive and more inclusive sense, which seems closer to reality than the staged and exclusive one heard today. Examples abound: In 1948, an Israeli intelligence officer, Shmarya Guttman, was involved in the occupation of the Palestinian Arab town of Lydda and the subsequent expulsion of its inhabitants. Benny Morris describes it:

> All the Israelis who witnessed the events agreed that the exodus, under a hot July sun, was an extended episode of suffering for the refugees, especially from Lydda. Some were stripped by soldiers of their valuables as they left town or at checkpoints along the way. Guttman sub-

sequently described the trek of the Lydda refugees: "A multitude of inhabitants walked one after another. Women walked burdened with packages and sacks on their heads. Mothers dragged children after them. . . . Occasionally, warning shots were heard. . . . Occasionally, you encountered a piercing look from one of the youngsters . . . in the column, and the look said: "We have not surrendered. We shall return to fight you." For Guttman, an archaeologist, the spectacle conjured up "the memory of the exile of Israel" at the end of the Second Commonwealth, at Roman hands.[13]

Morris continues this description:

> One Israeli soldier from Kibbutz Ein Harod, a few weeks after the event, recorded vivid impressions of the thirst and hunger of the refugees on the roads, and how "children got lost" and of how a child fell into a well and drowned, ignored, as his fellow refugees fought each other to draw water. Another soldier described the spoor left by the slow-shuffling columns, "to begin with [jettisoning] utensils and furniture and in the end, bodies of men, women and children, scattered along the way." Quite a few refugees died—from exhaustion, dehydration and disease—along the roads eastward, from Lydda and Ramle, before reaching temporary rest near and in Ramallah. Nirm al Khatib put the death toll among the Lydda refugees during the trek eastward at 335; Arab Legion commander John Glubb Pasha more carefully wrote that nobody will ever know how many children died.[14]

In the weeks that followed, a leader of the Mapam party, Meir Ya'ari, lamented: "Many of us are losing their human image. . . . How easily they speak of how it is possible and permissible to take women, children and old men and to fill the roads with them because such is the imperative of strategy. And this we say, the members of Hashmer Hatzair, who remember who used this means against our people during the Second World war. . . . I am appalled."[15]

Of course, many of the atrocities had little need of direct comparison with ancient or even contemporary Jewish experience in order to have an impact on those whose history was filled with suffering. S. Kaplan wrote of the occupation of the Palestinian village Ad Dawayima, near Hebron, which had surrendered without a fight:

> The first wave of conquerors killed about 80 to 100 male Arabs, women and children. The children they killed by breaking their heads with sticks. There was not a house without dead, wrote Kaplan. Kaplan's informant, who arrived immediately afterwards in the second

wave, reported that the Arab men and women who remained were then closed off in the houses "without food and water." Sappers arrived to blow up the houses. "One commander ordered a sapper to put two old women in a certain house . . . and to blow up the house with them. The sapper refused. . . . The commander then ordered his men to put in the old women and the evil deed was done. One soldier boasted that he had raped and then shot her. One woman, with a new-born baby in her arms, was employed to clean the courtyard where the soldiers ate. She worked a day or two. In the end they shot her and her baby.[16]

The flight of villagers from Sa'sa was described in moving detail:

> They abandon the villages of their birth and that of their ancestors and go into exile. . . . Women, children, babies, donkeys—everything moves, in silence and grief, northwards, without looking to right or left. Wife does not find her husband and child does not find his father . . . no one knows the goal of his trek. Many possessions are scattered by the paths; the more the refugees walk, the more tired they grow— and they throw away what they had tried to save on their way into exile. Suddenly, every object seems to them petty, superfluous, unimportant as against the chasing fear and the urge to save life and limb. I saw a boy aged eight walking northwards pushing along two asses in front of him. His father and brother had died in the battle and his mother was lost. I saw a woman holding a two-week-old baby in her right arm and a baby two years old in her left arm and a four-year-old girl following in her wake, clutching at her dress.[17]

These atrocities and expulsions occasioned, some months later, a ministerial probe that was discussed in Mapam's executive body. At the start of the meeting, Benny Marshak explicitly asked that members refrain from using the phrase "Nazi actions." Later at a cabinet meeting, Aharon Cizling told the other cabinet members that "I couldn't sleep all night. . . . This is something that determines the character of the nation. . . . Jews too have committed Nazi acts."[18]

In all of this, something is happening that is both ancient and new. The references, in a time of crisis, to an ancient Jewish archetype of destruction, to the memory of the exile of Israel with the destruction of the Temple by the Romans in 70 of the Common Era, and to the Holocaust, which already in 1948 functioned as an archetype of destruction, are now being made in relation to the suffering of another people at the hands of Jewish people. This is intuitively understood, and even the desire to keep this connection from being spoken belied the obvious, that at least some Jews were seeing, in the Palestinian people, their own history. And, in observing that history, in sad and profound ways, they were recognizing that the history of Jews and Palestinians is somehow, in the expulsions and massacres, bound together.

But it is also clear, at the very beginning, that the ability to see this bond is intimately related to the ability to admit that Jews are no longer innocent, and this is precisely the most controversial issue. Thus, many, at the outset, wanted to change the intuitive language, and instead, to address procedural matters and long-range goals, in a sense, to bury the intuitive connection. In their minds, any comparison from within, or later from outside, placed the legitimacy of Jewish empowerment in question. And, too, it cast doubt on the entire policy of separating the two communities, which gained strength as the war continued and Israel was, to a large extent, emptied of Palestinians.

One cannot help but hear, as these actors saw with their own eyes, the tension between the prophetic—questioning power—and the process of normalization—adjusting for the obvious excess, though continuing pursuit of the general goal. For those who pursued normalization, the time had come for Jews to grow up and to suppress the ancient and contemporary images of destruction that define a landscape better forgotten.

Decades later, the connection of Palestinian and Jew can still be found lurking beneath the surface of power politics. After the first Palestinian uprising began, Amos Kenan, a columnist for the Israeli daily, *Yediot Aharonot*, wrote an essay titled "Four Decades of Blood Vengeance" that takes on the quality of a dialogue with George Habash, head of the Popular Front for the Liberation of Palestine, whom he met in 1948 when the Israeli army conquered Lydda.

Kenan was a soldier who, as a part of the invading and occupying force, kept Palestinian Arabs at a distance. Habash, whose ailing sister lived in Lydda, managed to avoid security and visit her. Habash's sister was thirty years old, married, with six children, and at that point dying. A medical doctor, Habash diagnosed her disease and prescribed the appropriate medicines, but because Lydda was under curfew with no local pharmacies and no access to the outside, his sister died three days later. Because of the curfew, it was impossible to bury her properly, and so Habash dug a grave with his own hands and buried his sister in her own backyard. When the curfew was lifted, the survivors of the village, Habash and his sister's six children included, were transferred to temporary prison compounds and later expelled to Amman, Jordan.

Kenan recalls his days of guard duty in Lydda as essentially uneventful and in some senses comical, both because of the lack of military preparedness of many of the military personnel, some of whom had recently arrived from Eastern Europe, and the quality, or lack thereof, of the weapons. Since most of the inhabitants of Lydda had fled before the Israel occupation, there were few people to guard. In short, they had a typical military life with much standing around, gossiping, and the inevitable boredom. And it was typical in other, more horrifying ways as well:

> In the afternoon, those of us who couldn't take it any more would steal off to Tel Aviv for a few hours, on one excuse or another. At night, those of us who couldn't restrain ourselves would go into the prison compounds to fuck Arab women. I want very much to assume, and perhaps even can, that those who couldn't restrain themselves did what they thought the Arabs would have done to them had they won the war.

> Once, only once, did an Arab woman—perhaps a distant relative of George Habash—dare complain. There was a court martial. The complainant didn't even get to testify. The accused, who was sitting behind the judges, ran the back of his hand across his throat, as a signal to the woman. She understood. The rapist was not acquitted, he simply was not accused, because there was no one who would dare accuse him. Two years later, he was killed while plowing the fields of an Arab village, one no longer on the map because its inhabitants scattered and left it empty.[19]

Kenan then begins to write about blood vengeance, and about how difficult it is to square accounts. What he does know is that many have sought and taken revenge, and, to his mind, all the vengeance has already come:

> Both you and I, George, have already taken vengeance—before and during and after the fact. And both you and I have not taken pity on man or woman, boy or girl, young or old. I know that there is not much difference between pressing a button in a fighter plane and firing point blank into the head of a hostage. As there is no difference between a great massacre that was not meant to be and one that was meant to be. There is no distinction between justice and justice or between injustice and injustice, as there is no difference at all in what people—weak, transient beings, assured of the justice of their ways and their deeds—are capable of doing to people who are in sum exactly like themselves.

> Tears filled my eyes, George, when I read for the first time in these forty years how your sister died. How you dug her a pit with your own hands in the yard of her house in the city of Lydda. I reach out with an unclean hand to your hand, which also is not clean. You and I should die a miserable natural death, a death of sinners who have not come to their punishment, a death from old age, disease, a death weak

and unheroic, a death meant for human beings who have lived a life of iniquity.[20]

Two other stories from the Palestinian uprising make this connection between Palestinian and Jewish history in relation to the Holocaust. The first story dates from January 1988, one month after the Palestinian uprising had begun, when an Israeli captain was summoned to his superior. The captain was given instructions to carry out arrests in the village of Hawara, outside Nablus. The arrest of innocent young Palestinians is hardly out of the ordinary, but the further instructions provided to the officer—what to do to those Palestinians after their arrest—was disturbing. His conscience would not allow him to carry out these instructions unless he was directly ordered to do so. Having then received the direct order, the captain, with a company of forty soldiers, boarded a civilian bus, arriving at Hawara at eleven o'clock in the evening.

The local muhktar was given a list of twelve persons to round up, which he did, and the twelve sat on the sidewalk in the center of the village, offering no resistance. Yossi Sarid, an Israeli politcal analyst, describes what followed.

> The soldiers shackled the villagers, and with their hands bound behind their backs they were led to the bus. The bus started to move and after 200–300 meters it stopped beside an orchard. The "locals" were taken off the bus and led into the orchard in groups of three, one after another. Every group was accompanied by an officer. In the darkness of the orchard the soldiers also shackled the Hawara residents' legs and laid them on the ground. The officers urged the soldiers to "get it over with quickly, so that we can leave and forget about it." Then, flannel was stuffed into the Arabs' mouths to prevent them from screaming and the bus driver revved up the motor so that the noise would drown out the cries. Then the soldiers obediently carried out the orders they had been given: to break their arms and legs by clubbing the Arabs; to avoid clubbing them on their heads; to remove their bonds after breaking their arms and legs, and to leave them at the site; to leave one local with broken arms but without broken legs so he could make it back to the village on his own and get help.[21]

The mission was carried out; the beatings were so fierce that most of the wooden clubs used were broken. Thus was born the title of the article detailing this action, "The Night of the Broken Clubs."

The second story occurred just months after the beatings had begun, when Marcus Levin, a physician, was called up for reserve duty in the Ansar prison camp. When he arrived, Levin met two of his colleagues and asked for information about his duties. The answer: "Mainly you

examine prisoners before and after an investigation." Levin responded in
amazement, "After the investigation?" which prompted the reply,
"Nothing special, sometimes there are fractures. For instance, yesterday
they brought a twelve-year-old boy with two broken legs." Dr. Levin
then demanded a meeting with the compound commander and told him,
"My name is Marcus Levin and not Josef Mengele, and for reasons of
conscience I refuse to serve in this place." A doctor who was present at
the meeting tried to calm Levin with the following comment: "Marcus,
first you feel like Mengele, but after a few days you get used to it."
Hence, the title of an article written about the incident, "You Will Get
Used to Being a Mengele."[22]

The references in these articles to the night of broken glass,
"Kristallnacht," and to the Nazi physician Mengele, as a way of seeing
contemporary Jewish Israeli policy and activity, are startling. The resistance on the part of the Jewish community to what one might call the
Nazi analogy is understandable and so strong as to virtually silence all
such references. Yet, during the brutal attempt to suppress the
Palestinian uprising, in fact, from the very beginning of the Jewish struggle for statehood in Palestine in the 1940s and continuing to the present,
the connection between the Jewish experience of suffering in Europe and
the Palestinian experience of suffering at the hands of the Jewish people
in Palestine and Israel has been, and continues to be, repeatedly made by
Jewish Israelis.

What are we to make of these references?

First, it is important to see that they are not primarily comparisons
between Nazi and Israeli behavior, though some of the behavior may in
fact be comparable. Second, these references are not attempts to further
political objectives, such as promoting one political party over another or
challenging the legitimacy of the state of Israel, though clearly they sub-
vert partisan and bipartisan policies of Israel that lead to these incidents.

Rather, the force of the Nazi reference involves and moves beyond
comparison and politics and represents an intuitive link between the historic suffering of the Jews and the present suffering of Palestinians. It
further represents an implicit recognition that what was done to the Jews
is now being done by the Jews to another people. At the same time, the
connection of Jewish and Palestinian suffering is pre-political and pre-
ideological; that is, it operates in a terrain filled with images of Jewish
suffering, which remain untouched by the "realities" of the situation,
with the need to be "strong," or even with the communal penalties for
speaking the truth.

We might say that the Nazi reference represents a cry of pain and a
plea to end a madness that was visited upon Jews for millennia and now
is visited by Jews upon another people; thus, the vehemence with which
such analogies are met when spoken, almost as if a blunt instrument is

needed to repress the memories and the aspirations of the Jewish people to be neither victim nor oppressor.

Could it be said that it is impossible today to understand the Jewish liturgy of destruction, the burning of the Temple, the death of the martyr, and the pogrom, the events of exile and Holocaust, unless Jews include, as intimate partners, those people that Jews have expelled, tortured, and murdered as well—those who, for most Jews, exist without names and histories, the Palestinian people?

It could be that here, in an inclusive liturgy of destruction, lies the possibility and the hope of moving beyond the peripheral and the superficial into an engaged struggle—on behalf of the history of the Jewish and the Palestinian people. Might Jews be liberated from policies and attitudes that, when understood intuitively, are a betrayal of Jewish history, but have been seen as weakness, lack of political maturity, or even self-hate? Jews would then be released from theologies, Holocaust and fundamentalist, that now serve as ideologies that close off critical thought and serve the powerful.

To pursue connectedness means a serious reevaluation of parts of Jewish history, but can this painful task be accomplished without the voices and the faces of those whom Jews have initiated into the liturgy of destruction? Can Jews see themselves and their history in a new light without hearing and taking seriously the history and the struggle of the Palestinian people?

Yet, even in recent Jewish theological writing, there is a noticeable absence of Palestinians, and when they are mentioned it is almost exclusively within a Jewish critique rather than as independent theological voices. In Emil Fackenheim's book, *What Is Judaism? An Interpretation for the Present Age*, his first book after moving to Israel, he does not mention Palestinians even one time. In a massive compilation of essays on critical concepts, movements, and beliefs edited by the late Arthur Cohen and Paul Mendes-Flohr, and titled *Contemporary Jewish Religious Thought*, in 1,076 pages, Palestinians are mentioned less than five times.

When Wiesel and Greenberg do mention Palestinians, as they do infrequently, Palestinians exist primarily within the Jewish framework of interpretation. As Greenberg writes, in a tone typical of Jewish writing even when partially sympathetic to Palestinian aspirations, "Ideally, the Palestinians should earn their way—all the way to statehood— by peaceful behavior and policies." Or more to the point: "The Palestinians will have to earn their power by living peacefully and convincing Israel of their beneficence or by acquiescing to a situation in which Israel's strength guarantees that the Arabs cannot use their power to endanger Israel." By banishing Palestinians from the internal landscape of Jewish history, Israel remains essentially innocent. But, from a Palestinian perspective, who is in need of protection, Israelis or Palestinians? And who, with the experience of the last century on balance, needs assurance?[23]

Wiesel's most extensive discussion of Palestinian issues, in the form of a letter "To a Young Palestinian Arab," also bears scrutiny in this regard. Wiesel begins his letter with an outstretched hand, promising sincerity, which is the only path for those who have suffered. Facing that pain, Wiesel plans to "judge myself as well, since someone else's suffering always puts us to the test." In order to engage in a dialogue, Wiesel counsels the putting aside of politics as a confusing and superficial labyrinth.

To be sure, the arguments on both sides are valid; the Palestinians can invoke Palestine's Muslim past as Wiesel can speak of the Jewish past that preceded it. The injustices endured by Arab refugees in 1948 can also be countered by the Jewish suffering in the Holocaust. But the injustice endured by the Arabs is. for Wiesel. the responsibility of the Arabs themselves: "Your own leaders, with their incendiary speeches, their virulent fanaticism. If only they had accepted the United Nations' resolutions on the partition of Palestine, if only they had not incited the Arab population to mass flight in order to return 'forthwith' as victors; if only they had not attempted to drown the young Jewish nation in blood; if only they had taken into account Jewish suffering, also the Jewish right to also claim its sovereignty on its ancestral land. . . . For thirty years Israel's peace initiatives were ignored; Israel's appeals for mutual recognition were denied; Israel's conciliatory moves were rejected."

As for the Jews who emerged "from the darkest recess of history, from the most hidden marshes of man's and God's imagination," they chose to "opt for man" rather than vengeance. For Wiesel, those who went to Palestine did so to relive an ancient dream together, with the Palestinian people, not to displace them.

What then divides Wiesel and his Palestinian brother? The use of suffering against others: "Ask your elders and mine; they will tell you that in the immediate postwar years in Europe—in Germany, Hungary, Poland and elsewhere—there were countless collaborators who had every reason to be afraid. But they were not harmed—not by us. And those neighbors of ours who had been present at our agony and had pillaged our homes, sometimes before our eyes, went on living and drinking and sleeping as though nothing had happened. We could have lashed out against them—we did not. We consistently evoked our trials only to remind man of his need to be human—not of his right to punish. On behalf of the dead, we sought consolation, not retribution."

The Palestinian Arabs, he implied, had done the opposite. Though Wiesel felt responsible for what happened to Palestinians, he cannot abide by what Palestinians had done with their anger:

I feel responsible for your sorrow, but not for the way you use it, for in its name you have massacred innocent people, slaughtered children. From Munich to Maalot, from Lod to Entebbe, from hijacking to hijacking, from ambush to ambush, you have spread terror among unarmed civilians and thrown into mourning families already too often visited by death. You will tell me that all these acts have been the work of your extremist comrades, not yours; but they acted on your behalf, with your approval, since you did not raise your voice to reason with them. You will tell me that it is your tragedy which incited them to murder. By murdering, they debased that tragedy, they betrayed it. Suffering is often unjust, but it never justifies murder.[24]

Here is a simple and crucial error in logic that is almost systematic in Jewish analysis—when Palestinians, even as supposedly addressed in a letter, are essentially absent. For the Palestinians, the crucial connection in this story is not how Jews reacted in Europe to their former conquerors, but how they acted as they themselves became conquerors in Palestine and Israel.

Wiesel's desire to move beyond the confusion of politics is easily stated when the configuration supports Jewish empowerment. But a Palestinian might respond that a face-to-face discussion can only take place in an authentic way if the political situation is changed. Without politics the Palestinian is consigned to Jewish turf. But implicit is Wiesel's condemnation, as vengeful, of the political and sometimes bitter struggle of a displaced people. The Palestinians might reverse Wiesel's framework and speak about a highly organized terrorism against the Palestinian people.

But how can Jews know how Palestinians might respond? And how can Jews in Wiesel's sense judge themselves as well—because someone else's suffering always puts us to the test—if Palestinians are absent from our history and theology? Or if they are simply interpreted within the Jewish framework? Who, then, is to challenge the Jewish framework of renewal if not one who has suffered under its heel?

Credit can at least be given to Wiesel and to Greenberg for mentioning Palestinians and engaging issues that might one day lead beyond monologue to a genuine dialogue. How is it possible, at this late date, for two prominent theologians, David Hartman, a Jewish Israeli, and Michael Wyschogrod, an American Jew, to publish full-length monographs on the present and future of Jewish belief and activity without mentioning Palestinians, as if they did not exist?

And would one think it possible that, despite Wiesel's earlier letter to the Palestinians and his dialogue on the uprising (already discussed), and despite Greenberg's attempts to engage Palestinians in his work "The Ethics of Jewish Power," their most recent works—published after the uprising had begun and attempting to define a Jewish liturgy of destruction—apparently do not even allude to Palestinians?

It is fascinating that both books encourage Christian involvement in commemorating the Holocaust, even Christian liturgies centered on the Holocaust. They recognize that those who were the oppressors must incorporate their victims into their sacred liturgy, but that recognition carries no inkling that Jews face a similar task with regard to Palestinians.[25]

Still, the problem is not just an absolute absence of Palestinians—for as we have seen, on the intuitive level Palestinians are ever-present—but rather, their banishment from the ideological and theological articulation of Jewish expression; that is, Zionist ideology and Holocaust theology represses, even at this late date, the deepest intuitions of the Jewish people.

Envisioning a Common History

But ultimately, the challenge of Jewish dissent during this period is to see the uprising, in historical perspective, as a continuation of Palestinian suffering rather than as something new and unprecedented. Thus, the Palestinian uprising provides Jews with the possibility for viewing the renewal of Jewish life in Palestine and Israel as a historical event a century in duration, and therefore, allowing fundamental judgments to be made concerning that history, judgments that can contribute to choices for the future.

Recent books reflecting other than the standard history, written by Jewish Israelis and published before the uprising, assume new importance within the context of the uprising. In a sense, they help place the uprising in context as almost inevitable, or at least understandable, within the framework of the birth of Israel. They challenge the myth of the state's origins and, thus, the myth of Israel's original innocence. To do this is to challenge the theory that Israel's present problems and methods of dealing with those problems are aberrational, simply to be corrected by self-adjustment. Rather, they point to a flawed beginning, to inherent contradictions that are manifested in the uprising today. Together with the outrage expressed by Schindler, Hertzberg, Lerner, Shahak, and others, these books make clear the implications, at least for now, of the tradition of dissent.

A polemical but essentially accurate framing of the issue, *The Birth of Israel: Myths and Realities*, was written by Simha Flapan, who was born in Poland and emigrated to Palestine in 1930. Flapan, who died in April 1987, just as his book was going to press, had a long and distinguished career as a writer, publisher, peace activist, and educator. From 1954 to

1981, he was national secretary of Israel's Mapam party and director of its Arab Affairs department.

In his previous book, *Zionism and the Palestinians, 1917–1947*, Flapan traced the evolution of the Jewish and Arab conflict as it developed in the pre-state period. Flapan's next book, which turned out to be his last, was supposed to survey the next stage of the Israeli-Palestinian conflict, beginning with Israel's War of Independence in 1948 and ending with the 1967 war. But his concentration on the years 1948–52 as the formative years of Israeli statehood came about, strangely enough, because of Menachem Begin's challenge to massive antiwar protest during the Lebanese war.

In defending the actions and aspirations surrounding the invasion of Lebanon, Begin claimed continuity with David Ben-Gurion's policies of 1948, as Israel's first prime minister. Among other things, Begin cited Ben-Gurion's plan to establish a homogeneous Jewish state by dividing Lebanon, setting up a Christian state north of the Litani River, and destroying Arab villages within the borders of Israel and expelling their inhabitants during the 1948 war.

Because the 1948 war had never been a subject of controversy, and the difference between the "defensive" War of Independence and the offensive invasion of Lebanon was clear, and further, because Ben-Gurion and Begin had always been enemies, and because, at least for most progressive Israelis, the Likud's policies and vision clearly represented a break with traditional Labor aspirations, Begin's claim of continuity came as quite a shock to Flapan and others. And it represented a challenge as well. For Begin was claiming to be carrying out, in an open way, what was there from the beginning; Ben-Gurion, and, by implication, the Labor party, from then to the present, had resorted to subterfuge.

For Flapan, the uncovering of the origins of the state to dispute or verify Begin's claims was essential to understanding the course of the Jewish-Palestinian conflict leading up to and including the Lebanon War—and surely the Palestinian uprising, which erupted months after Flapan's death.

The historical parallel of the War of Independence and the Lebanon war, and, by extension, the Palestinian uprising, raised for Flapan the following questions: "Was the policy of the Zionist leadership in 1948 and that of Israel's subsequent leaders actually aimed at attaining a homogeneous Jewish state in the whole or most of Palestine? If this was the case, then the attempted destruction and further dispersal of the Palestinian refugees in Lebanon appears to be a more advanced application of the same policy. Does this mean that the socialist leadership of the Jewish community in 1948 and their successors up until 1977—when Begin's party came to power—were no different from their hated Revisionist rivals on this issue? And even more frightening, to what extent does the growing support for the theocratic racist Rabbi Meir Kahane—who talks openly of deporting the Palestinians from Israel and the West Bank and Gaza—have its roots in the events of 1948?" Flapan continues:

> Like most Israelis, I had always been under the influence of certain myths that had become accepted as historical truth. And since myths are central to the creation of structures of thinking and propaganda, these myths had been of paramount importance in shaping Israeli policy for more than three and a half decades. Israel's myths are located at the core of the nation's self-perception. Even though Israel has the most sophisticated army in the region and possesses an advanced atomic capability, it continues to regard itself in terms of the Holocaust, as the victim of an unconquerable, blood-thirsty enemy. Thus whatever Israelis do, whatever means we employ to guard our gains or to increase them, we justify as last-ditch self-defense. We can, therefore, do no wrong. The myths of Israel forged during the formation of the state have hardened into this impenetrable, and dangerous, ideological shield. Yet what emerged from my reading was that while it was precisely during the period between 1948 and 1952 that most of these myths gained credence, the documents at hand not only failed to substantiate them, they openly contradicted them.[26]

For Flapan, these were less abstract theories to be debated than a personal challenge to the naiveté and ignorance of a person committed to the Zionist ideal since his childhood in Poland in the post-World War I years.

Flapan's book traces several myths central to understanding the origins of Israel and the present predicament facing Israel. These myths are crucial to the entire premise of Holocaust theology: that Zionists accepted the United Nations partition plan of 1947 as a compromise by which the Jewish community abandoned the concept of a Jewish state in the whole of Palestine and accepted the right of the Palestinians to their own state; that Palestinian Arabs rejected partition and responded to a call for all-out war on the Jewish state, forcing Jews into a military conflict; that Israel, as a "numerically inferior, poorly armed people in danger of being overrun," faced and defeated a military giant composed of the entire Arab world bent on destroying the embryonic state and expelling its inhabitants; and finally, that the flight of the Palestinians before and after the establishment of the state of Israel was prompted by Arab leadership as a temporary measure, that they were to return with the victorious Arab armies, and that, despite those efforts, Jewish leaders tried to persuade the Palestinian Arabs to remain in Israel.

Contrary to these assumptions, Flapan's research shows the reality to be either more complex or completely different. According to Flapan, from the beginning, Israeli policy was to thwart the emergence of a Palestinian state through secret agreements with the leaders of Transjordan, who were interested in creating a Greater Syria. The majority of Arabs did not respond to the call for a holy war against Israel; instead, many Palestinians, at leadership and grass-roots levels, tried to find an accommodation with the new Israeli state, an effort that was undermined by the Israeli government's opposition to the creation of a similar Palestinian state. Arab states aimed to prevent the agreement that might lead to a Greater Syria rather than liquidate the Jewish state. Furthermore, Israel was on the defensive only for the first month of the war and, for the remainder of it, had superiority in weapons and armed forces. Finally, the flight of Palestinian Arabs was prompted by Israel's political and military leaders, who "believed that Zionist colonization and statehood necessitated the transfer 'of Palestinian Arabs to Arab countries.'"

From these understandings of the myths and realities of Israeli history, Flapan concludes that there is a clear line of continuity between Ben-Gurion and Begin, the War of Independence and the Lebanon war, and, by extension, the then current prime minister, Yitzhak Shamir, and the uprising: the identification of Palestinians as the enemy; the Israeli army confronting not only soldiers but a civilian population; and the subsequent dehumanization of the Israeli soldiers through brutality and violation of elementary human rights.

Still, the end of this cycle, the brutalization of Israel's soldiers, cannot occur without dehumanizing the enemy, and, here, the continuity is again clear. Ben-Gurion described the Palestinian Arabs as the "pupils and even the teachers of Hitler, who claim that there is only one way to solve the Jewish question—one way only: total annihilation." Begin described the Palestinian fighters as "two-legged animals" and compared the bombings of Beirut, the stronghold of Yassir Arafat, with the bombings of Berlin, the last fortress of Adolph Hitler.

The last element of this cycle, the philosophy of expulsion promulgated by Meir Kahane then and others today, was already in place in 1948, though expressed in the more benign terms necessary for the creation of a homogeneous Jewish state. Thus, for Flapan, a fundamental contradiction exists from the beginning with Ben-Gurion and continues through Begin and Shamir, that is, the desire to build a democratic Jewish society in the whole, or in most, of Palestine.[27]

The strength of Flapan's work rests in his framing of the issues and their patterns of continuity. The details of the history, which in the main confirm Flapan, can be found in works of younger historians like Avi

Shalim's *Collusion Across the Jordan*, Ilan Pappé's *Britain and the Arab-Israeli Conflict, 1948–1951*, Tom Segev's *1949: The First Israelis*, and Benny Morris's *The Birth of the Palestinian Refugee Problem, 1947–1949*.[28]

The latter two books are crucial to undermining Jewish naiveté about the creation of the state of Israel, and they point to the continuity of policies faced by Jewish dissenters today. Morris's book, for example, outlines, in great detail and complexity, the mass movement of Palestinians, estimated between 600,000 and 760,000 people, from their homes, villages, and cities during the war and the creation of a refugee population as an unexpected, but generally welcomed, bonus for the new Jewish state. This exodus was initially instigated by some regular and irregular Jewish forces, through the massacre of Deir Yassin in 1948, for example, which carried a lesson to those Palestinian Arabs who stayed behind at the end of the war. There was also "Plan D," in which Jewish brigade- and battalion-level commanders were given "carte blanche to completely clear vital areas: it allowed the expulsion of hostile or potentially hostile Arab villages."

During the early part of the war, there was never any official decision to expel Palestinians; no plan or policy was articulated. But according to Morris, it was "understood by all concerned that, militarily, in the struggle to survive, the fewer Arabs remaining behind and along the front lines, the better, and, politically, the fewer Arabs remaining in the Jewish state, the better. At each level of command and execution, Haganah officers 'understood' what the military and political exigencies of survival required."

By the second half of the war, the readiness to expel grew, both because of the unforeseen possibility, as a result of the first waves of the Palestinian exodus, of an almost completely Jewish state, and because of the length and bitterness of the war itself. Still, the reality of expulsion was not announced as policy: "Ben-Gurion clearly wanted as few Arabs as possible to remain in the Jewish state. He hoped to see them flee. He said as much to his colleagues and aides in meetings in August, September and October."

As Morris understand it, "No expulsion policy was ever enunciated and Ben-Gurion always refrained from issuing clear or written expulsion orders; he preferred that his generals 'understand' what he wanted done. He wished to avoid going down in history as the 'great expeller' and he did not want the Israeli government to be implicated in a morally questionable policy. And he sought to preserve national unity in wartime." By the end of the war, another as yet unannounced policy went into effect: except for a few notable exceptions, and despite tremendous international pressure, the Palestinians who left what became the state of Israel would not be allowed to return.[29]

Tom Segev provides an account of the human side of the creation of the Palestinian refugee population and the way Jews in power handled the question of expulsion. In a Ministerial Committee for Abandoned Property meeting of July 7, 1948, Segev cites the following dialogue between Eliezer Kaplan, minister of finance, and Behor Shalom Shitrit, head of the ministry for the minorities.

> E. Kaplan reported that the conquest of Lydda and Ramlah has now, for the first time, confronted us with the problem of possessing an area occupied by a very large number of Arabs. The total number of inhabitants in these two towns and the adjoining villages is estimated at several tens of thousands.

> B. Shitrit had "visited occupied Ramlah and observed the situation close up. The army proposed to capture all the men who are capable of bearing arms (except for those who signed the letter of surrender), take them as far as the Arab border and set them loose. Mr. Shitrit contacted the Foreign Minister and asked him to formulate a policy. The Foreign Minister's reply was that those inhabitants who wished to remain could do so, provided the State of Israel did not have to support them. Those who wished to leave could also do so."

> E. Kaplan "discussed the problem of the population of Ramlah and Lydda with the Minister of Defense [Ben-Gurion] and received an answer which to a certain extent contradicts that of the Foreign Ministry. The Minister of Defense replied that the young men should be taken captive, the rest of the inhabitants ought to be encouraged to leave, but those who remain, Israel will have to provide for."

Aharon Cizling, minister of agriculture, also made the following comments when informed of murderous acts and rape committed by Israeli soldiers:

> I've received a letter on the subject. I must say that I have known what things have been like for some time and I have raised the issue several times already here. However after reading this letter I couldn't sleep all night. I felt the things that were going on were hurting my soul, the soul of my family and all of us here. I could not imagine where we come from and to where we are going. . . . I often disagreed when the term Nazi was applied to the British. I wouldn't like to use the term, even though the British committed Nazi crimes. But now Jews too have behaved like Nazis and my entire being has been shaken. . . . Obviously we have to conceal these actions from the public, and I

agree that we should not even reveal that we're investigating them. But they must be investigated.[30]

This history is relevant to Jewish dissent because the essential contradictions posed by the historical analysis are, in essence, posed today, four decades after the creation of the state of Israel. Moreover, they were posed initially three decades before the state was established. This history is relevant also because it undermines the themes of innocence and redemption central to Holocaust theology, and therefore, can provide a bridge of understanding between Jews and Palestinians, if its reality is recognized at any deep level. Perhaps the challenge that faces Jewish dissenters today is that of achieving that depth of understanding, which will also give rise to a call for repentance.

But this history is particularly relevant because important sectors of the Jewish community refuse to understand the present situation. Alongside the progressive response to the Palestinian uprisings has been a conservative and chilling defense of Israel's innocence, and this, too, can be seen in statements made in paid advertisements in *The New York Times* over the years.

Clearly, after the first months of the first uprising, these statements began to predominate, with their essential call to support Israel against its enemies, variously defined as Palestinians, the P.L.O. leadership, Yassir Arafat, the Arab states, the national network news anchors, and self-deluded Jews. As Michael Lerner wrote his lead editorial in March 1988, labeling the occupation immoral and stupid, a rally in support of Israel was publicized and a welcome message to Prime Minister Shamir on his visit to the United States was included under the title "Territory for Peace—Bad Deal: International Conference—A Trap." Believing that Israel had a historically legal and moral right to "Judea, Samaria, Gaza and the Golan Heights," the signed message applauded "the dignified and principled manner in which you have performed your duties as leader of the Jewish state," and prayed for the success of Shamir's visit, assuring him that the American people were with him.[31]

Two months later, in May, a wealthy Jewish man born in Poland, Jack Mondlak, whose entire family perished in the Holocaust, wrote of his early life in Poland and the anti-Semitism in the "attacks, pogroms, humiliation and sense of terror that all Jews knew." Mondlak's concern was focused on the relation of the Holocaust to Israel when, in the present crisis, the existence of Israel was being debated and slandered in the press and when some Jews were attempting to undermine Israel by distortion and unjust charges:

Shame on you "Concerned Jews"! You have added heavily to Israel's burden. You accuse Israel of having lost its soul because you have lost your nerve. You have maligned Israel but in so doing you have revealed the emptiness of your Jewish commitment. Israel, a nation that has made huge strides in medicine and science, deserves no rebuke from you. Israel, which has illuminated the Middle East with a spirit of democracy, needs no lesson from you who would stifle her voice. Israel, which has demonstrated unparalleled restraint in the face of those who would destroy her, should be a source of pride to every Jew—yes, even including you. I see again the shadows of the Holocaust which began with the assassination of character and ended with physical extermination. We should not take this threat lightly. We should not blind ourselves again.[32]

The themes that emerge in the inclusive liturgy of destruction often assume a dialectical form. Jewish renewal is haunted by the prospect of creating new victims. Jews' own history of victimization is shadowed by the present reality of power, and fear of imperiling the Jewish community is confronted with the need to question Jewish power. The larger Jewish community suppresses the direction of this evolving inclusivity that seeks to revitalize the Jewish witness to the world.

The Jewish rendition of history has traditionally been expressed in ethics and critical thought, rather than statehood and political power. Too often, the discussions framed by history are argued within the parameters set by Jewish institutions and the state of Israel itself. Thus, the inclusive liturgy of destruction is being recognized by some Jews *and* remains ineffectual. The fears expressed in reaction to the inclusive liturgy of destruction—often even by the historians themselves—of recreating a climate of anti-Semitism, also continues, to circumscribe the ability to speak and act without equivocation.

The Revenge Must Stop

As the second Palestinian uprising continued in 2002, Sara Roy wrote a short opinion piece for her local newspaper. Her title: "The Revenge Must Stop." Though deemed "too personal" by the editors (it remains unpublished to this day), Roy's writing testifies to the complexity of the issue of Israel/Palestine for Jews.

A child of Holocaust survivors, Roy tells the story of her mother and her mother's sister who had just been liberated from the concentration camp by the Russian army. The Nazi officials and guards who ran the camp had been captured, and the surviving inmates were given free reign to do whatever they wanted to their German persecutors. Many survivors threw themselves upon the Germans, injuring many and killing others.

Roy's mother and aunt witnessed this revenge and fell into each other's arms sobbing. Roy's aunt, who had trouble standing, grabbed "my mother as if she would never let go," saying to her, "We cannot do this. Our father and mother would say this is wrong. Even now, even after everything we have endured, we must seek justice, not revenge. There is no other way."

In her moving portrait of her mother and aunt, Roy reveals, in an intimate way, the struggle that Jews undergo to find their voice of dissent. Roy crosses the most intimate boundaries of personal violation when she suggests the meaning of her story: "Peace for Israelis and Palestinians has a price: an end to occupation, an end to Israeli settlements, the establishment of a viable Palestinian state, Jerusalem as the capital of both states, and a mutually acceptable resolution of the Palestinian refugee issue." Without this, Roy concludes, "the violence and revenge will continue with more shedding of innocent blood on both sides. As my aunt said long ago, 'There is no other way.'"[33]

The victims of violence can react in different ways, and certainly the desire for vengeance—the vivid scene of Holocaust survivors beating and killing their former tormentors—is understandable. Who could judge such a reaction? And yet, the haunting scene of two women struggling to hold themselves upright physically and psychologically is breathtaking. Justice, not revenge, is the way. The lesson of the Holocaust is to end the cycle of violence and atrocity. There is no other way.

One hears Roy's anguish, as the next generation, as a child of Holocaust survivors, that the cycle of violence and atrocity continues. Could it be that Roy seeks the end of this cycle as a way of somehow bringing healing to her mother and aunt, whose only solace could be that their suffering was not in vain?

Another Jewish voice is the Israeli journalist Amira Hass. Writing for the progressive Israeli newspaper *Ha'aretz*, she is the only Israeli journalist who lives in and reports from the Palestinian territories. Like Roy, she sees Barak's offer as far from generous, for it kept "intact the largest Israeli settlements and their connecting roads." The overall consequences of decades of Israeli settlements are, for Hass, clear, allowing Israel to "create the infrastructure of one state, stretching from the Mediterranean to the Jordan River."

Hass details the result of these policies: "Alongside the flourishing green and ever-expanding Israeli-Jewish outposts—well maintained by Israeli policies and laws—is a Palestinian society subject to the rule of military orders and restrictions, its dense communities (including those in East Jerusalem) squeezed into small areas, served by miserably maintained roads and an insufficient water supply system." Like Roy, Hass is a witness to the occupation and provides a warning of what has already come into being. "Anger has accumulated in every Palestinian heart," Hass writes, "over the scarce water, over each demolished house, over the daily humiliation of waiting for a travel permit from an Israeli officer. A small match can cause this anger to explode, and in this past year, it has."

But, Hass has something else in common with Roy. Like Roy, she is a child of Holocaust survivors. In fact, Hass was formed by the stories of the Holocaust she heard from her parents as a child. Of all the many accounts, one stood out: "On a summer day in 1944, my mother was herded from a cattle car along with the rest of its human cargo, which had been transported from Belgrade to the concentration camp at Bergen-Belsen. She saw a group of German women, some on foot, some on bicycles, slow down as this strange procession went by and watch with indifferent curiosity on their faces. For me, these women became a loathsome symbol of watching from the sidelines, and at an early age I decided that my place was not with the bystanders."

In the end, Hass' desire to live among Palestinians stemmed "neither from adventurism nor from insanity, but from the dread of being a bystander, from my need to understand, down to the last detail, a world that is, to the best of my political and historical comprehension, an Israeli creation." For Hass, the territories represent the central contradiction of the creation and expansion of Israel—"our exposed nerve"—and she quickly found that "something special" connected her to refugees and the camps in which they lived. "I felt at home there," Hass writes, "in the temporary permanence, in the longing that clings to every grain of sand, in the rage that thrives in the alleyways. Only gradually, and just to a few friends in Gaza and Israel, did I begin to explain that it was my heritage, a singular autobiographical blend passed on by my parents, that had paved my way to the Gaza Strip."[34]

Both Roy and Hass, through their political analyses, also know something else: that Israel, as a nation-state, has over the decades, and with incredible, one might say brilliant, political, military, economic and technological skill, pursued a policy of occupation and settlement that insures that the cycle of violence and atrocity will continue. Despite intermittent lulls, peace talks, cease-fires and hopeful signs, all of these punctuated by suicide bombers and armed incursions, Israel's full withdrawal and the creation of a viable Palestinian state, with Jerusalem as a joint capital of Israel/Palestine, for which Roy and Hass so desperately hope, is a dream that is likely not be realized in their lifetime.

CHAPTER 6

Liberation Struggles
and the Jewish Community

It is perhaps an oddity of history that the Exodus and the prophetic stories the Jewish people formed and bequeathed to the world are being
taken seriously by contemporary Christians in a way that is increasingly
difficult for the Jewish community to understand. As the Jewish people
learn more and more about the trappings of power, a prophetic
Christianity is emerging from powerless Christians of Latin America,
Africa, Asia, and North America.

Rooted in impoverished communities and inspired by the gospel
proclamation of justice and peace, a new understanding of Christianity
has emerged, one that adopts a preferential option for the poor and advocates liberation from oppressive social structures. The recently empowered contemporary Jewish community, however, appears fearful—and
perhaps threatened—by such a prophetic revival within Christianity, for,
in its use of the Exodus and the prophets, Christian liberation theology
speaks for those on the underside of history, the marginalized and the
oppressed.

The Jewish tradition is atrophying under the mantle of political
empowerment. Could it benefit from a sympathetic dialogue with this
movement? Perhaps such a dialogue would enhance our understanding,
not only of those struggling under oppression, but also of our own history. At the same time, since oppression characterizes much of our own
story, our solidarity might add our experience to those who struggle
today.

The revival of the Exodus and prophetic traditions in Christian theologies of liberation is itself heir to a long history of interpreting
the Exodus within political movements. As Michael Walzer, a Jewish

political thinker, demonstrates, in his study of the Exodus in Western history, reference to the Exodus in protest and radical movements is so common that its absence is the exception. It figures prominently in such diverse settings as the political argument of the radical monk Savonarola, who preached twenty-two sermons on the Book of Exodus in the months before his execution; the self-understanding of the English Puritans on their "errand into the wilderness"; and the writings of the early socialist Moses Hess.[1]

Much of the theoretical grounding for this Christian renewal is expressed in Black, Latin American, and Asian liberation theologies. A brief review of representative figures of these movements helps illustrate the revival of these themes from the Hebrew Scriptures.

Liberation Theologies from Around the World

When James Cone, the first person to articulate a theological component of the Black Power movement in the 1960s, searched for a definition of a Christianity which supported the "complete emancipation of black people from white oppression by whatever means black people deem necessary," he found little support in the otherworldly Jesus of white European and American Christianity. Theologians who analyzed the idea of God's righteousness were far removed from the exigencies of daily life. This had the effect of supporting a racist society where "people suffer and die for lack of political justice."

An African-American theologian has a task far beyond theological disputation and speculation. As Cone articulates in his groundbreaking 1969 book, *Black Theology and Black Power*, African-American theologians want to know what the gospel has to say to a person who cannot get work to support his or her family because the society is unjust. "He wants to know what is God's Word to the countless black boys and girls who are fatherless and motherless because white society decreed that blacks have no rights. Unless there is a word from Christ to the helpless, then why should they respond to him? How do we relate the gospel of Christ to people whose daily existence is one of hunger or even worse, despair? Or do we simply refer them to the next world?"

For Cone, the answer is found in the biblical concept of the righteousness of God. This concept refers less to abstract speculation about the quality of God's being, which is commonly found in Greek philosophy, than to God's activity in human history, in God's desire for the oppressed to be free:

> Israel as a people initially came to know God through the Exodus. It was Yahweh who emancipated her from Egyptian bondage and subsequently established a covenant with her at Sinai, promising: "You have

seen what I did to the Egyptians, and how I bore you on eagles' wings and brought you to myself. Now therefore, if you will obey my voice and keep my covenant, you shall be my own possession among all peoples. . . . You shall be to me a kingdom of priests and a holy nation" (Exod. 19:4–6). Divine righteousness means that God will be faithful to his promise, that his purposes for Israel will not be thwarted. Israel, therefore, need not worry about her weakness and powerlessness in a world of mighty military powers, "for all the earth is mine" (Exod. 19:5). The righteousness of God means that he will protect her from the ungodly menacing of other nations. Righteousness means God is doing justice, that he is putting right what men have made wrong.[2]

Cone's exploration of the Jewish Scriptures provides a key to the understanding of his people's history and of contemporary hopes for liberation. In *The Spirituals and the Blues*, Cone demonstrates that the central theological concept in the Black spirituals is the divine liberation of the oppressed from slavery. According to Cone, the spirituals show that the slaves believed that God did not create Africans to be slaves and that slavery was in fact "irreconcilable with their African past and their knowledge of the Christian gospel." Instead, they portray a God who is involved in the history of a struggling people: the deliverance of the children of Israel from bondage in Egypt is also the story of deliverance of an African people enslaved in America:

> O freedom !
> O freedom!
> O freedom over me!
> An' befo' I'd be a slave,
> I'll be buried in my grave,
> An' go home to my Lord an' be free.
>
> My Lord delivered Daniel,
> Why can't he deliver me?
>
> When Israel was in Egypt's land,
> Let my people go;
> Oppressed so hard they could not stand,
> Let my people go;
> Go down, Moses, 'way down in Egypt's land;
> Tell ole Pharaoh
> Let my people go.[3]

The critical task of a Black theology of liberation is to break through the status-quo-reinforcing Christianity held by white America. Cone is

energized by the fact that his insights are grounded in the expressions of
the history of his people. But for Christians, the ultimate foundation is
the life and meaning of Jesus Christ, and often, Jesus is seen as otherworldly, divorced from the political realm. Cone addresses this issue by
placing Jesus in continuity with the Exodus and prophetic traditions.

For Cone, the central theme of the Jewish Scriptures, involvement in
history and the liberation of the people, is the key to understanding Jesus.
Jesus' reading Isaiah's prophecies of messianic justice in the Nazareth
synagogue represents, for Cone, the scandal that the "gospel means liberation, that this liberation comes to the poor, and that it gives them the
strength and courage to break the conditions of servitude." This is the
meaning of incarnation: "God in Christ comes to the weak and the helpless, and becomes one with them, taking their condition of oppression as
his own and thus transforming their slave-existence into a liberated existence."

Incarnation is followed by death and resurrection and, for Cone,
Jesus' earthly life achieves a radical significance not possible without that
death and resurrection. The cross and resurrection mean that Jesus' ministry with the poor "was God himself effecting his will to liberate the
oppressed. The Jesus story is the poor person's story, because God in
Christ becomes poor and weak in order that the oppressed might become
liberated from poverty and powerlessness. God becomes the victim in
their place and thus transforms the condition of slavery into the battle
ground for the struggle of freedom." This is what the resurrection of
Jesus means: "The oppressed are freed for struggle, for battle in the pursuit of humanity."[4]

Cone places Jesus in continuity with the Jewish Scriptures; he also
places Jesus in the dynamic of the Exodus and the prophets, a dynamic
which brings the message of liberation to the fore. The genius of Cone's
theology, like that of his struggling ancestors, is that he rarely mentions
Jesus alone, but rather, in the company of Moses, sent by the God of the
Exodus and of the prophets.

At the same time as Cone was thinking through the theological
dimensions of Black Power in America, the struggle for justice in Latin
America was developing a theological voice. At the Second General
Conference of Latin American Bishops at Medellin, Colombia, in 1968,
the situation of Latin America was described as one of injustice and
despair that "cried to the heavens." The Exodus paradigm was invoked:

> Just as Israel of old, the first People (of God), felt the saving presence
> of God when He delivered them from the oppression of Egypt by the
> passage through the sea and led them to the promised land, so we also,
> the new People of God, cannot cease to feel his saving passage in view

of true development, which is the passage for each and all, from conditions of life that are less human, to those that are more human. Less human: the material needs of those who are deprived of the minimum living conditions, and the moral needs of those who are mutilated by selfishness. Less human: the oppressive structures that come from the abuse of ownership and of power and from exploitation of workers or from unjust transactions. More human: overcoming misery by the possession of necessities; victory over social calamities; broadening of knowledge; the acquisition of cultural advantages. More human also: an increase in respect for the dignity of others; orientation toward the spirit of poverty; cooperation for the common good; the will for peace. More human still: acknowledgment, on man's part, of the supreme values and of God who is their source and term. More human, finally, and especially, faith, the gift of God, accepted by men of good will and unity in the charity of Christ, who calls us all to participation, as sons, in the life of the living God who is the father of all men.[5]

Three years later, in 1971, Gustavo Gutierrez, a Peruvian priest and theologian, published his seminal work *Teologla de la liberacion, Perspectivas*. The English translation, *A Theology of Liberation: History, Politics and Salvation* appeared in 1973. Central to Gutierrez's thesis is that faith in God is intimately linked with works in behalf of justice. In fact, God is a liberating God who acts in behalf of struggling peoples and encourages them to act in their own behalf as well. According to Gutierrez, biblical faith is "faith in a God who reveals himself through historical events, a God who saves in history," and the Exodus is the prime example of such historical activity:

The liberation of Israel is a political action. It is the breaking away from a situation of despoliation and misery and the beginning of the construction of a just and fraternal society. It is the suppression of disorder and the creation of a new order. The initial chapters of Exodus describe the oppression in which the Jewish people lived in Egypt, in that "land of slavery" (13:3; 20:2; Deut. 5:6): repression (1:10–11), alienated work (5:6–14), humiliations (1:13–14), enforced birth control policy (1:15–22). Yahweh then awakens the vocation of a liberator: Moses. "I have indeed seen the misery of my people in Egypt. I have heard their outcry against their slave masters. I have taken heed of their sufferings, and have come down to rescue them from the power of Egypt. . . . I have seen the brutality of the Egyptians towards them. Come now; I will send you to Pharaoh and you shall bring my people Israel out of Egypt." (3:7–10)

Like Cone, Gutierrez sees the Exodus event as paradigmatic for the present. "It remains vital and contemporary due to similar historical experiences which the people of God undergo."[6]

It is within the dynamic of the Exodus and the prophets that the historical Jesus can be recovered in his political dimensions. Gutierrez sees Jesus as a person who confronted the established political and religious powers of his day. As Jesus criticized inauthentic religion, he proclaimed his opposition to the rich and powerful as a radical option for the poor. Jesus' trial was a political one: "Jesus died at the hands of the political authorities, the oppressors of the Jewish people."

Though Jesus did not place himself within any one political faction, the gospel stories point to a deeper political reality. For Gutierrez, the life and preaching of Jesus postulate the search for a new kind of person in a qualitatively different society. Although the kingdom must not be confused with the establishment of a just society, this does not mean, in Gutierrez's mind, that the kingdom is indifferent to this society. Instead, the announcement of the kingdom "reveals to society itself the aspiration for a just society and leads it to discover unsuspected dimensions and unexplored paths. The kingdom is realized in a society of brotherhood and justice." It is this realization that opens up the promise and hope of complete communion of all persons with God.[7]

The use of the Exodus and of the prophets is not limited to African-Americans and Latin Americans. The African continent has been touched by theologies of liberation, most notably in South Africa. Starting in June 1985, as the South African crisis was intensifying, a series of meetings of theologians and church leaders took place in the heart of Soweto, its purpose to chart a course of action for Christians in the perilous waters of apartheid and the state of emergency. The meetings resulted in "The Kairos Document," published in September 1985, described by the authors as an "attempt by concerned Christians in South Africa to reflect on the situation of death in our country." Such reflection produced a critique of the current theological models used by the church to resolve the problems of South Africa. Further, there was an attempt to develop an alternative biblical and theological model that would lead to forms of activity designed to affect the future. Not surprisingly, the authors found the Hebrew Scriptures to have much to say about their present situation, especially as seen through the Exodus experience:

> The description of oppression in the Bible is concrete and vivid. The Bible describes oppression as the experience of being crushed, degraded, humiliated, exploited, impoverished, defrauded, deceived and enslaved. And the oppressors are described as cruel, ruthless, arrogant, greedy, violent and tyrannical and as the enemy. Such descrip-

tions could only have been written originally by people who had had a long and painful experience of what it means to be oppressed. And indeed nearly 90 percent of the history of the Jewish and later the Christian people whose story is told in the Bible, is a history of domestic or international oppression. Israel as a nation was built upon the painful experience of oppression and repression as slaves in Egypt. But what made all the difference for this particular group of oppressed people was the revelation of Yahweh. God revealed himself as Yahweh, the one who has compassion on those who suffer and who liberates them from their oppressors. 'I have seen the miserable state of my people in Egypt. I have heard their appeal to be free of their slave-drivers. I mean to deliver them out of the hands of the Egyptians. . . . The cry of the sons of Israel has come to me, and I have witnessed the way in which the Egyptians oppress them. (Ex. 3:7–9)[8]

Christians throughout Asia are also exploring liberation themes. One example is that of Korean Christians, who are finding the Hebrew Scriptures important to their own identity and crucial to the development of minjung theology. "Minjung" is a Korean word combining two Chinese characters: "min," translated as "people," and "jung," translated as "the mass." Thus, "minjung" means "the mass of the people," or "mass," or simply "the people."

As the Korean theologian Suh Kwang-Sun David describes it, minjung theology grew from the experience of the people laboring under an unjust political regime, and thus, contains a socio-political biography of oppressed Korean Christians. "Theology of minjung is a creation of those Christians who were forced to reflect upon their Christian discipleship in basement interrogation rooms, in trials, facing court-martial tribunals, hearing the allegation of prosecutors, and in making their own final defense. They reflected on their Christian commitment in prison cells, in their letters from prison to families and friends, in their readings of books sent by friends all over the world, in their unemployment, in their stay at home under house arrest, while subject to a twenty-four-hour watch over their activities, and during visits with their friends. Out of that suffering and struggling, Korean Christians want to speak of what they have learned and reflected upon theologically, and to share this with others who in their own social and political context are searching for a relevant theology in Asia."[9]

Though, in the Jewish Scriptures, there is no exact parallel for the term minjung, scholars have searched the experience of the early Hebrews and have found similarities. Moon Hee-Suk Cyris begins an extended analysis of the similarities between the Exodus tradition and the minjung by showing that, in essence, the Jewish Scriptures are the history of belief about the minjung's liberation movement, as well as a creedal statement about their original status as bearers of the image of God in the creation narrative in Genesis. When, later, the minjung are economically under the dominion of the upper class and the powerful, the Jewish Scriptures describe the minjung subjectively, calling them the people of God, and thus, making them the subjects of history. Therefore, the meaning of minjung in their relation to God and their welfare becomes God's concern.

Cyris's conclusion is that the minjung of today are in the midst of an Exodus/prophets paradigm and that the three characteristics of Moses, Amos, and Micah—that is, living and identifying with the people, becoming advocates for the oppressed, and remaining commoners rather than professional prophets—are relevant today. "Like Moses, Amos, and Micah, we in Korea must resolve to follow the footsteps of the true prophet living among our oppressed people and standing against political, social, and economic oppression. To work for the transformation of our society is to participate in the task of ushering in the Kingdom of God."[10]

A Palestinian Theology of Liberation

Just as the history of Jewish suffering prompted extended theological reflection in the Jewish community on the themes of survival and the Christian theologies that oppressed Jews, the Palestinian struggle with Israel has also prompted theological reflection by Arab and Palestinian Christians on their own situation and that of their oppressors. Though this theology is specifically for the Christian community affected by the power of Israel, it is also addressed to the Jewish community in Israel and around the world, as a critical assessment of those aspects of Jewish theology and activity that oppress the Palestinian people. At the same time, Arab and Palestinian Christians are also addressing their Western Christian brothers and sisters, whom they find culpable in the oppression of both Jew and Palestinian. Here we find a theology of liberation that both implicates the oppressor and envisions a path beyond oppression.

Just days after the 1967 war ended, for example, a working group of Christian theologians, which included Father George Khodr, metropolitan of Mount Lebanon and professor of Arab civilization at the Lebanese University, the Reverend Samir Kafity, Martine Albert Lahham, and Father Jean Corban, issued a memorandum whose title posed a question, "What Is Required of the Christian Faith Concerning the Palestine Problem?" For the Christian faithful, they hoped to shed light on three matters: the facts of the present situation and what led to them, revelation of the Bible concerning the ideals of Judaism and Zionism, and ideas on a just solution to the Palestinian problem.

For the Christian theologians gathered together, the present state of crisis between Israel and Palestine began with the destruction of the Temple and the consequent expulsion of the bulk of the Jewish community from Palestine. Over the centuries, the desire to return to Jerusalem was incorporated into Jewish prayer and ritual. This longing is, to their mind, worthy of respect in the "name of freedom of the spirit."

However, the transformation of a religious aspiration into a political claim made the return itself ambiguous. Clearly, the impetus for Zionism was a history of violent anti-Semitism in the Christian kingdoms of Europe, something virtually unknown in the Arabic world since the seventh century, and repentance for Christian "unfaithfulness to the gospel" is essential. The problem is the transference of the sin from West to East; Western Christians are enjoined to search for a solution to anti-Semitism, rather than allowing the entire weight to "hang on the innocent population of Palestine."[11]

The early Jewish settlers were accorded the same welcome that other religious refugees were, but the politicization of the settlement, with the decline of the Ottoman Empire and the Balfour Declaration of 1917, changed the settlers from a refugee population to a political force. When European anti-Semitism reached its "hysterical climax" in the Nazi persecution, the Jewish communities of Eastern and Central Europe should have been reintegrated into those societies, as others were who had been victims of the Nazis.

Theses states refused to do that, and the result is the extension of injustice: "Because the Christians of Europe and America denied their responsibility for a million Jews who were their brothers, they threw one million Arabs out of their homeland of Palestine. 'What have you done to your brother?' In rejecting one million Jews and in despoiling one million Arabs, the Christians of the West have committed a double crime which cries to heaven for redress."

The newly founded state of Israel continued the injustice by refusing to integrate a million refugees whom they had "driven from their homes and lands." This defiance represented, for the theologians, a racist attitude that Christian conscience could not accept: "As long as the Israelis want to found a state based on this kind of racism, it will continue to be the duty of all Christians to oppose it."

To these theologians, the 1967 war demonstrated, once again, the violence inherent in a Zionist state that displaced the Palestinian people. After the war, three hundred thousand new refugees had been created, and a cycle of violence, physical and spiritual, was escalating. Threats of extermination and anti-Semitic demonstrations in some countries, and anti-Arab pronouncements in others, needed to be condemned "without reserve." Anti-Semitism produced Zionism; Zionism produces new waves of anti-Semitism, which in turn strengthens Zionism. All of this, according to the memorandum, was built on a fundamental confusion, a confusion between the well-being of the Jewish people and the interests of the state of Israel. Here, these theologians approach what for them is the central political, but also theological, problem, that is, the confusion between the Jewish people and the state of Israel and between Judaism and Zionism.

From the biblical perspective, there is, according to these theologians, little confusion. The Jews are a people chosen by God, a consecrated people, a nation of priests, whose vocation is to live out in their own history, the history of the whole of humanity. In this way, the Jewish people is prophetic, a witness of God among the nations, chosen to serve the "Salvation of Humanity" rather than to establish itself in any particular national way. Here, the comparison is made between the vocation of the Jews and the vocation of the Church; the Church is also called to serve the world, rather than to enfold itself in a particular race or nation. The creation of an exclusively Jewish state of Israel violated God's plan for the Jews, just as the creation of exclusively Christian states, historically and in the present, violates the calling of the Church.

What is the solution for the Palestinian people? First of all, it lies in the Christian uncovering of the true vocation of the Jews, that is, spirit rather than nation building and in the integration of Jewish citizens by all nations. The second aspect involves the acceptance of all the inhabitants of Palestine—Christians, Muslims, and Jews—of an ethnic, religious, and social pluralism. This pluralism, which moves beyond the simple tolerance of minorities, is the modern equivalent of universalism. The embrace of their true vocation will move Jews to integrate all Palestinian refugees, to make reparation toward them as certain states have done toward Jews, to accept all the inhabitants of Palestine as citizens with full and equal rights. In doing this, the Jewish community will promote active participation in the political life of Palestine, without any discrimination, will use all available resources for the development of all the citizens, and finally, will submit to all international decisions regarding Israel and Palestine.[12]

Seven years later, in 1974, Gabriel Habib, one of the founders of the Middle East Council of Churches, refused an invitation to present a paper at the International Symposium on the Holocaust, held at the Cathedral of Saint John the Divine, and, at the last moment, sent a message instead. The message expresses similar themes, but with a greater sense of urgency, and identifies the Western and Zionist character of the discussion, especially as reflected by the Christians and Jews invited to the conference.

According to Habib, the symposium was limited to Jewish and Christian views, as they had developed in Europe and North America since World War II, and left out Eastern Christians and Muslims as well as Jews of Middle-Eastern background. Though sensitive to Jewish suffering in the West, the symposium posed the problem—Jewish suffering and empowerment—in a way foreign to the East. For Habib, this formulation's lack of balance was a cause of division, both among Christians in the West and East and among Jews, whose life in the West and East has differed considerably: "Spiritual Zionism has been emptied by a temporal Zionism, and the traditional Judaism of the East has been subjugated to the technological Jewish ethos of Europe and America. In the conflict within Judaism, we strongly ally ourselves with those Jews who promote a sense of belonging to a common Judeo-Arab community, free from all discrimination. We are thus in accord with the line of Jewish thinkers and militants reaching from Ahad Ha'am to Judah Magnes, Henrietta Szold, and the Ihud movement, without forgetting Simone Weil (La Pesanteur et la Grace, chapter on Israel)."

In a particularly insightful conclusion, Habib sees the need to develop a critical conscience at the center of Judaism to correct the direction in which Western European and American Jews have led the whole of Judaism—away from solidarity with the oppressed. One way Habib sees to create this critical conscience in Western Christians, as well, is to open a new dialogue with the East, especially with Muslims. This would help Westerners break out of their "fallacious, anachronistic, and provincial situation and put an end to the fatal epoch of Auschwitz, opening the way, in Palestine, to a new era. Jerusalem will be the symbol of this new era, for all those who claim it as their mother—not through blood, but through faith and hope in a just and human world."[13]

The most recent theological development among Palestinian Christians is the call for a Palestinian theology of liberation in Naim Stifan Ateek's book, *Justice and Only Justice: A Palestinian Theology of Liberation*, published in 1989 in response to the first uprising. Here again are theological reflections formulated on the other side of the crucible of Jewish power, yet providing Jews insight into the consequences of the power they wield. Ateek, like the Christian theologians and Habib, seeks, in his own way, a path for Palestinians and Jews beyond opposition and destruction.

Ateek is an Anglican priest and was then canon of Saint George's Cathedral in Jerusalem; he starts his book with an all-too-familiar story. He was born in Beisan, Palestine, twenty miles south of the Sea of Galilee. Ateek's father was born in Nablus and, in the 1920s, left for Beisan to establish himself as a silver and goldsmith. Brought up in an Eastern Orthodox church and later active in the Anglican church, Ateek's father was a pious believer and a successful businessman.

When the Jewish soldiers occupied Beisan, Ateek was eleven years old, and both Muslims and Christians fled their homes in fear that what had been done in Deir Yassin might be done to them. Friends pleaded with Ateek's father to go and to take his ten children with him, lest they be murdered. Those who stayed were ordered to leave upon threat of death: the Muslims were sent across the Jordan River; the Christians were taken on buses to Nazareth, as yet unoccupied, where they were unloaded and abandoned.

Several months later, Jewish soldiers occupied Nazareth, and Ateek's father hoped to be able to return to Beisan. As the exile became permanent, there was really no choice for him: at the age of 57, Ateek's father had to begin again. The story of the family's expulsion recalls again the liturgy of destruction:

> My father asked us to carry with us whatever was lightweight yet valuable or important. The military orders were that we should all meet at the center of town in front of the courthouse, not far from my father's shop. My oldest brother and sisters had each carried a few items to the center of town, hoping to leave them there and return to the house for more. Yet when they got to the courthouse, they found that the soldiers had fenced in the area so that whoever reached there was not allowed to leave again. I recall that my father and mother were quite upset because my brother and sisters had not returned. I was asked to run and hurry them back. So I ran to the center of town, only to be caught with them; the same thing happened to both my father and mother when they came themselves. I discovered later—I was not told at the time—why my parents were so terribly anxious: they realized that in one of the baskets left in front of our house to be picked up after was some of the gold we were trying to take with us. In another basket was some fresh bread my mother had been baking that morning when my father came home with the bad news. My brother Michael was worried about a small Philips radio—one of his most precious possessions—that he had bought just before his marriage. When the soldiers occupied Beisan, they ordered people to turn over their radios. It was so difficult for my brother to part with his radio that he hid it in the garden.[14]

Ateek's theology begins with the expulsion and continues with what, at first glance, seems a sense of conflicting realities that similarly inform his theology—a Palestinian who is at the same time an Arab, a Christian, and an Israeli. After tracing the history of the suffering of the Jews in Europe as a prelude to Zionist colonization and occupation of Palestine, Ateek systematizes the history of Palestinian Israelis in four time periods:

1948–55, a people in shock; 1956–67, a community resigned; 1968–88, a nation awakening; 1988—the uprising. The road traveled between 1948 and today can be seen in two passages from Ateek's book; the first is from 1948, the second from 1988:

1948
Israel's Palestinians were stunned when, within a short period, they had become a minority in their own land. The catastrophe was too great to be believed. Intense bitterness and hatred also developed. On the one hand, profound feelings of recrimination against both the Arab countries and the Zionists were constantly, although privately, expressed. On the other hand, divided families were trying to establish contact with their relatives. Thousands of people attempted to cross the armistice lines in order to be reunited with their families or to return to their homes. Moshe Dayan estimated that between 1949 and the middle of 1954 there was an average of one thousand cases of infiltration per month along the various frontiers, this at the risk of being killed, jailed, or in most cases thrown back across the border.

1988
Within a forty-year period, Palestinian Arabs in Israel have moved from humiliation and shock to despair and resignation and on to raised consciousness and awakening. From isolation and resignation and on to raised consciousness and awakening. From isolation and fragmentation to entity. From a people robbed of its very identity to one that has regained it. If the establishment of the State of Israel was the thesis of the Holocaust, then the uprising of 1988 was the beginning of a process antithetical to the 1948 tragedy of Palestine. Even if the uprising is momentarily quelled, it will remain a turning point in the awakened consciousness of the Palestinians, bringing a new understanding of themselves and a new view of Israel. In fact, Palestinians have already started dating events as pre- or post-uprising. Undoubtedly, a new period in their long struggle for justice and peace has begun.[15]

Ateek sees many problems ahead. Over the years, Palestinian Christians in Israel, a double minority within the Palestinian Muslim ethos and the Jewish state, have struggled to find their identity and voice. In some ways, their leadership has been woefully inadequate, though some improvement, in recent years, justifies a certain optimism in Ateek's view of the potential for action by the churches. However, the beleaguered Christian minority in Israel, and in the West Bank and Gaza as well, has found little support from Western Christians. On the contrary, theological liberals like Paul van Buren and fundamentalist Christians like Jerry Falwell have, to Ateek's mind, ignored and denigrated Palestinian Christians, in effect warning them that to oppose their own displacement is to sin against the resurrection of Israel, which is God's desire.

The Bible, too, is problematic, especially as it is often used against Palestinians by Jews, in Israel and outside, as well as by Western Christians and their missionaries. The term Israel itself becomes ambiguous when it is applied to contemporary life. What does the verse "Blessed be the Lord God of Israel, for he has visited and redeemed his people" mean for Palestinians today? To which Israel is it referring and to whose redemption? Because of the biblical emphasis on Israel and the contemporary reality of Israeli occupation, Ateek sees the state of Israel as a "seismic tremor of enormous magnitude that has shaken the very foundation" of Christian belief. Thus, a major task of Palestinian theology of liberation is to liberate the Bible for Palestinian use, a task that begins with biblical understanding of the land and of justice.[16]

Looking at the Bible from these perspectives, Ateek finds Zionism and the state of Israel wanting. From the biblical perspective, the land belongs to God and to the people who live on the land, according to their ethical stance. Power is to be used to implement justice; the existence of the poor and displaced signifies abuse of power and, therefore, a break with God. It is with the poor and the oppressed, the Palestinians, that God sides.

For Christians, the way out of the cycle of violence is nonviolent resistance, as exemplified by Jesus and embodied, in many ways, in the Palestinian uprising. Ateek sees nonviolence as both prophetic and peacemaking, combining the elements of justice and mercy and asserting the strength of Eastern Christianity, which is pre-Constantinian in its situation as a powerless minority. The center of this resistance should uphold Ateek's major premise of a solution for Israelis and Palestinians, that Palestine is a country for both the Jews and the Palestinians. Though the ideal would be "one united and democratic state for all Palestinians and Jews," Jewish fears of becoming a minority and of annihilation makes this impossible; thus a two-state solution is the only alternative offering justice and the possibility of peace and stability. For Ateek, this position, of the Palestinian leadership and the people themselves, represents a paradox; the two-state solution wanted by Jewish settlers in the first place and rejected by the Palestinians is now being offered by the Palestinians and rejected by the Israelis.

To build acceptance of this two-state solution, new attitudes must be adopted by both communities. To begin, Palestinians must acknowledge the reality and significance of the Holocaust to the Jewish people:

The Palestinians need to become really conscious of and sensitive to the horror of the Holocaust, Nazi Germany's attempt to exterminate the Jews. Granted, the Holocaust was not a Middle Eastern phenomenon, and the Palestinians had nothing to do with it; nevertheless, we need to understand the extent of the trauma for the Jews. Our need to be educated in this matter is similar to that of the Eastern Jews, the Sephardim, for whom the Holocaust was also not part of their frame of reference. Admittedly, we as Palestinians have refused to accept, much less internalize, the horrible tragedy of the Holocaust. We have resisted even acknowledging it, believing that we have been subjected to our own holocaust at the hands of the Jews. Many Palestinians have doubted that the Holocaust even occurred; they could not believe that those who suffered so much could turn around and inflict so much suffering on the Palestinians. We have also refused to admit or acknowledge its uniqueness, pointing to the attempt to destroy the Assyrian and Armenian Christians in this century.

Be that as it may, a new attitude is expected of us vis-à-vis the Holocaust. We must understand the importance and significance of the Holocaust to the Jews, while insisting that the Jews understand the importance and significance of the tragedy of Palestine for the Palestinians.

For their part, Jews have to admit that they have wronged the Palestinian people:

The new attitude of the Israeli Jews toward the Palestinians should be simply this: We are sorry that we came to you with arrogance and a feeling of superiority. We came with good and not so good reasons. But we are now here in the land. Forgive us for the wrong and the injustice that we have caused you. We took part of your country. We ignored you. We pretended that you did not exist, or even worse, that you did not matter. We stereotyped you, convincing others that you are all terrorists. We have refused to recognize that you have any rights, while we insisted that you should recognize and legitimate our right to your land. We have insisted, and convinced the United States and others to insist, that you recognize our claim to your land. And amazingly, many governments in the world have agreed with us. We have refused to negotiate with your representatives, rejecting them as terrorists. Here, too, we have extracted a pledge from the United States government that it will not negotiate with your representatives. We have done this and much more. We have wronged you. Now, we

recognize that the healthiest solution to any conflict is the use of negotiation and compromise, as opposed to power, repression, and control.
We are willing to negotiate with your representatives, the P.L.O., and
we choose to live in peace with you. We want to stay a part of the
Middle East. We want to live among you, Muslims and Christians.
Your own country of Palestine today used to be our country two thousand years ago. We still have many cherished historic memories that
keep pulling us to it. It is our "holy land," too, our "promised land."
There is room for both of us here.[17]

Ateek's analysis brings forward, into the present, many of the central
themes of Arab and Palestinian Christians, and those of Palestinians with
Muslim backgrounds analyzed earlier, as they have witnessed the slow
but sure process of destruction. The images are difficult for Jews: that of
occupying the land, uprooting a people, creating ghettos, expelling, rap-
ing, torturing, murdering. We see a theological struggle to separate that
which part of the Jewish community insists is inseparable—Judaism and
Zionism—and a call for the reemergence of the prophetic Jewish tradition, in their eyes essentially non-statist. The return of the Jews to
Palestine, legitimated by Jewish and Western Christian theology, is
unfair and unjust—in short, a disaster for the Palestinian people. Rather
than aberrational, the brutality of the occupation army is in continuity
with Zionist policy from the beginning, a reality Palestinians know intimately in their history and bodily.

From the beginning of the twentieth century and now into the
twenty-first, theirs has been a liturgy of destruction as well, ignored by
much of the world. There is also a call for confession of past and present
injustices as if this, rather than the disappearance of Israel, might allow a
path of reconciliation to emerge. To be sure, the state of Israel, in and of
itself, is a symbol of oppression for Palestinians, but the hope is that the
people of Israel and Palestine, Jew, Christian, and Muslim, will overcome
what the state represents and live together in a unity characterized by
mutual respect, diversity, and pluralism.

What does this emerging Christian theology have to say to Jewish
theology? To begin with, it reminds Jews of a time when the possibility
of theological legitimation of a state was a debatable proposition in the
Jewish community. It also seeks to clarify a crucial issue that has been lost
to that legitimation; that is, the state of Israel was formed outside the
arena of contemporary Jewish suffering, in Palestine rather than in
Europe. Why should the Palestinian people suffer for the recognized sins
of Europe?

While recognizing the tragedy of the European catastrophe for the
Jews, Arab and Palestinian Christian theologians separate the settling of
Jewish refugees from the establishment of an exclusive Jewish state.

Rather than logically expressing an evolving history within the Middle East, the movement of refugees into a state repeats a pattern of Western colonialism in which "inferior" indigenous peoples are displaced. In doing this, the refugees pervert the idealistic rhetoric of saving a remnant people and oppress another people.

Arab and Palestinian Christian theology has much to say to the shifting perspective of a Jewish theology that now, for the first time in two thousand years, is called to legitimate, rather than to confront, state theology. If, in Holocaust theology, Jews continue their tradition of confronting the world with the suffering imposed on the Jewish people, the Jewish tradition of dissent, especially after the uprisings, forces Jews to confront one another. With Arab and Palestinian Christian theology, for the first time, others confront the world and the Jewish people with the suffering caused by Jewish power. Thus, beyond the specifics, Christian theology emanating from the Middle East is a challenge and a warning: Jews are becoming everything against which they protested.

Just as the Holocaust has reached liturgical expression, the Palestinian tragedy has achieved a like expression. We have analyzed David Roskies's version of a Jewish response to destruction—the recalling of the ancient archetypes, the reunification of diverse classes and religious and nonreligious sensibilities in the European ghettos, the movement from a literature of consolation to a literature that prompts action, even uprising. This is occurring today among those who live on the other side of Jewish power. In fact, for Palestinians, the Jewish liturgy of destruction has come to legitimate that which it originally resisted: statelessness, deportation, murder. Thus, Palestinians insist that the Jewish liturgy of destruction be complemented by a similar Palestinian liturgy.

That liturgy, inclusive of Palestinian and Jew, might be exemplified in the statement of Mubarak Awad, a Palestinian Christian advocate of nonviolent resistance, upon his deportation from Israel in June 1988:

> I am a Palestinian in an enemy court.
>
> I am a Christian in a court of Jewish justice.
> I am from occupied Jerusalem in an Israeli High Court.
>
> I accepted to come to court knowing all the odds. I gave you legitimacy and recognized you as a State and recognized your High Court of Justice because I am searching for true peace. Only peaceful means can achieve peace. If peace is the sign of victory, victory has to be for both Palestinians and Israelis. Both must be winners; there can be no losers. This would be the great measure of justice.

Moral and judicial responsibility is not a historical or religious debate. It is the reality that I face today with the rest of the Palestinian people. You have the power, the law and the gun pointing in my face. I am armed with hope, truth and nonviolence pointing toward your conscience. If the uprising will not open your eyes and soul to tell you we need freedom I don't know what will.

I am here to fight my deportation order. Uprooting me from my family, land, friends and culture is a disgrace. As a government Israel is doing all it can to rid Palestinians from their land. It is deliberate, through unjust laws that we can't change, with tricks and unfair practices. You are depriving me of my basic human and religious rights.

As a Palestinian I never hated you. I don't hate you now. And I will never hate you.

But as a Jerusalemite I am telling you—I will be back.[18]

The liturgy of destruction heard from the Palestinian side confirms the initial and ongoing Jewish intuition that Palestinians are as intimate to Jewish history as Jews are to Christian history. The victors in Israel, like the victors in Europe, create a history that is univocal in its outlook and violent in its expression. After the celebration of victory, its hollowness becomes evident, the oppression of others more obvious. The search begins for a way back to the community vocation that affirms rather than destroys.

The original desire to be neither victim nor oppressor returns, yet, paradoxically, the critical thought necessary to break through the ideologies and theologies that legitimate power rest with the defeated and marginalized. Thus, the renewal of Christianity in the West rests, to a large extent, in Jewish hands, that is, with those who lived on the other side of Christian power. It is the Jewish people who provide insight into the betrayal of Christian witness.

What is startling for Jews, as indeed it was at first for Christians, is that today Palestinians call the Jewish community to account. For they have lived on the other side of Jewish power and see through the ideological and theological justifications of their oppression. For Christians, after the Holocaust, the German Catholic theologian Johann Baptist Metz wrote, "We Christians can never go back behind Auschwitz: to go beyond Auschwitz if we see clearly, is impossible for us by ourselves. It is possible only together with the victims of Auschwitz." For Jews today it might be said, "We Jews can never go back behind empowerment: to go beyond empowerment, if we see clearly, is impossible for us by ourselves.

It is possible only together with the victims of our empowerment, the Palestinian people."

Thus, the inclusive liturgy of destruction sees the history of Palestinian and Jew as now intimately woven together, the bond of suffering as the way forward for both peoples. From this vantage point, Mubarak Awad's pledge that he will one day return to Jerusalem should be seen as a hope for the Palestinian people and for the Jewish people as well.

Four Elements of a Jewish Response

1. Wrestling with Christian Theologies of Liberation

The reactions of the Jewish community to the emergence of liberation theology, as intimated earlier, have been diverse, from ignorance to curiosity to critique and dismissal. To the curious, liberation theology represents the possibility of a politically active force for uplifting poor and oppressed people, though for the curious, their knowledge of Christianity (and of Judaism, too) is often limited, and thus, they observe from a distance. For Jewish theologians and institutional leaders, the rise of liberation theology can be more difficult: some see this revival as an ancient form of Christian triumphalism returning in a new guise. At the same time, for many Jews, liberation theology's call for societal transformation presages chaos; they fear such restructuring can lead only to totalitarian regimes.[19]

There is another element here as well. In most liberation theologies, the Jewish Exodus is used as a paradigm of revolution, but contemporary Jews are nowhere to be found in the writings of the theologians. This continues an age-old Christian tradition of seeing the Jewish people as bequeathing the "Old Testament" and Jesus, and then disappearing from history, their mission accomplished. The use of the Jewish story is coupled with our historical invisibility. Too often, liberation theologians often miss an element crucial to the Exodus story itself: that it has a history of interpretation by the people who lived the story and those who live today.

The movement to place Jesus within the history of the Jewish people—which is at the same time the rescuing of Jesus from the otherworldliness of various Christian traditions—also opens once again the horrible landscape of the crucifixion. For Jews, of course, the accusation of responsibility for crucifying Jesus is an indelible mark of the last 1,900 years—years which culminated in the death camps of the Nazi period. And since that time, ecumenical relations have been predicated on the removal of that stigma, which, to some extent, has been accomplished since Vatican II. But some liberation theologians, in their description of the historical Jesus, come dangerously close to posing this problem again. This, combined with a militant Christian social movement, understandably arouses Jewish concern. The sign of the cross as a banner for social reform is greeted with both skepticism and fear.[20]

Moreover, the ecumenical movement over the last thirty years has primarily taken place among educated white middle- and upper middle-class Christians and Jews, who have vested interests in continuing the political status quo. The rise of liberation theology questions the religious integrity of these Christians, who base their faith on cultural symbols and ritual assent rather than on socio-political transformation. Have Jews been talking with people whose Christianity is now being challenged?

The ironic twist is that, despite the Holocaust, many Jews are now quite comfortable with the institutional church. Moreover, they are extremely uneasy with grass-roots Christian movements. This comfort is bound up with preferring known religious affirmations to the unknown, but also with the institutional protection sometimes afforded the Jewish community by Catholic and Protestant institutions that have moral and political leverage in Western societies. That some unfamiliar configuration of Christianity and Christian institutions might emerge raises the level of Jewish anxiety.

The most frightening aspect for parts of the Jewish community, however, is the Third World character of liberation theology and its emerging cross-cultural solidarity. Charges of imperialism and neocolonialism are part and parcel of these movements, and the United States is a frequent target in their critique. At the same time, Israel is heavily involved on the side of the government in some of the areas where liberation struggles are the strongest and most symbolic, as noted earlier. Thus, the fear that movements of liberation will not only be critical of America but also of Israel leads some to accuse these movements of anti-Semitism.

In a more significant way, the theological reflections of the Jewish community after the Holocaust do not resonate with triumphal language in the theological realm. On the one hand, the Exodus—God who rescues the people from bondage—is contradicted by the Holocaust event; on the other hand, the need for empowerment renders prophetic voices naïve and even dangerous. If Christians have appropriated the Jewish Exodus and the prophets, without reference to the contemporary heirs of the Hebrew Scriptures, it is also true that the Jewish community, because of our history, has been reluctant to claim its own heritage.

It is clear, then, that the impasse between the Christian theologies of liberation and the Jewish community is multifaceted and complex, with many strains and tensions that will exist into the future. The question, it seems, is not how to go beyond the tension but how to move constructively within it. The choice to be with and for the empire in this struggle seems, on the face of it, to be safer and less complex: to choose to move with those who seek community is to promote a configuration that may change both the Christian and the Jewish perception of the world and of ourselves. By placing ourselves in the struggle for justice, we of the Jewish community may discover the other side of our own history.

At the outset it seems that the theological task of dialogue, between the post-Holocaust Jewish community and the emerging theologies of liberation, is framed in confrontation: a God unable to rescue the people within the Holocaust versus a God leading the people to freedom and justice. Or, if Israel is a redemptive sign, somehow connected to God, the connection remains hidden while the Christian theologians of liberation boldly announce the building of God's kingdom.

And yet, when analyzed more closely, the triumphal strain in liberation theology is increasingly countered by strains of doubt in religious language. For the liberation of the oppressed, like the experience of the concentration camps, is not a superficial testimony to religious certainty. Rather it is a test of God's fidelity and of human struggle, characterized by abandonment and death.

To those in the struggle for liberation, theological language is increasingly found wanting. Joan Casañas, a Spaniard and longtime resident of Chile, describes the gap between revolutionary activity and theological language in a fascinating essay, "The Task of Making God Exist." Casañas begins with the question "Activist, What Do You See in the Night?" and cites a conversation with Christian activists after the overthrow of Salvador Allende's government in 1973, shortly before the massacre of the Chilean people began. After discussing the importance of religious language and of the Christian faith of the majority of Chileans, they reached a conclusion: "There is no need to tell the people that God is with them, that God will help them to overcome the right-wing plot; that God is their friend and will save them. For the more a people becomes organized and fights for socialism, the more it realizes that no one outside its world, not even God, is doing anything on behalf of the people's liberation other than what the people itself is doing. It would be better for us to be silent about what God is and what God can do."

The problem is that most theologians, even liberation theologians, want to mold the experience of those who struggle for justice into theological categories to which the people themselves no longer relate. But activists want to know "what we are living through and seeing, and what has been given to us in the present; not what we have been 'taught' as being 'good,' and what we have 'assented to' with 'religious' fidelity." For Casañas, a concrete example of this is the prayer of petition:

> Many individuals and groups of proven praxis in revolutionary faith, and with obvious practical love for the oppressed lived in openness to the transcendence proposed by the gospel, do not feel comfortable with a prayer that consists in asking for things from God, even though those things may be justice or the strength to fight for it. . . . A little old woman from the Christian community in my neighborhood, a working woman who had been exploited all her life and who was very much aware of the nature of the conflict in our society, remarked at a community faith celebration, "Yes, we have asked God often to let justice come and let Somoza go, but God does not listen at all." I think this checks, or even checkmates, the most brilliant pages of theology, as far as talk about God and God's treatment of us is concerned. Hers was not the sarcasm of the rationalist spinning theories about God, but the disappointment of the poor exploited person who has nothing against God, but who senses that God should be something other than what has generally been thought and taught.[21]

At the same time that Casañas rejects talk of God's omnipotence, he also rejects the more recent theories of the crucified God, who refuses to act with force and instead suffers with the people until liberation. The reason for the rejection of this theological category is similar to that which motivates a rejection of prayer of petition: revolutionary activists do not see this kind of God in the night.

For Casañas, direct knowledge of God is impossible, especially in an unjust society. Those who affirm God's presence in an unjust society often see God as a legitimator of that injustice—but can that conception of God be accepted? Theism becomes a form of idolatry, a worship of false gods. In this case, a certain atheism is necessary, a refusal to believe in a God who sanctions oppression. Still, the theologians who recognize most theism as idolatrous continue to place limitations on those who explore God through revolutionary activity:

> When those who fight and die today for real, concrete justice—the justice that capitalism impedes—do not speak of God and, for example, do not experience God as Father, it is thought and said, even in the most "advanced" theology or pastoral writing, that something is lacking in them. It is said that they must be "evangelized," that we have a "message" to give them, that we know something about God that they do not know. It seems to me that we are involving ourselves in a serious contradiction between knowledge acquired through conscious practice and knowledge acquired through learned and religiously accepted truths. . . . If many of those fighting and dying selflessly for the people's liberation (that is, placed in the practical life-situation

acknowledged to be optimal for "knowing God") have not discovered that "God exists" and is "Father," is it not possible that this "message" that "God exists" and is "Father" may not be as profound, at least in its formulation, as it has generally seemed to us? Has what many activists have not discovered by giving their lives for the oppressed been discovered by a Videla, a Pinochet, a Somoza, or the bishops who honor them? Has some "apostle" told it to them, and they believed it with all their mind and heart? Is it so easy to know something about God in a world where injustice is so rampant?[22]

What Casañas is describing is a new understanding of fidelity, a broadening of language and conceptualization in the struggle for justice. Under such conditions, the certainty of God falls away, though the absolute refusal of God is also questioned. For some, religious tradition does nothing but hinder the revolutionary struggle; others admire its continuity among the people as a source of strength in adversity; still others see tradition as providing clues to a possible reconstruction. Casanas's point is that those who struggle in the present proceed with the insights that are bequeathed within the moment, and that entering the depths of history is the way of fidelity:

> There is the Colombian guerrilla fighter who often prays the rosary with some of his comrades. And there is the guerrilla fighter who rejects all sentiments of a religious nature, or even an openness to transcendence, because of the great fear he has of succumbing to rapture that would curtail his involvement in the struggle. And there is the one who seems cold and insensitive to anything that might be a symbol, or poetry, or a mystique, but who readily and sincerely adapts to whatever the circumstances require for liberating efficacy. And there is the Montonero leader who, after years in jail and exile, attended a Mass on the fourth anniversary of the assassination of Miguel Enriquez and stated publicly that the fact that he, the Montonero, was able to escape from jail and from Argentina was "a gift from God" (and no one dared ask him what the death of Miguel Enriquez was, on the part of God). There was another one, who did not attend that Mass, because for tactical reasons he feared his presence would be interpreted as a compromise with the religious language and symbolism that, for him, mask a kind of magic. And there was the one who attended for the sake of solidarity, observed, listened, and departed, saying that all this was not so bad, that there was something authentic about it, but that it had been expressed better by the "unbelieving" relatives and political leaders who had spoken at the Mass than by the priests with all their homilies and prayers.[23]

As Casañas moves from a triumphal Christianity to one which is open to the insights which come from struggle and death, the Jewish experience of the Holocaust comes into view. Though faith did not disappear in the Holocaust, certainty did, and the Exodus and prophetic traditions are confronted with a horror which shatters ancient precepts and beliefs. If Casañas starts with the question "Activist, what do you see in the night?", the Holocaust raises a similar question for the Jewish victims: "What did you see in the night?"

It is possible that, by recounting the night vision of the Holocaust victims, we might be able to provide the basis for a dialogue with those who, today, are peering into the darkness with fear and trepidation? Could it be that we are not alone in the night but are joined by sisters and brothers in a new continuity of struggle and affirmation, a retrospective solidarity across religious and geographic boundaries, which might portend a flesh and blood solidarity for the future? As we probe the night together, perhaps we can begin to imagine a broader tradition of faith and struggle, which is confessional for past atrocities, is bold in allowing the experiences of peoples to speak, unfettered by religious or political constraints, in short, one that allows the reality of the night to speak.

As with the night of which Casañas speaks, the night of Holocaust is ever present. The darkness contains many peoples. They are different— each with their own history and voice; they are also similar—pertaining to oppression and resistance, abandonment and affirmation, prayer and negation. But in the night, if just for a moment, they are one.

Consider the reality of death and abandonment, first from a Jewish mother of Eastern Europe, then from the eyes of a pastoral worker in Guatemala:

Eastern Europe
When I came up to the place we saw people naked lined up. But we were still hoping that this was only torture. Maybe there is hope— hope of living. . . . One could not leave the line, but I wished to see— what are they doing on the hillock? Is there anyone down below? I turned my head and saw that some three or four rows were already killed on the ground. There were some twelve people amongst the dead. I also want to mention what my child said while we were lined up in the ghetto, she said, "Mother, why did you make me wear the Shabbat dress; we are going to be shot," and when we stood near the dug-outs, near the grave, she said, "Mother, why are we waiting, let us run!" Some of the young people tried to run, but they were caught immediately, and they were shot right there. I had my daughter in my arms and ran after the truck. There were mothers who had two or three children and held them in their arms running after the truck. We ran all the way. There were those who fell—we were not allowed to

help them rise. They were shot right there wherever they fell . . . When we all reached the destination, the people from the truck were already down and they were undressed—all lined up. All my family was there—undressed, lined up. The people from the truck, those who arrived before us. . . .

When it came to our turn, our father was beaten. We prayed, we begged with my father to undress, but he would not undress, he wanted to keep his underclothes. He did not want to stand naked. Then they tore off the clothing of the old man and he was shot. I saw it with my own eyes. And then they took my mother, and she said, let us go before her; but they caught mother and shot her too; and then there was my grandmother, my father's mother standing there; she was eighty years old and she had two children in her arms. And then there was my father's sister. She also had children in her arms and she was shot on the spot with the babies in her arms. . . .[24]

Guatemala

All day long we were fleeing. We ran seeking the ravines. We brought all the injured from the other villages; there were many. The largest number were women and little children. We hid in the mountains, but the women wore clothes of many colors, and from the helicopters they could see us very well. We saw the helicopters begin to fly in circles, surrounding us all. They began to machine-gun the people. The only way of saving ourselves was to run to the ravine and throw ourselves into it, which was quite steep. We began to run and run to the mountain, falling and falling. The small children ran alone. They were being left behind, getting lost among so many people; and all shouted, "Mama, Mama." One woman cried; she cried a lot, talking in the language of Quiche. I didn't understand well what she said. Someone said to me, "She's crying because her child was killed." I had seen the little child. She had been born 15 days earlier. The woman had carried the child on her back. She fell when she was running, and she fell on the child and it was killed. She said, "God is going to punish me. I have a great sin on me because I have killed my child." A woman said, "God is not with us, God has abandoned us. If we haven't done anything bad, if we haven't asked for so much, why does God abandon us now?"[25]

Commonality can be found in resistance as well. During the Somoza dictatorship, two Nicaraguan peasants discuss their movement toward armed resistance, as does a Warsaw ghetto fighter:

ALEJANDRO: "One sentence here is very clear: 'Therefore do not fear the people.' The fear you have is that they're going to do you some harm. And when are they going to do you harm? When you're against certain systems, certain injustices. That is, we're absolutely forbidden to be afraid of telling the truth, of being against anything that will endanger us, even our lives. It's clear that for the sake of justice we have to risk even our bodies. They can kill the body but they can't kill the cause for which we fight. And it spreads even wider: The Gospel tells us some words here in secret that we're supposed to shout."

Another boy said: "I think like you, Alejandro, that here, the government we have in Nicaragua, it does whatever it wants with us, with the people, and because we're afraid we don't fight against these injustices. According to what it says here we shouldn't be afraid of that, because if they're doing an injustice to the people we should fight. And all right, let's die, the body isn't worth anything and they can destroy our bodies but not our souls. It seems to me then that we ought to fight and not submit."[26]

The Warsaw ghetto fighter writes:

The number of our losses, that is, the victims killed by shooting and by the fires, in which men, women and children have been consumed, is immense. Our last days are approaching. But so long as we have arms in our hands we will continue to fight and resist. We have rejected the German ultimatum demanding our capitulation. Aware that our day is at hand, we demand from you to remember how we were betrayed. What we have experienced cannot be described in words. We are aware of one thing only: what has happened has exceeded all our dreams. The Germans twice ran from the ghetto . . . I have the feeling that great things are happening, that what we have dared is of great importance. Beginning with this evening we are passing to partisan tactics . . . Keep well, my dear. Perhaps we shall meet again. But what really matters is that the dream of my life has come true. Jewish self-defense in the Warsaw Ghetto has become a fact. Jewish armed resistance and retaliation have become a reality. I have been the witness of the magnificent heroic struggle of our Jewish fighters.[27]

Prayer becomes an act of affirmation, a prelude to martyrdom. As told by an eyewitness, Shlomo Zlichovsky, a Polish Jew and a teacher, prepared for his death in much the same way as did Salvadoran Archbishop Oscar Romero.

The eyewitness writes:

Then, as the last preparations were being made for the hanging, I, too, looked into the face of Shlomo Zlichovsky. It was smiling with joy. I stood in the crowded place, in the midst of many humiliated Jews. But suddenly a spirit of encouragement passed over all of us. The gallows were standing in a row, under each of them a chair in readiness. The Germans were in no hurry. A pity to waste a single moment of the "entertainment." But Shlomo Zlichovsky, still singing, urged them on: "Nu!" (come on already), and jumped on the chair in order to put his head into the hanging loop. Some moments passed. We all held our breath. Deathly silence came over the market place, a silence that found its redemption as Shlomo Zlichovsky's mighty voice was shattering it in his triumphant Shema Yisra'el. We were all elevated; we were exalted. We shouted . . . without a voice; cried . . . without tears; straightened up . . . without a movement; and called, called altogether in the innermost recesses of our souls: *Shema Yisra'el* ("Hear, O Israel: The Lord your God, the Lord is One").[28]

Romero writes:

My life has been threatened many times. I have to confess that, as a Christian, I don't believe in death without resurrection. If they kill me, I will rise again in the Salvadoran people . . . If they should go so far as to carry out their threats, I want you to know that I now offer my blood to God for justice and the resurrection of El Salvador. . . A bishop will die, but the church of God, which is the people, will never perish.[29]

The commonality found in the night does not mitigate the unique quality of historical events, nor does it encourage a superficial universalism. Entire books are written about the absolutely unique quality of the Jewish Holocaust. But, is not the loss of life during the African slave trade, estimated to be in the millions, a unique event of mass death, a holocaust, as it were, of immense proportions for the African people then and now? For the Guatemalan peasant, particularly the indigenous Indian population, the continuing slaughter of its people and the decimation of native peoples in the Americas over the centuries is a unique event of mass death as well.

Western Jews have participated in and benefited from these events of violence and atrocity. America may be seen as a haven for Jewish people, but this can hardly be said for the Native American and the African-American. Further, the present also produces a startling picture: we, as Jews, continue to benefit from a racist society in America and are building such a society in Israel. To an alarming degree, we have supported policies in the United States and Israel that assure continued atrocities in Central America and South Africa.

The role of the United States in the atrocities of Central America and in support of the apartheid regime in South Africa is well documented. But the Israeli role is relatively unknown in the Jewish community, though it, too, is documented. Such operations were often unannounced and covert, dictated by the needs of survival.

As we have seen, there are Jews who speak and write about these policies as forms of complicity with evil and as a denigration of our own people. If we are going to learn how to see the suffering of other peoples in the night, as we so well see our own, we need to be honest about our own present contribution to that suffering. And if it is true that the language of the Exodus and the prophets rings hollow in our experience of Holocaust, it is difficult to search for a new religious language, while at the same time we contribute to the suffering of others.

The late Victor Perera, a Sephardic Jew, who grew up in Guatemala and lived in Israel, detailed Israeli involvement in Guatemala in the 1970s and 1980s. As summarized by Jane Hunter in her monthly research report, *Israeli Foreign Affairs*, Perera presents a vivid account of the suffering of the Guatemalan people: the family of four, killed with an Uzi submachine gun for inquiring after the disappeared; the genocidal assault on the Mayan Indians, the highlands where they are concentrated, "emptied" in a scorched-earth campaign to purge guerrilla "contamination." At the same time, his article details the scope of Israeli assistance to the Guatemalan regime.

- The major arms deliveries of Galil assault rifles, Arava counter-insurgency airplanes, armored cars and assorted gear that kept the military in its bloody business after the Carter Administration, hoping to bring about an easing of human rights abuses, banned military aid to Guatemala.

- The installation of the computer system which kept track of "subversive elements" and the computer system—this one made by the major electronics firm, Tadiran, which has also brought high technology to the white minority in South Africa—which measures the usage of water, electricity and telephone, enabling the military to pinpoint and raid houses where there is a high level of activity.

- The training of soldiers loyal to Gen. Efrain Rios Mott in his overthrow of the previous military government and in his Plan Victoria 82, the infamous scorched-earth and forced-resettlement campaign to exterminate an insurgency

deeply anchored in the largely Indian Guatemalan peas-
antry.

- The training and inspiration of Guatemalan military officers in structuring the new "model villages" which, along
with mandatory civil defense patrols, are designed to exercise total control over residents.[30]

Israel did little better in relation to Nicaragua. After supporting the
Somoza dynasty for close to thirty years, including weapons sales right
up to the end of Anastasio Somoza's reign in 1979, Israel began as early
as 1983 to aid the counter-revolutionaries, responsible for the death of
more than 12,000 Nicaraguan citizens. Some examples follow.

- In July, 1983, Pastora received 500 AK-47 rifles from Israel
via Venezuela. These weapons came from a large stash
Israel had captured in Lebanon in 1982.

- In July, 1983, Reagan Administration officials revealed that
Israel had assented to an American request and had recently
begun to supply arms captured in Lebanon—artillery
pieces, mortar rounds, mines, hand grenades and ammuni-
tion—to Honduras.

- In April, 1984, US officials in Honduras confirmed that the
Contras received arms from Israel, and five months later
Washington officials again noted that the Contras had
"received official and private aid from Israel" and other
countries. *Time* reported that "Israel funnels arms to the
Contras through the Honduran Army" and, according to
the respected *Latin American Weekly Report*, the CIA had
been footing the bill for all of the Israeli arms shipments.

- The Contras also had the benefit of Israeli intelligence
experts, "retired or reserve Israeli army commandos . . .
hired by shadowy private firms." Recruiters in Israel were
offering top dollar—$6,500 to $10,000 a month for this
work.[31]

By the mid-1980s, when American aid to the counter-revolutionaries
began to run out, the government of Israel increased its support, including the addition of Israeli military advisors.

The relationship between Israel and apartheid South Africa was
older and even broader: it included cooperation in economic, military,
nuclear, scientific, and academic affairs, as well as in the areas of energy,

tourism, culture, sports, transportation, agriculture, and intelligence. Of all the cooperative enterprises, the military link was the most important to South Africa.

Although Israel once stated that it was abiding by the 1977 United Nations embargo on arms to South Africa, by 1983, it was widely known that Israel was violating the agreement. As Jane Hunter documents, South Africa bought Israeli weapons, including attack boats equipped with ship-to-ship missiles, patrol boats and jet fighters, radar stations, electronic fences, infiltration alarm systems, and night-vision apparatus. At the same time, South Africa made a major commitment to help finance Israeli weapons systems, including the Lavi, Israel's fighter bomber for the 1990s. Israelis trained South Africans in everything from naval construction to counter-insurgency techniques and "observers have noted striking similarities between Israeli and South African techniques."

Cooperation between Israel and South Africa in developing a nuclear capability was significant for many years and continued until the collapse of the apartheid regime. In the 1980s, Shimshon Zelniker, then head of social studies at the Labor Party's college, met with future Nobel laureate Bishop Desmond Tutu and other Black leaders in South Africa. In an article published in the *Jerusalem Post*, Zelniker reported that the Black leaders had "lambasted" Israel's collaboration with the white minority regime, and they spoke of similarities between South African apartheid and the plight of the Palestinians on the West Bank and Gaza. Bishop Tutu wondered how Jews could seek a monopoly of the Holocaust and, at the same time, refuse to understand the fascist nature of apartheid.[32]

It is important to understand the massive shift in Jewish perspective that Bishop Tutu suggests, in noting Israel's support of the apartheid regime, and it is true for the cases in Guatemala and Nicaragua, cited earlier, though, unfortunately, this hardly exhausts Israel's foreign policies worthy of mention in this regard. The three major reasons for such policies relate to economics, defense, and the increasing surrogate role for United States interests—no doubt a reasonable return payment for massive United States aid to Israel over the years.

Yet, mention survival as a reason for supporting Hitler during Holocaust, or even remaining silent or neutral for whatever reason, and one is quite correctly condemned. Even the Americans who helped to liberate the concentration camps are criticized for not actively committing themselves to a policy of rescuing Jews, and the Jewish community itself in America and in Palestine is not spared investigation on this count. And yet, for reasons of state, the Israeli government, aided and abetted by many American Jews, pursued policies which seem, to the oppressed, to be quite similar. Bishop Tutu immediately recognized a similarity between the Jewish Holocaust and apartheid, and yet, it is no longer obvious to many in the Jewish community, at least in practical political and military actions.[33]

In religious terms, the inability to see the connection between our own suffering and the suffering of others may be related to a contemporary form of idolatry, an ancient Jewish insight that, like the Exodus and the prophets, has atrophied in the contemporary Jewish community and has been reclaimed by Christian liberation struggles.

Idolatry has at least two aspects: the problem of cultic images of God and the worship of other, false gods. Pablo Richard, a Chilean biblicist and sociologist, understands the first aspect of idolatry as a radical call to liberation found in the Exodus story. Affirmation of the transcendence of God is, at the same time, an affirmation of God's plan to liberate the people. A refusal to work for liberation is an act of idolatry—not the idolatry of false gods, but the idolatry that is possible only from within the worship of the true God. "In Exodus 32, God reveals his transcendence as God the liberator, and not a God who consoles the oppressed so that they will accept their condition as an oppressed people. The veneration of God as consoler is idolatry. The seat or throne of this god—where he reigns or manifests his presence to the people—is gold, and gold is the symbol of domination." At the same time, the oppressor is seen as an idolater as well: both the oppressed and the oppressor "practice an idolatry that deforms and perverts the revelation of the liberating transcendence of God."

The prophets embody the critique of the second aspect of idolatry, refusing to worship false gods. The false gods are domination and excessive materialism; they take on a transcendent quality which displaces the liberating God. According to Richard, Isaiah 46:1–7 illustrates this understanding, the central idea being that the idolatrous have to "carry" their idols, whereas believers are carried, lifted, and liberated by Yahweh.

Christian Scriptures continue and further the understanding of idolatry, and Richard sees the transcendent presence of God in humans, in nature, and in history as the most radical critique of idolatry. This transcendent and liberating presence of God in history is antagonistic to all idolatrous practices and all fabrication of idols, because now God's liberating deeds in history have been revealed. On the other hand, idolatry is revealed through the destruction of human beings and of nature, to the extent that human beings make idols that allow them to manipulate powers and values, to use them against other human beings.[34]

The most interesting aspect of Richard's and of other Christian liberation theologians' discussions of idolatry is that they find idolatry in the Bible to be intimately linked to situations of political oppression. The refusal to be idolatrous is the refusal to place systems of domination over the human quest for compassion and solidarity. Stated another way,

Christian liberation theologians assert that the God we worship is not defined by the prayers we say or the words used to justify activities in the world, but that the activity itself defines our God and commitment.

When we face a system of domination whose rationale assumes a transcendent quality, the only honest response is to refuse to "worship" or participate in that system. Thus, the refusal to be idolatrous can be seen as the willingness to be a-theistic. The question of idolatry, then, often does not begin with affirming transcendence but with breaking away from a false transcendence, which legitimates oppression. Idolatry distorts judgment; breaking with idolatry opens the possibility of clarity and justice.

There is no doubt that parts of the Jewish community have our own recently acquired idols: unbridled capitalism, jingoistic patriotism, and national security. These trends have grown after September 11th. We are increasingly taught to "believe" in America and Israel rather than to embrace critically diverse Jewish communities. A high-ranking officer of a major Jewish denomination remarked once that Israel is a God in the Jewish community—and so it has become. That is why a rational discussion of Israel is so difficult today.

Irving Greenberg's sense of Israel as a religious category describes the situation and yet portends doom. Could atheism toward Israel be a path of fidelity in which our own community is brought to account? In this crucial time, the refusal to make of Israel an idol may be a gesture of humility and hope rather than an unforgivable sin for which excommunication is the only answer.

Instead of being divisive, the refusal to engage in idolatry might actually begin healing our community; it might serve as a bridge between religious and secular Jews among whom the question shifts from belief in God to the values of a good and just life that we can mutually affirm. At the same time, the refusal of idolatry might become a bridge to other suffering communities where we together begin to emphasize the most powerful statement of Irving Greenberg, that after the Holocaust "no statement, theological or otherwise can be credible if it is not credible in the presence of burning children."

"Burning children" at once becomes the central critique of unjust power and the path to a new form of solidarity. According to Greenberg, the victims ask the world above anything else "not to allow the creation of another matrix of values that might sustain another attempt at genocide." Is this not the place of meeting that demands an opening to other struggles, an opening that at the same time calls us to the depths of our own history?

2. *Listening to the Witness of Etty Hillesum and Martin Buber*

Years after the liberation of the camps, Elie Wiesel wrote, "Were hatred a solution, the survivors, when they came out of the camps, would have had to burn down the whole world." In fact, the world had already been burned down, and the survivors inherited a world emptied of values and much goodness, though the victors had difficulty recognizing the new landscape.

Hannah Arendt, in her book *The Origins of Totalitarianism*, saw this clearly when she wrote of the end of Western civilization and the traditions that gave rise to and guided it. For Arendt, the Judeo-Christian traditions, as well as the humanist tradition, collapsed in the death camps of Nazi Germany: they not only failed to prevent this catastrophe; they in many ways contributed to the impetus for mass death. Because of this a new foundation for civilization was needed, and Arendt called for a consciously created philosophical and political structure that would renew— or at least make possible again—a civilization worthy of the name.

Yet, almost a half a century later, the difficulty of such an enterprise is ever-present. In fact, many see the possibility of a new foundation in the renewal and transformation of the traditions that failed and are in disarray. Christian liberation movements are desperately and courageously addressing this question, and though they are a distinct minority among Christians, can one doubt that they are the hope of the future?

A new Christian witness not only confronts its own propensity for domination; it lends strength, courage, and insight to other struggling communities, as we have seen. Still, it is critical to understand that Christian renewal did not come simply from within, but rather, arose in dialogue with suffering communities, including the Jewish community, that posed unequivocally the critique of domination, which could no longer be denied. Christian movements today are authentic only insofar as they carry the memory of their Jewish victims with them.

As we have seen, the Jewish tradition is hardly free from the onslaught of contemporary history; it struggles within the dialectics of Holocaust and empowerment, survival and ethics, exile and renewal. A strength, deservedly seen as remarkable, has emerged from the Holocaust world. At the same time, we find a profound unease, often covered over with militant rhetoric and accusation.

Proud of our achievements in economics and science, celebrating our new-found military prowess, we nevertheless feel the ground giving way beneath our feet. Togetherness is stressed as an ideal unto itself, while grafted to it is a profound sense of loneliness. Those Jews who struggle for renewal often do so without religious language, or in a language that has hardly confronted the night. The religious language of empowerment is important, but it lacks the ability to critique; the religious language of renewal is neo-orthodox or fragmented, spoken to a small audience or in pre-Holocaust symbols that, in view of our contemporary history, are less and less adequate.

The voices of ethical concern, such as Shorris and Feuerlicht, are warnings to be taken seriously. They place ethical teaching in contact with everyday reality. Christian liberation movements are of help, if we are humble enough to listen; recognition of the commonality of night, of the innocent suffering, is crucial. Ultimately, however, these are clues to a reconstruction that is only on the horizon, feared by some, expected by others, and yet unnamed.

Our history bequeaths the dialectic of Holocaust and empowerment, as well as the tension and arguments found within it. But what are the borders of this dialectic for which the forces of renewal reach? Is there a way to move within and beyond the now articulated tripartite reality of Holocaust, empowerment, and renewal that elicits articulate rhetoric while allowing the present neoconservative direction to continue and perhaps even to accelerate?

In a sense we have already suggested a way to challenge the Jewish community to move forward, by virtue of solidarity with those who suffer. The desire to be in solidarity does not eliminate the dynamics of the Jewish community, but places them in a different perspective. It has the possibility of moving us beyond isolation and liberal concern into an active community that finds its way by means of concrete acts of justice. Thus, a new reference point emerges, and solidarity becomes the watchword.

Solidarity is the movement of the heart, mind, and body toward those who are suffering. Though often seen as a movement outward toward others, as something added on to a fulfilled life, solidarity actually is a journey to ourselves as well. It is an attempt to reclaim our own humanity, bruised and alienated when our lives are built on the exploitation of others. This is true of a solidarity with our own community as well, for the journey toward others is at the same time a journey toward the foundations of one's own community.

One can posit the opposite: a person or community that refuses solidarity ultimately refuses itself. The Constantinian synthesis of church and state speaks clearly in this area: when Christianity became the empire's religion, it lost its soul. The Nazis became mirror images of the victims they created: lonely, anonymous, dehumanized. In a very different way, we see this possibility in the Jewish community today, as empowerment overshadows the prophetic until it is banished, and with it a founding block of the Jewish spirit.

Solidarity also means the willingness to enter into history with authenticity and fidelity. Entry into history is the willingness to engage in a critical dialogue with economic, social, political, and religious issues. Put simply, the critical dialogue is ongoing: sometimes decisive, other times indeterminate. Rarely is there one answer; rather, there is a series of questions and decisions to be thought through and acted upon.

A lived witness means to make a choice within the critical dialogue, to plant one's feet without all the answers, to choose a way of life in the mix of history. The critical dialogue informs lived witness with an open invitation to continue the search; the lived witness deepens the dialogue with a reality which calls forth commitment. Critical dialogue and lived witness are both individual and communal. The community can encourage or discourage individuals to enter into history, and the community itself can undergo the process of critical dialogue and lived witness, though this is rare.

Whether a person or community views the present as a hostile environment to be transcended and defeated, or as a locus for solidarity, dialogue, and lived witness depends, in large measure, on how the past is viewed. The past is alive in the present through memory and myth; past events influence the life of a people as these events take on a formative character. The Holocaust and the founding of the state of Israel are two such formative events for the Jewish people.

While it is true that these two events, because of their power, broke through tradition as it had been given, they are now part and parcel of a new tradition. Tradition always has a tendency to become, in the words of Walter Benjamin, a Jewish philosopher, "a tool of the ruling classes"; that is, it begins to lose its power as a motivator toward solidarity. The events themselves critique injustice, displacement, and murder, even though time and human agencies dull the critical edge: they may approve what they once critiqued. Hence Benjamin's comment: "In every era the attempt must be made anew to wrest tradition away from a conformism that is about to overpower it."

For Benjamin, this is the task of the historian, who, recognizing that the "image of enslaved ancestors" allows both hatred and a spirit of sacrifice, seeks to recover the past as an impetus for solidarity in the present. Benjamin writes: "The past carries with it a temporal index by which it is referred to redemption. There is a secret agreement between past generations and the present one. Our coming was expected on earth. Like every generation that preceded us, we have been endowed with a weak Messianic power, a power to which the past has a claim. That claim cannot be settled cheaply." Benjamin concludes, "Only that historian will have the gift of fanning the spark of hope in the past who is firmly convinced that even the dead will not be safe from the enemy if he wins. And this enemy has not ceased to be victorious."

Thus, for Benjamin, the past, as recalled in the present, has two possibilities: to legitimate or to critique unjust power. The tendency is to conformism, but this robs the past of its authenticity and, in so doing, robs the dead of their voice. Certain actions, although performed in behalf of persecuted persons, actually serve to affirm the persecutors.

The task of the historian is to allow the voices of the suffering to be heard, particularly by their children, who, while venerating their oppressed ancestors, tend to ignore their cries by persecuting others. The memory of enslaved ancestors thus subverts traditions of conformism to power. Empowerment is possible, but those who are empowered must bear in mind that solidarity with those suffering in the present is the only link to those suffering in the past, and that to ignore or cause suffering is to lose the raison d'etre of empowerment.

Even more dangerous is the emerging solidarity that follows: solidarity with other victors. Benjamin writes that "all rulers are the heirs of those who conquered before them" and "whoever has emerged victorious participates to this day in the triumphal procession in which the present rulers step over those who are lying prostrate." That is why the historian regards it as his or her task to "brush history against the grain."

For Benjamin, the recovery of suffering is subversive and is carried out by those willing to brush against the grain of acceptable speech and activity. Conformism is the way of betrayal; fidelity is the critique of the victorious, by way of committed thought and activity that takes seriously the dead and those dying in the present. Not surprisingly, it is this difficult struggle to be faithful that, for Benjamin, is the stirring of theology, "the straight gate through which the Messiah might enter."[35]

To recover the memory of suffering is to probe again what is now assumed, to analyze what has been elevated to the sacred. We are alerted to a diversity where we now see only monolith; we uncover paths untraveled, though once suggested. The present loses its univocal quality as the choices of the past are brought into view.

The understanding of fidelity is broadened considerably, and the possibility of reconciliation emerges. Reconciliation is understood here not only in terms of the enemy, but in terms of oneself and community. Past and current events take on a new shading where forgiveness, as well as humility, is possible. Such memories challenge the victim and the victor alike, even when they seem to have changed places. Reconciliation portends transformation.

The tension between empire and community has surfaced in every age. "Empire" goes beyond an individual's attempt to dominate, control, or manipulate others for survival and affluence; it represents the organization of this impulse and the creation of structures that ensure a pattern of dominance and control. "Community" moves in another direction. Equality, cooperation, and mutuality in decision making become the goals, and structures are created that foster creativity rather than domination. Rarely, however, is either empire or community perfectly realized. Where domination is the organizing principle, those who seek community become the way of the future; where community is primary, the will to dominate remains.

In a small, but nonetheless intense, way, we can see how this dialectic of empire and community is being played out in contemporary Jewish life. Though there are many reasons why the Jews have survived in desperate circumstances, it seems that the will to community is preeminent among them. The post-Holocaust world, however, is a unique place with different demands for survival. Many fear the Jewish people cannot survive without empire.

Over against this view, many reassert that the values of Jewish life are the Jews' essential witness to the world, and that without such a witness, Judaism ceases to be Judaism. The forces of renewal see no choice but to balance the survival of the Jewish people with the preservation of its essential message of community. Those forces assert that survival and preservation of Judaism's essential message are ultimately one and the same: there is no meaningful survival without a deepening of the witness its message offers to the world.

Two figures who challenge present Jewish sensibilities are Etty Hillesum and Martin Buber. As persons living within the formative events of contemporary Jewish life, the Holocaust and the founding of the state of Israel, they viewed their situations quite differently from the way Jewish consensus allows today.

Hillesum elicits a spirituality that is difficult for us to understand. She evokes a familiarity with God that major theologians of our community find almost impossible. Hillesum seems almost to accept the fate of her people as inevitable or, perhaps more accurately, rises to heroic stature within the parameters of the moment. Though in and around the borders of her life we hear the familiar refrain "Never Again," we also hear other voices, including the poetic and the language of God. She is shocking in her simplicity, in her acceptance, and in her prayer.

Buber, on the other hand, as an exile from Germany and a settler in Palestine, is a voice of empowerment, though in tones less familiar to us today. Buber was a great biblicist, philosopher and educator, but, what concerns us here, is his unequivocal stand for rapprochement with his Arab neighbors. Buber's theology underlay these positions and was equally scandalous: one of the most famous religious Jews in the world rarely attended synagogue, and he understood that deed and encounter called for confederation with, rather than domination of, the Arab population.

Etty Hillesum was born on January 15, 1914, in Middleburg, Holland, where her father, Dr. L. Hillesum, taught classical languages. Dr. Hillesum was an excellent and disciplined scholar who prized an orderly life, while Etty's mother, Rebecca Bernstein, was passionate and driven; having fled Russian pogroms, she migrated to the Netherlands. Though the marriage was quite tempestuous, Etty and her brothers, Mischa and Jaap, were intelligent and gifted. Mischa was a brilliant musician, considered to be one of the most promising pianists in Europe, while Jaap discovered some new vitamins when he was a teenager and later became a doctor. Etty took her first degree in law at the University of Amsterdam and then enrolled in the Faculty of Slavonic Languages. When the Second World War broke out, she had already turned to the study of psychology.

At the time she started writing her diaries, Holland was increasingly under the domination of Nazi Germany, and with Holland's surrender in the spring of 1940, Germany began to isolate the Dutch Jews. Despite resistance to those measures by the Dutch, Jews were gathered into ghettos and work camps. In the spring of 1942, Jews were forced to wear the Star of David, and wholesale deportations began. Westerbork, a transit camp in the east of the Netherlands, was designated as the last stop before the extermination camp, Auschwitz.

By July 1942, Hillesum found work as a typist in a department of the Jewish Council, a body formed at Nazi instigation to handle Jewish affairs. In essence, the Nazis gave orders to the Council and then let it decide how to implement them. Fourteen days after she started work, Hillesum volunteered to go with the first group of Jews to Westerbork. As the editor of her diaries, J.G. Gaarlandt, writes, "She did not want to escape the fate of the Jewish people. She believed that she could do justice to life only if she did not abandon those in danger, and if she used her strength to bring light into the life of others."[36]

From August 1942 until September 1943, Hillesum remained in Westerbork camp with a new job in the local hospital. Because of a special permit from the Jewish Council, she was able, on occasion, to travel to Amsterdam, where she brought letters and messages to people and was able to procure medicines for the camp. Though her health was poor and friends encouraged her to escape, she refused. On September 7, 1943, Hillesum—along with her parents and brother, Mischa—was transported to Auschwitz, where she died on November 30. Her parents and Mischa died there too; her other brother, Jaap, survived the camp but died returning to Holland.

Hillesum's diaries are filled with passion and an almost mystical simplicity. Her spirituality is eclectic and beautiful, though in some ways disturbing. Rilke and Dostoevsky are her spiritual guides, as are the Jewish and Christian Scriptures. In a harrowing time, Hillesum is open to the world, unafraid of exploring its treasures. Suffering and beauty, existing side-by-side, encourage reflections on life and destiny. Throughout, her guide is compassion, though increasingly a compassion tried through fire.

The testimony of such a life is startling. On June 25, 1942, Hillesum reflects on Nazi brutality:

> They are merciless, totally without pity. And we must be all the more merciful ourselves.

> That's why I prayed early this morning: "Oh God, times are too hard for frail people like myself. I know that a new and kinder day will come. I would so much like to live on, if only to express all the love I carry with me. And there is only one way of preparing the new age, by living it even now in our hearts. Somewhere in me I feel so light, without the least bitterness and so full of strength and love. I would so much like to help prepare the new age."

> That's how it went, more or less, my prayer this morning. I suddenly had to kneel down on the hard coconut matting in the bathroom and the tears poured down my face. And that prayer gave me enough strength for the rest of the day."[37]

It is within the context of her time that Hillesum's prayers continue and deepen. In Westerbork, on August 18, 1943, just three weeks before her death, she wrote:

> My life has become an uninterrupted dialogue with You, oh God, one great dialogue. Sometimes when I stand in some corner of the camp, my feet planted on Your earth, my eyes raised towards Your Heaven, tears sometimes run down my face, tears of deep emotion and gratitude. At night, too, when I lie in my bed and rest in You, oh God, tears of gratitude run down my face, and that is my prayer. I have been terribly tired for several days, but that, too, will pass; things come and go in a deeper rhythm and people must be taught to listen to it, it is the most important thing we have to learn in this life. I am not challenging You, oh God, my life is one great dialogue with You. I may never become the great artist I would really like to be, but I am already secure in You, God. Sometimes I try my hand at turning out small profundities and uncertain short stories, but I always end up with just one single word: God. And that says everything and there is no need for anything more.[38]

Hillesum's prayers to God are filled with questions. God may be powerless to help the Jewish people, but can Jews help God? Here a mystical element becomes central. Her diary entry of July 12, 1942, begins with this meditation:

Dear God, these are anxious times. Tonight for the first time I lay in the dark with burning eyes as scene after scene of human suffering passed before me. I shall promise You one thing, God, just one very small thing: I shall never burden my today with cares about my tomorrow, although that takes some practice. Each day is sufficient unto itself. I shall try to help You, God, to stop my strength ebbing away, though I cannot vouch for it in advance. But one thing is becoming increasingly clear to me: that You cannot help us, that we must help You to help ourselves. And that is all we can manage these days and also all that really matters: that we safeguard that little piece of You, God, in ourselves. And perhaps in others as well. Alas, there doesn't seem to be much You Yourself can do about our circumstances, about our lives. Neither do I hold You responsible. You cannot help us but we must help You and defend Your dwelling place inside us to the last.[39]

If Hillesum had isolated herself from her people, these prayers, even her dialogue with God, would sound empty, almost arrogant. Their power comes from the commitment for which she gave her life. For Hillesum. it was quite simply being faithful:

I shall always be able to stand on my own two feet even when they are planted on the hardest soil of the harshest reality. And my acceptance is not indifference or helplessness. I feel deep moral indignation at a regime that treats human beings in such a way. But events have become too overwhelming and too demonic to be stemmed with personal resentment and bitterness. These responses strike me as being utterly childish and unequal to the fateful course of events. People often get worked up when I say it doesn't really matter whether I go or somebody else does, the main thing is that so many thousands have to go. It is not as if I want to fall into the arms of destruction with a resigned smile—far from it, I am only bowing to the inevitable and even as I do so I am sustained by the certain knowledge that ultimately they cannot rob us of anything that matters. But I don't think I would feel happy if I were exempted from what so many others have to suffer. They keep telling me that someone like me has a duty to go into hiding, because I have so many things to do in life, so much to give. But I know that whatever I may have to give to others, I can give it no matter where I am, here in the circle of my friends or over there, in a concentration camp. And it is sheer arrogance to think oneself too good to share the fate of the masses.[40]

For many Jews, these prayers are impossible to utter after Auschwitz; yet, they were offered on the rails to Auschwitz and, no doubt, in the camp as well. To be sure, her understandings are disturbing: is her God the God of the Exodus, or the God of Rilke? Passages from the Christian Scriptures are evoked, and though she herself does not indicate a preference, Christians reading her diaries might find a latent follower of Jesus. Her journey, however, yields much more than these retrospective problems.

There is no hint from Hillesum that the suffering of her people is justified or divinely ordained, but there is a sense that fidelity within suffering opens the possibility of a new age. Barbarism is overwhelming; to hold on to the human, to acknowledge beauty, to continue to pray is to begin the transformation of travail into goodness.

For Hillesum, Jews are not going like lambs to the slaughter, as is often said today. Instead, we find unfolding a witness to the degradation and possibility of the human. The fate of the Jewish people, already decided by forces beyond their control, has an inner meaning that only the experience of suffering can impart. Martyrdom occurs without bitterness and with a commitment beyond ordinary comprehension. To accompany her people, to continue to pray, to listen to the stories of her compatriots is to resist the ultimate triumph of Nazism with every fiber of her being. For Hillesum, resistance unto death is the preparation for a future beyond Nazism.

It is in the midst of suffering and commitment that Hillesum understands the beauty of creation and the goodness of life. The Kingdom of Death remains, though permeated with the sacredness of creation. Is this a contradiction that cannot now be spoken, or a paradox that bespeaks a healing that opens levels of understanding beneath a justifiable internal and external hardening?

Survival as a people is nowhere mentioned in the diaries; perhaps this is presumed. Empowerment seems farther from her mind. Is it that she does not realize the extremity of the situation of Jews worldwide, or can she even imagine an empowered Jewish presence in Palestine?

Whatever the answer, Hillesum's central theme is witness, not empowerment. Can we speak of this emphasis today without hesitation and shame, as if her view was naïve and even dangerous? Even most difficult is Hillesum's emerging sense of forgiveness that undergirds her refusal to hate even the enemy. Her solidarity with the Jewish people extends to those caught up in a system that dehumanizes and, in effect, murders the conquerors as well. Hillesum's March 21, 1941, extended diary entry is, in the face of her impending death, as remarkable as it is controversial:

> What a bizarre new landscape, so full of eerie fascination, yet one we might also come to love again. We human beings cause monstrous conditions, but precisely because we cause them we soon learn to

adapt ourselves to them. Only if we become such that we can no longer adapt ourselves, only if, deep inside, we rebel against every kind of evil, will we be able to put a stop to it. Aeroplanes, streaking down in flames, still have a weird fascination for us—even aesthetically—though we know, deep down, that human beings are being burnt alive. As long as that happens, while everything within us does not yet scream out in protest, so long will we find ways of adapting ourselves, and the horror will continue. Does that mean I am never sad, that I never rebel, always acquiesce, and love life no matter what the circumstances? No, far from it. I believe that I know and share the many sorrows and sad circumstances that a human being can experience, but I do not cling to them, I do not prolong such moments of agony. They pass through me, like life itself, as a broad, eternal stream, they become part of that stream, and life continues. And as a result all my strength is preserved, does not become tagged on to futile sorrow or rebelliousness.

And finally: ought we not, from time to time, open ourselves up to cosmic sadness? One day I shall surely be able to say to Ilse Blumenthal, "Yes, life is beautiful, and I value it anew at the end of every day, even though I know that the sons of mothers, and you are one such mother, are being murdered in concentration camps. And you must be able to bear your sorrow: even if it seems to crush you, you will be able to stand up again, for human beings are so strong, and your sorrow must become an integral part of yourself, part of your body and your soul, you mustn't run away from it, but bear it like an adult. Do not relieve your feelings through hatred, do not seek to be avenged on all German mothers, for they, too, sorrow at this very moment for their slain and murdered sons.

Give your sorrow all the space and shelter in yourself that is its due, for if everyone bears his grief honestly and courageously the sorrow that now fills the world will abate. But if you do not clear a decent shelter for your sorrow, and instead reserve most of the space inside you for hatred and thoughts of revenge—from which new sorrows will be born for others—then sorrow will never cease in this world and will multiply. And if you have given sorrow the space its gentle origins demand, then you may truly say: life is beautiful and so rich. So beautiful and so rich that it makes you want to believe in God."[41]

Hillesum's journey is recalled here, not because it was or should be paradigmatic for the Jewish people, but because it brushes against the grain of acceptable testimony. As Wiesel asserts, the Jewish survivors did not find hatred a solution. However, it is also true that the path to God and the possibility of forgiveness have been difficult, if not impossible. How do we trust a God who could not or did not deliver us from the death camps? How can we possibly forgive those who constructed the camps with their own hands, often with an incomprehensible joy? Certainly there are no answers here, only the willingness to allow disparate voices to be heard in their authenticity. Hillesum's is a lonely voice, though to be sure not the only voice that exists on the borders of our understanding of the Holocaust.

Martin Buber was another such voice on the periphery of Jewish consciousness and activity, though, from a certain vantage point, it may be hard to discern him as anything if not central to the Jewish community.

Born in 1878 to a wealthy Austrian family, by the 1930s, Buber was well known throughout Europe as a Jewish theologian and scholar. As the Nazi period began, Buber became an outspoken opponent of Hitler and finally left for Palestine in 1938. His journey there was, in the first instance, forced by Nazism, though Zionism was hardly new to him. From the early part of the century he perceived the need for the revival of Jewish culture in the ancient home of the Jewish people. His Zionism, however, had a striking caveat: the success of the Jewish return to Palestine would be measured by relations with the Arab population. For Buber, Palestine was to be shared by those who returned and those indigenous to that land.

The case for the Jewish return to the land is made over and over again in Buber's works. One example is his testimony, in March 1946, before the Anglo-American Inquiry Committee formed to explore the British Mandate, specifically the plight of Jewish survivors of the Nazi Holocaust and the possibility of their immigration to Palestine.

Buber begins by relating modern political Zionism to the ancient birth of the Jewish people. For Buber, modern political Zionism was prompted and intensified, but not caused, by modern anti-Semitism. Zionism attested to the unique connection of a people and a country. The Jewish people were created by the power of a tradition founded on the promise made to them during their wanderings in the desert: the promise of Canaan as their "heritage." According to Buber, this tradition was decisive for the history of humankind in that it "confronted the new people with a task they could carry out only as a people, namely to establish in Canaan a model and 'just' community." Later the prophets interpreted this task as obliging the community to carry social and political justice throughout the world.

Thereby the most productive and most paradoxical of all human ideas, messianism, was offered to humanity. Buber believed that this messianism placed the people of Israel in the center of an "activity leading towards the advent of the Kingdom of God on earth," an activity calling forth the cooperation of all humanity. Though it oriented all peoples and every generation to contribute to the upbuilding of a messianic future "within the people that had created it, this idea grew to a force of quite peculiar vitality." Though Jews were driven out of their promised land, they "survived nearly two millennia by their trust in their return, in the fulfillment of the promise, in the realization of the idea. The inner connection with this land and the belief in the promised reunion with it were a permanent force of rejuvenation for this people, living in conditions which probably would have caused the complete disintegration of any other group." From this analysis flows what Buber considers to be the three irreducible demands of Zionism. First, the freedom to acquire land in sufficient quantity to bring about a renewed connection with the "primal form of production," from which the Jewish people had been separated for centuries and without which "no original spiritual and social productivity can arise." Second, a powerful influx of settlers, especially of youth, to strengthen and revive the work of reconstruction and to protect it from the dangers of stagnancy and isolation. Third, self-determination of the Jewish community about its way of life and about the forms of its institutions, as well as an assurance for its unimpeded development as a community.[42]

For Buber, these demands also produced obligations: justice for and within a community must be carried out without threatening the rights of any other community. Independence of one could hardly be gained at the expense of another. "Jewish settlement must oust no Arab peasant, Jewish immigration must not cause the political status of the present inhabitants to deteriorate, and must continue to ameliorate their economic condition." Buber saw the aim of a regenerated Jewish people in Palestine as twofold: to live peacefully with the inhabitants of the land and to cooperate with Palestinians in opening and developing the land. As Buber wrote, "Such cooperation is an indispensable condition for the lasting success of the great work of the redemption of this land."[43]

Buber saw the cooperative basis as offering room for both the Jewish and the Palestinian people, and though this necessitated autonomy, the demand for a Jewish state or a Jewish majority was of less importance. Though as many Jews as possible were needed, it was not in order to establish a majority against a minority. The need was for a "solid, vigorous, autonomous community, but not in order that it should give its name to a state; we need it because we want to raise Israel and Eretz Israel to the highest level of productivity they can be raised to." Buber believed that the new situation demanded new solutions "beyond the capacity of the familiar political categories." That is why Buber desired an "internationally guaranteed agreement between the two communities . . ., which defines the spheres of interest and activity common to the partners and those not common to them, and guarantees mutual noninterference for these specific spheres."[44]

Early on, Buber saw two opposing tendencies within Zionism that correspond to two different interpretations of the concept of national rebirth. The first was to understand national rebirth as the intention to restore the true Israel, where spirit and life would no longer be separated as in the Diaspora. Rather, spirit and life would come together in Israel's ancient homeland. The second saw rebirth as normalization: the need for land, language, and independence such as any nation needed.

For Buber, this latter interpretation displayed an interest in acquiring the commodities of nationhood but failed to consider the important questions: How will people live with one another in this land? What will people say to one another in the renewed Hebrew language? What will be the connection of their independence with the rest of humanity? Two conflicting tendencies were inherited from ancient times: "the powerful consciousness of the task of maintaining truth and justice in the total life of the nation, internally and externally, and thus becoming an example and a light to humanity; and the natural desire, all too natural, to be 'like the nations'." According to Buber, the ancient Hebrews never succeeded in becoming a normal nation. Two weeks after the Proclamation of Independence in May 1948, Buber reported, "Today Jews are succeeding at it to a terrifying degree."[45]

Buber continued to protest Israeli nationalism until his death in 1965. While it is true that he was never alone in his hopes and disappointments, Buber can honestly be seen as an exile in a land he participated in building. His confederationist and bi-national proposals fell on deaf ears. By the end of Buber's life, his vision of religious socialism was hardly understood or considered.

Though dissenting minorities within Israel continue to criticize their government's policies, the road taken by the state of Israel is quite different from the one proposed by Buber. His understandings are regarded as utopian, untenable, and even dangerous for a modern state. The security of Israel is defined as distinct over and against that of the Palestinian people, and since the 1967 war, new territories have been acquired. Normalization continues unabated, as the arms industry becomes the leading earner of foreign currency; the foreign-policy involvements in the Middle East and elsewhere would have horrified Buber in their magnitude and cynicism.

Buber's understandings challenge the contemporary Jewish community in many ways. For Buber, the return to Palestine is a spiritual act, in a religious category, as it were, the essence of which is regeneration rather than survival. Regeneration occurs in relation to history, to the land, and to the people who inherited the land; autonomy signals authenticity and the ability to enter into relationship, rather than the ability to go it alone. Regeneration represents the rebirth of Jewish witness and values: survival without witness can only be seen as failure.

To be sure, Buber's thought raises many questions. Buber assumed the right of Jews to become an autonomous force in Palestine; but was this possible in the historical situation without a state and its concomitant militarization? Friendship and cooperation are built on mutual give and take; but did either the Jews or the Palestinians, at that moment of history, have the inner resources to come into relation?

Most of the Zionists were secular Jews and saw religion as a bulwark against change. Could Buber's religious socialism have appealed to a people longing to reclaim itself within the realm of economics and politics? The inhabitants of Palestine also raised questions: Was not Buber's sense of Jewish mission really the continuation of European colonialism, albeit in a more friendly manner? Though less than most settlers, Buber retained a sense of paternalism toward his Arab neighbors, and his sense of development, though socialist and decentralized, was still based on a European rather than on a Middle-Eastern model.

As with Hillesum, the questions remain and the answers are less important. The memory of Martin Buber brushes recent Jewish history against the grain. He represents a choice as yet untaken, a path almost disappearing from view. Can his understandings be broached in the Jewish community today, or is his life a dangerous memory better left alone? Still, he represents the possibility of reconciliation with the Palestinians, as well as with our own history. Buber calls for a fundamental turning away from domination to relation, which is at the same time peace with the Palestinian people and a recovery of the Jewish witness in Israel and Palestine. Buber's voice, however, extends far beyond the Middle East. Would not his views, like Hillesum's, call for a reevaluation of Jewish understandings in North America as well?

Buber's understanding of empowerment, as intimately linked with solidarity, is bound to the reality of God, and here, Buber is at his most challenging. For Buber, tradition names God too easily, objectifying what is mysterious and nameless. In his pre-Holocaust writings, Buber seeks to establish for the Jewish people an existential relation with God through exploration of subjectivity and nature. God is revealed to the person through history, individually and in community. God calls for teshuvah, repentance and turning toward self, neighbor, and nature. The human responds with decisions and deeds that illustrate teshuvah. A path is before us; it is up to us to choose it. Even as we move in another direction, the path remains to be chosen again. The path is a form of solidarity with creation and history; the locus of fidelity becomes a "mysterious approach to closeness."

The post-Holocaust theology Buber posits is less certain than his previous theology, though the basic outlines remain the same. The difficulty of belief is understandable, and to force belief is dishonest. Still, the path of trust and solidarity remains, and righteous activity may once again bring the center of Jewish life into focus. For who has banished God if not humans themselves?

"Such is the nature of this hour," Buber wrote, "But what of the next?" For Buber, it was a modern superstition that the character of an age acts as fate for the next. "One lets it prescribe what is possible to do and hence what is permitted. One surely cannot swim against the stream, one says. But perhaps one can swim with a new stream whose source is still hidden? In another image, the I-Thou relation has gone into the catacombs—who can say with how much greater power it will step forth! Who can say when the I-It relation will be directed anew to its assisting place and activity!" Buber believed that the most important events in history called individuals and communities to new beginnings. This was true today: "Something is taking place in the depths that as yet needs no name. Tomorrow even it may happen that it will be beckoned to from the heights, across the heads of the earthly archons. The eclipse of the light of God is no extinction; even tomorrow that which has stepped in between may give way."[46]

Could it be that the reestablishment of trust will allow the difficult post-Holocaust questions to be raised again in a spirit of search and fellowship? The eclipse of God, felt by women and men of our age, is a reality, which, if unaddressed, allows the carnage to continue. Could solidarity be a response to this eclipse that one day may allow the question of God to be raised in a different, more relevant way?

3. Envisioning Jerusalem as the Broken Middle of Israel/Palestine

There is no doubt that the path of solidarity that Hillesum and Buber suggest is a difficult one, especially when the lessons of Jewish history counsel against it. After the Holocaust and the struggle to establish an autonomous presence in Palestine, trust is often seen as naïve and dangerous. Still, Hillesum and Buber caution us that hatred and isolation lead to bitterness without solace and, ultimately, to survival without witness.

The fact that within the Holocaust and the founding of the state of Israel there were Jews who prayed and struggled, dissented and trusted, reminds us that generosity often occurs in the most unexpected places—when we are least secure—and that, paradoxically, the hardening occurs when the community achieves power. Surely the demands are different within empowerment, but the raison d'etre of empowerment found in the struggle and generosity of enslaved ancestors is in danger of being lost.

The lives of Hillesum and Buber echo the challenge of Walter Benjamin to rescue tradition from conformity to power, a power that becomes the tool of the ruling class. They suggest that to move from one oppression to another, in spite of the rationale, is to forget our history and, ultimately, to denigrate ourselves as a people.

Today we desperately need a new angle of vision, and thus, the reconstruction of Jewish life begins with the forgotten and the peripheral, with the unasked questions and the assumed answers. Hillesum and Buber provide this different angle of vision because they carry within them parts of our heritage that languish in the present. They embody a language of the heart formed in the midst of Jewish history, a language almost frightening to speak of today.

If it is true, however, that the way back is covered with the blood of our ancestors, a future without the possibility of God and of reconciliation is bleak indeed. Could Hillesum and Buber and the many others like them provide, in Benjamin's words, the "weak messianic spark" of which we are in such great need and through which a renewed Jewish life might emerge?

Within the cycle of dislocation, settlement, wars, uprisings, torture, and poisonous demonization of the adversary, it seems an impossible task to envision such a messianic spark. For what can that mean in such a situation?

Perhaps such a spark can be ignited by demystifying the "other," by living together and by searching for an ordinary way of life, rather than for *the* solution.

The challenge seems to be somewhere else, to uncover the myth, but in the broader pursuit of finding a middle ground between opposing sides. Over time the middle ground will take on a life of its own, thus establishing a basis from which the next steps can be taken. New questions arise from this middle, which will ultimately displace aspects of the original myths or transform them into new configurations.

The deliberate and unconscious myths are still in need of exposure, but, when new ground is reached, their importance and the need to defend them is diminished. In this sense, Rabin's rhetoric, though contradicted by his actions, may be used as a bridge to that middle to which he pointed, but did not reach. Though his intentions are important to investigate, they are less important than the hope that he outlined. Hope can be seen as the next arena of the struggle to move beyond the present. The next arena will likely also hold its myths and become a place from which further struggle is needed.

The solution in its finality always eludes us as we move toward an ever evolving middle ground. As the late Jewish philosopher Gillian Rose remarks, the middle is always broken and with reason. Life itself is broken, and the images, philosophies, ideologies, and theologies we create are flawed. From Rose's perspective, the attempt at closure through the elimination or purification of the myths, half-truths, and lies, covers over that which one sought to eliminate. Something less than the purification should be attempted, that is, the need to build upon a "broken middle," which recognizes myths *and* history, flaws *and* movement, injustice *and* the pursuit of justice, the fears within each community *and* the possibility that fears can be overcome in the process of forging a new relationship.[47]

To approach the broken middle in Israel/Palestine is to face the difficult subject of Jerusalem. Jerusalem stands for a diverse array of symbols and realities to Jews and to Palestinians. For some Jews, Jerusalem represents the hope of return, nurtured for almost two thousand years of exile. In this sense, Jerusalem is a religious and national symbol, whose power cannot be overestimated. Other Jews, while embracing both the religious and national symbolism, see Jerusalem as the geographic center of an empowered and expanding Israel. Jerusalem is to them as much present as future. With the prayers of return having been realized, the challenge now is to Judaize the city and expand its boundaries.

Though rarely spoken or written about, there are Jews in Israel and elsewhere who are wary of Jerusalem, with its history of religious fanaticism, its Middle Eastern flavor, and the present-day religious and settler movements that have flourished since the Israeli annexation of Jerusalem following the 1967 war. The cities of Jerusalem and Tel Aviv still define a fundamental fracture in Israeli society. Jerusalem denotes a religious and continually expanding Israel, Tel Aviv a more European, secular, and limited state.

Palestinians are also intimately involved in the question of Jerusalem. Jerusalem is central to their history, as a religious site of prayer and pilgrimage for both Muslims and Christians. It is also a sign of their defeat and displacement, as the annexation of Jerusalem has had the effect of denying Palestinian governance and, at the same time, through demolition of Palestinian housing and land confiscation, steadily decreasing the number of Palestinians living in Jerusalem.

Jerusalem has been, and remains today, the intellectual, cultural, and economic center of Palestinian life. The end of Jerusalem as a Palestinian place of prayer and activity divides the Palestinian population, north and south, east and west; hence, the segmentation and ghettoization which has increased in the past decades. For Palestinians who look to Jerusalem as a religious symbol, as well as for those who see the city in secular, economic and cultural terms, the loss of Jerusalem is devastating.

Without seeking to universalize or romanticize the experience of Jews and Palestinians, it is important to realize the commonality of how Jerusalem functions in the imaginations of both peoples. Both Jews and Palestinians see Jerusalem in symbolic and practical terms. Religious Jews and Palestinians are drawn to Jerusalem for religious reasons, while secular segments of both peoples have more mixed feelings about the city. Secular Jews and Palestinians may be drawn to Jerusalem for historic, economic, or political reasons, yet they tend to be ambivalent, sometimes stridently so, about the religious militancy that is part of Jerusalem's past and present.

For both peoples, Jerusalem represents destruction, exile and hope for restoration; though the messianic message continues to emanate from this ancient city, the cycle of domination and destruction is evident in the very architecture of the city. For can Jews and Palestinians be unaware that the one who controls Jerusalem today is the same one who is exiled tomorrow?

The broken middle is found here, in the myths, historical experiences, common aspirations, the attraction to, and ambivalent feelings about, the city, which is called holy and eternal. The fact is that Jews and Palestinians are now living side by side in a proximity which has engendered suspicion and bloodshed, but which could also provide a visible, bodily encounter with those who are primarily known as the "other."

The broken middle recognizes the "other" as a challenge and possibility to fulfill aspects of the internal longing and needs of each people while respecting and seeking to understand and facilitate the longing and needs of the "other." Both peoples have claims, have suffered, and seek dignity and justice. Both histories have been broken in the twentieth century, and both have struggled for a rebirth that is whole and complete.

Clearly, the Palestinians have failed in this effort of rebirth, with loss of land, swelling refugee populations, and loss of a meaningful sovereignty. In a physical sense, Jews have succeeded in reversing losses, and some even hail the foundation of Israel, with its capital in Jerusalem, as the beginning of redemption. Yet, it is difficult to accept the redemption of one people at the expense of another. It is difficult to celebrate the Jewish return to Jerusalem when Palestinians are relegated to segregated precincts, ghettos if you will, like those that too often have formed the landscape of Jewish history.

Perhaps, then, the broken middle begins with the hope of return and the failure of both peoples to achieve the result they aspired to historically and in the present. Or, it could encompass the terrible result of achieving an end that includes the conquest and displacement of the "other," furthering the cycle of displacement and death, calling into question the moral worth of victory.

It is difficult to envision how Jews and Palestinians can be healed of their trauma by inflicting wounds on one another. Rather the opposite is the case: the wound inflicted on the other deepens the trauma of the initial injury. Thus, the broken middle includes hope, failure, a desire to end the cycle of destruction, and the realization that a true healing of a people can only come by including the "other" as significant in one's own hopes and aspirations.

It may be that opting for the broken middle begins the dissipation of the "other" as "other," and that the commonality initially recognized becomes the life of a community in the making. The "other" becomes the neighbor, who begins to share a common life and, in so doing, both embark on a new history with its own symbols, aspirations, ambivalence, and failures.

To many Jews, the thought of a new community brings fear of a final assimilation, as if a life without barriers might make Jewish identity unattractive. The fear is that there is little that is compelling left to Jewish life and that another people might replace that attraction. In Israel/Palestine, the fear is also cultural, as if a European Jew is somehow lost to the Jewish community because of involvement with Palestinian and Arab culture. Since a majority of Jews in Israel are of Arab and North African descent, this possibility invokes fear only insofar as Jewish life is defined by European background and culture.

If Jewish and Palestinian cultures come into close contact and intermingle freely and on an equal basis, do European and American Jews fear that the Western orientation of Israel will disappear in favor of a new configuration of an Arab/North African Israel/Palestine? Since the Holocaust is so central to the European experience, but peripheral to Jews of Arab and North African descent, this shift in consciousness might mean that the narrative of European Jewish suffering will be displaced as the guiding principle of Israel.

The broken middle, while attentive to history, does not freeze that history or seek to develop an orthodox theology beholden to it. Rather, the broken middle seeks to recognize the openness of history by addressing the next questions which face a people; it refuses to allow past suffering to be used as a shield against accountability in the present. Though the broken middle refuses utopia, it also refuses paralysis and the pretense of innocence.

The broken and the middle become a path where the future is worked out with reference to the past, present, and future. The connection among the three may be obvious, for it is difficult to see how a people can arrive at a destination, and how that arrival can be understood with any depth, unless the connection of past and present is understood.

Yet, the connection is neither linear nor preordained. Rather, the future always involves new elements and configurations, and, though preservation and continuity may remain a goal of some, even to the point of inventing a mythic continuity where little or none exists, a new reality has already come into being.

It is important to note that, when there is freedom to choose, Jews choose, even after the Holocaust, to live in a democratic and secular framework in contact with other cultures and religions. That is, Jews continue to hope for a society and a way of life beyond what they have known, and they continue to pioneer new realities in their own life and in the cultures in which they live.

Holocaust survivors who remained in or returned to Europe after the war, and American Jews who continue to live in America, despite the availability of Israel, attest to this determination to live in the broken middle. To live among Christians, with their symbolism, theology, and culture after the Holocaust event, so intertwined with Christian complicity, is an example of the choice of the broken middle. It is difficult to propose honestly that the stakes of a wager on the broken middle in the Middle East are higher than those of a wager on a civilization that burned Jewish bodies day and night for years.

The passions that have been raised in the decades-old struggle between Jews and Palestinians are important to identify and affirm. Clearly both sides feel in need of protection, and this includes the need for physical safety. The particularity of each culture has been under assault in this century, and the necessity of insuring a sense of cultural continuity is as important as the political structures which insure the physical integrity of each community

In the broken middle, healing and the future of the Jewish and Palestinian communities must have a structural base from which to evolve. With regard to Jerusalem, this might mean a dual governing entity that allows autonomy for each community, and a larger entity which provides joint governance of the city. Jerusalem becomes the capital of Israel and Palestine and, over time, the capital of Israel/Palestine. The city remains undivided, and the possibility of the resurgence of Palestinian life comes into being.

It is here where the difficulty is found. Despite the ebb and flow of agreements and rhetoric, a structural division is in place which separates Jews and Palestinians. The broken middle cannot be one that accepts this division or the future that this structure envisions for both communities. With reference to Jerusalem, the present political, military, cultural, and population configurations must be equalized, or at least allowed a process which will, in a relatively short time, provide a rough parity between the two communities. This means, among other measures, increasing the Palestinian population of Jerusalem, as well as housing main political institutions of the Palestinian government there.

From Jerusalem, further expansion of the agreement can occur that will include, in a structured and orderly way, Palestinians within Israel and Palestinian refugees around the world. For to achieve a broken middle, their inclusion and return must be recognized as part of the brokenness of the past and present, so as to become part of the future. Ignoring these realities is to mistake the rhetoric of peace for a future beyond the past; the difficult realities will remain, only to paralyze Jews and Palestinians in a cycle from which there is little chance of escape.

Azmi Bishara, a Palestinian who is also an Israeli citizen and a long-standing member of the Israeli Knesset, understands the limits of the present agreements as catalysts for the revival of the binational idea once current in Jewish and Palestinian circles. To achieve this binationalism in the future, Bishara envisions the need to mobilize Palestinian and Israeli democratic forces who champion binational values over narrowly nationalist values: "We will have to point out to the Israeli Left that its current slogan of separation . . . is actually a racist slogan: it legitimizes Israel's ongoing domination of another people; it legitimizes the idea that Palestinians are a demographic threat. In its stead, we must propagate political programs that emphasize the genuinely binational values of equality, reciprocity and coexistence."

Bishara echoes the words of Judah Magnes when he wrote to a friend in 1929: "It must be our endeavor first to convince ourselves and then to convince others that Jews and Arabs, Moslems, Christians and Jews have each as much right there, no more and no less, than the other: equal rights and equal privileges and equal duties." For Magnes, this was the sole ethical claim for Jewish life in Palestine, for without this equality, the quest for a Jewish homeland would turn into a nightmare. The vision of Magnes and Bishara could prompt a search for the broken middle to be found in the ancient city of Jerusalem.[48]

4. Embracing a Revolutionary Forgiveness

Today the hope of Isaiah seems distant, almost unrealizable. The memory of the dissenter Martin Buber or even that of David Ben-Gurion, much closer in time and relevance, seem distant as well. Yitzhak Rabin is likewise a distant figure, part of the founding generation whose ideals and sins are forgotten.

The state of Israel has come to a place where even the rhetoric of justice is seen as a sign of weakness, and the possibility of a shared future of justice and peace for Jews and Palestinians is spoken about in memory.

At the same time, a new complication has arisen with the failure of Palestinian leadership to mobilize Palestinian society and institute a democratic and open society. Some Palestinians have equated the Israeli occupation with their own leaders, portraying those Palestinians who have returned from exile as the new occupiers. Corruption and commercial monopolies, political authoritarianism and police brutality are charged by many.

Though the situation is unequal in power and possibility, clearly the dream of Palestinian empowerment is tempered by its reality. The arguments that have issued from this disappointment are tenacious, sometimes deadly, and, to Jewish ears at least, familiar. The late Edward Said's criticisms of Palestinian leadership are argumentative in an intellectual way and beyond. There is an anger that shouts betrayal, not only in a political sense of choosing the wrong direction, but in the more fundamental sense of betraying an entire people.

It is as if the struggle of Palestinians to create a new society that is faithful to their suffering has been lost. This is why Said's commentary is so passionate and his call to prepare the next phase of the struggle so clear. For Said, at least, the oppressive qualities of Israel remain in the new settlements that close the ring of settlements around Jerusalem, and in the continuing cleansing of Palestinians from East Jerusalem by confiscating Palestinian identity cards, depriving Palestinians of the right to live there.[49]

One wonders if this mutual disappointment, this passionate anger over the betrayal of both histories, will bring dissenting Jews and Palestinians into a new relationship characterized by sorrow and the hope of life within and beyond empowerment. Both Jews and Palestinians come to nation-state building late and under circumstances of distress and catastrophe. In different ways both are beginning to understand that empowerment, while necessary, is limited and helpful only when the basic elements of life are respected and supported.

Occupation of a land and a peoples' history, the diminution of the prospects for culture and justice, can come in many forms, foreign and internal. There can even be a collaboration between the two forces, so that empowerment may become another way of suppressing that for which both struggled. Those who realize the need and limitations of empowerment are, thus, in a new situation when the oppressor has changed clothing, or when the new configuration of power limits the possibility of a future worth bequeathing to the next generation. When this situation presents itself, those who recognize the limitations of the present situation must prepare and embody a new vision.

Surely the present power arrangements mitigate against the deepest values of Jewish and Palestinian culture and tradition. The result is an exilic condition of many Jews and of an increasing number of Palestinians. Thus, the meeting ground of those who worked for peace and justice during the years of the Palestinian uprising, a ground built around mutual recognition and support of a two-state solution, has shifted.

Large areas of Palestinian territory, supposed to be ceded to the Palestinians within the context of the two-state solution, have passed to Israeli sovereignty and are beyond the call of withdrawal. The fact is that a viable Palestinian state—a state in reality rather than rhetoric—is difficult to imagine. One might say that those who meet under the banner of "two states" harken back to a period of possibility that has already passed. The experience of those working for justice is that a new vision must emerge.

The meeting ground today is one of exile but also one with the possibility of becoming a new Diaspora. In their mutual flight, strangers may come to recognize each other in a new way. For more than fifty years the recognition has been immediate and unrelenting, as Jews and Palestinians have defined themselves against the enemy "other." This is crucial for authorities of both communities, and it is essential to legitimize state and communal violence. It is also important for the silencing of dissenters within both communities, as critical discourse is defined as traitorous.

The boundaries established by each community function to keep the "other" from discovering the oppressive aspects of one's own culture and power structure because they are shielded by representing the enemy as being outside. Crossing the boundary of Israel and Palestine allows the possibility of seeing the "other" reflected in one's own community, and thus, recognizing the "other" as more than stranger or, in an obvious way, reflecting back to their shared history and geography as possible intimates whose paths have crossed in enmity.

The point of recognition in the present is not found by reverting to the past, as if the reality of being "other" in history can be surmounted by dreaming a romantic past, but by recognizing the injustice of the past and present as throwing exiles together in contemporary life where a future project can be discovered. Returning to the past is another way of freezing history, as if Jews and Palestinians are just emerging from the era of colonialism and the struggle for independence.

The encounter now, with all its difficulty and suspicion, if taken on its own terms, is a way of moving forward within a common predicament. This will spur discussion on many topics, including the past, though the past will fade in priority as the present crisis is clarified. When the past is emphasized, even a dialogue in exile simply replicates old arguments and proposes truces while the future remains to be born. That is why the exile, even after some decades, continues to produce Jews and Palestinians who, while, to some extent sharing a similar plight and hope, remain strangers to one another.

When exiles begin to recognize one another, then a condition of flight gives way to the possibility of solidarity. The present situation opens toward a future where exiles form a Diaspora community. Whereas exile is a situation of flight and wandering, Diaspora is dispersion within the context of community; it is a movement away from empire and oppression toward the creation of a new matrix of values and institutions.

The past is brought with those who form the new Diaspora but only as possibilities, remnants, and small contributions to be combined, confronted, and transmuted with other pasts. The present defines the community more strongly than the past, as mutuality of experience is the guide for shifting through values and actions. Interaction in the present brings a recognition of parts of the past that must be jettisoned and those parts that have been abused and perverted, which might be preserved or reconfigured.

One thinks, here, of the sense of Jewish redemption in Israel and the desire among some Palestinians to reclaim all of Palestine. Though differing in duration and context, both claims are now disasters for those on the other side of the claims. If both are held as the highest value and are disasters then the very concepts themselves must be reevaluated. Furthermore, the recognition that disaster for the "other" is likewise disaster for those who make the claim is a humbling moment. This prompts a reevaluation that is itself a way of confession and reconciliation, especially when it is done in the face of, and with, the "other."

To move from exile to Diaspora, the possibility of forgiveness must be faced. Forgiveness as a mutual accounting of the past and the present frees the person and the community to the possibility of a new future, when authentic forgiveness is preceded by a confession that is searching and reflective, rather than simply damning and univocal.

Like the present, the past is complex in its various configurations, and its tendencies to violence and deceit confront the future hope. The tendency toward fidelity and betrayal are common patterns, even if adorned with specific symbols for particular epochs and peoples, and the very dichotomy itself may be part of the inability to move forward. Authentic forgiveness is mutual in that the cycle of fidelity and betrayal is identified and then seen in the larger context of a journey that is diverse in content and intent.

In this journey, the good and bad can be identified, but, unless a more complex and ambivalent picture emerges, unless the dichotomy of victor and victim gives way, then the past is woven into the present as the defining point of the future. At that point the victor and victim have too often changed places, for is it possible to condemn forever and maintain a reflective view on life that is self-critical? Can a future be created without the ability to forgive and be forgiven, and even to move beyond the need for forgiveness to see a depth of life from which we emerge and to which we seek to journey forward?

Carter Heyward, a Christian theologian, has emphasized the need for forgiveness as a way of embarking on a path toward justice and reconciliation. Heyward terms this path "revolutionary forgiveness," a process of forgiveness in which the righting of the wrong that has been done is given priority. The righting of wrong is itself a process of self-discovery and change, and becomes, with the act of forgiveness, a way of viewing the world as it is transformed in confession and justice.[50]

In this journey, a healing takes place within and between those who were once strangers and enemies. The vision of a just future is essential to enable forgiveness to realize its authenticity and to reach its revolutionary potential, for, without the movement toward justice, forgiveness is simply a piety without substance that leaves the world as it is. The freeing of the future, of course, means a forgiveness that interacts critically with the past and seeks to minimize that which originally gave rise to the offense in the first place.

In her philosophical writings, Hannah Arendt has also written about forgiveness as a way of entering public life with an orientation toward the future. Her caution about forgiveness is important here. For Arendt, there are some crimes in the public realm which are so heinous that they exist outside the framework of the human. Therefore, they cannot be forgiven.

One thinks of the Holocaust in this regard, and here, the challenge is simply to forge a path beyond the terrible nature of that atrocity. The tragedy of the Holocaust is exacerbated by the generation after the tragedy, not because it refuses to forgive, but because, in the holding up of that tragedy, self-critical reflection is diminished. The community chose a path that, to some extent, replicates that which violated the community in the past. Instead of embarking on a new venture, the Jewish community seeks survival and security in the most obvious of ways: territorial and national sovereignty.

The consequences for the Palestinian people are obvious, and the cycle of pain and suffering continues. One may argue that the pain of the Holocaust is extended to the Palestinians while the healing that Jews pursued through empowerment has been illusory. It may be that the cycle of dislocation and death continued by Jews after the Holocaust has increased the trauma of the Jewish people. Creating a future that anticipates the replication of the past is more than a refusal of forgiveness for an unforgivable event. Rather, it extends the unforgivable act to another people not responsible for the original injury.

The trap is obvious and one that Arendt knew only too well: life cannot be defined by the unforgivable or lived indefinitely within its shadow. The task is to move on with those who will journey with you, but first, the desire to move internally must be manifest. Carrying the Holocaust as a sign of distinction is a recipe for isolation and mistrust. Trust cannot be earned within the context of an event beyond even the ability to punish, nor can healing be achieved.[51]

Forgiveness is less a definitive act than a posture of critical reflection and openness to a future beyond the past. Arendt stresses that the act of forgiveness itself is a realization of the complexity and limitations of life, as well as a release from grief. Forgiveness has future consequences for identity, culture, and politics that cannot be known in advance. Insofar as forgiveness is possible within the movement of a new solidarity, the shared history of the adversaries remains so, but in a new configuration. In the West, the example of Jews and Christians after the Holocaust exemplifies this process. Once bitter adversaries, a new relationship of trust and mutuality has emerged. The transformed relationship is multifaceted and may involve, among other things, a solidarity against new "enemies." Clearly, part of the Jewish-Christian relationship in the present is an agreement to share the spoils of Western capitalism; in some quarters, Jews can be elevated into full participation in the white and Western domination over other races and cultures. Forgiveness, here, is a deal, to resolve one injustice and to unite to perpetrate further injustices with a clear conscience. The "other" disappears to create a different "other," one more convenient and more important in the present. Still, the new relationship may develop a critical matrix from which Jews and Christians can recognize a constantly devolving estrangement.

The task, then, is to be vigilant in recognizing that resolution of one enmity may lead to still another projection of otherness. Could such a forgiveness, a revolutionary forgiveness whose path is justice, give birth to an Israel/Palestine, where values formed in the Jewish and Palestinian exile help to create a political structure that gives voice to those values?

It is more than coincidence that has Yad VaShem within eyesight of Deir Yassin. Rather, a shared history and geography have brought this memorial and village together in proximity. Deir Yassin remains unmarked by a memorial: only with justice can such a memorial to the Palestinian catastrophe be erected. Yet at the moment of its building, both the Holocaust and the Palestinian catastrophe will begin to recede in memory. Or perhaps, the journey toward a shared Jerusalem and land will begin at both memorials with Jews and Palestinians commemorating both tragedies. New possibilities will emerge in this journey, as well as dangers, for a shared land will also be open to violation and injustice. The setting free from grief means a vigilance in the present, so that that which creates grief will not be repeated under *any* banner or ideology.

CHAPTER 7

From Holocaust to Solidarity

Jewish theology arises out of and is accountable to the experience of the people. Its function is threefold: to articulate significant moments in Jewish history; to become a guide for direction and choice in the present; and to provide the resources necessary to create a future for the Jewish people.

The present incorporates the past as a guide and witness. Memory serves as an anchor to those who have gone before us and as a critical reminder of the difficult path of fidelity. The future emerges from the binding together of memory and contemporary choice, sometimes in a slavish way, other times in the way of freedom.

While mooring us, the past can also set us free. Once we are sure of our origins, sure of who we are, this rootedness allows us to explore, to rethink, to move forward, even in dangerous times.

Theology that has arisen from the Holocaust experience is of over-whelming importance. Like Elie Wiesel, Richard Rubenstein, and Emil Fackenheim, Irving Greenberg quite rightly places the Holocaust along-side the Exodus event and the rabbinic interpretations in its scope and honesty. Many, perhaps a majority of Jews, preferred that the painful Holocaust would remain unnamed and that the abyss would fade from view. Similarly, the state of Israel was, in the beginning, opposed by some of the Orthodox and Reform Jews and by more than a few of the Conservative movement.

Until the 1967 war, American Jews approached Israel in the light of charity and of the bonds Jews feel with other Jews, but with nowhere near the uncritical consensus one sees today. Yet, Jewish theologians presented the story of Israel as intrinsic to the renewal of Jewish life. As theologians, they refused the pious sphere of prayer and good deeds and spoke publicly about the need for empowerment as a religious response to destruction.

However, along the way, the articulation of Jewish concerns and aspirations lost its edge. Perhaps the consensus that Holocaust theology responded to and helped to form blunted the theology's critical edge. Perhaps Holocaust theology is awaiting a new theology to continue the work it so nobly began. The Holocaust theologians were a daring generation, criticized and heralded; their legacy is a lasting one. They did not arise from the centers of Jewish power and influence, but from the periphery of organized Jewish life. They took the Jewish establishment by surprise and turned it upside down.

Today a new generation of Jewish theologians is needed. Buoyed by the evolving tradition of dissent and by the movements of ethical concern, informed by the witness of Etty Hillesum, Martin Buber, Sara Roy and Amira Hass, they, like the Holocaust theologians, must emerge from the periphery of Jewish life to challenge a consensus that admits of little dissent.

Yet, we should not be naïve. The difficulties are immense and have grown over the years. Israel has conquered Palestine; the ongoing peace processes and ultimate Palestinian statehood cannot hide the fact that Israel controls Palestine through military and economic power. This is a fact that is unlikely to be reversed in the twenty-first century.

The Wall of Separation, begun in 2002, is the most obvious and visible symbol of this control. Spanning the West Bank and literally walling-in Palestinian population centers, this concrete wall, twenty to thirty feet high, with sniper towers and electronic imaging systems, can only remind Jews of the ghettoization that we faced throughout our history. We have conquered a people and ghettoized them. This, too, is unlikely to be reversed in the twenty-first century.

This inversion of our history is now accepted by mainstream Judaism and Jewish leadership. It places a cycle of violence and atrocity at the very heart of our history and of our future. It diminishes the possibility of seeing Jerusalem as the broken middle of Israel/Palestine. It banishes revolutionary forgiveness to a marginality that may now be irretrievable.

The Challenges of a New Theology

Yet, though it seems impossible to reverse the trends in the Jewish community or to roll back Israeli power, we cannot simply accept this reality. The factual and conceptual understanding of the defeat of Jewish dissent cannot diminish the fact of the survival of the Jewish prophetic voice in our time.

The twenty-first century presents us with a series of challenges. Will the Jewish prophetic voice survive Jewish empowerment? Where will that voice be spoken and to whom? What words will be used? What texts will be cited? What punishments will be meted out? Will the prophetic word break through the numbness of the Jewish community? Can it transform the power of the Israeli state to the homeland vision of Judah Magnes and Hannah Arendt? Will that voice testify to the power of God or to God's inability to address unjust power? Will prophetic critique of injustice testify to God's renewed presence in the world or to his continuing absence so deeply felt by Holocaust theologians?

Though it is impossible to state definitively what kind of Jewish theology will emerge in the twenty-first century, major themes that have surfaced in our discussion of contemporary Jewish life are worthy of note. They help to define the parameters of Jewish theology, and thereby, may well, in coming years, elicit further clarification of the future of the Jewish community.

First, a contemporary Jewish theology feels a tension between particularity and universality, as a self-critical voice that comes from the depths of the Jewish tradition and seeks to serve the world. It must be distinctly Jewish in category and speech, yet generous toward other religious and humanist communities.

Second, Jewish theology needs to acknowledge that genuine affirmation comes only through critical discourse and responsible activity in light of historical events. It must seek to be present in history, rather than pretending to isolation or transcendence.

Third, Jewish theology has to emphasize inclusivity (e.g., religious and secular Jews, women and men), a search for a renewal of community life in the midst of Holocaust and empowerment, and the refusal to be silent despite pressure from political and religious neoconservatives for a moratorium on critique of the Jewish community.

Fourth, Jewish theology has no choice but to balance the survival of the Jewish people with the preservation of its message of community. It is compelled to assert that survival and preservation of its essential message are ultimately one and the same thing: there is no survival, in any meaningful sense, without a deepening of the witness its values offer to the world.

Fifth, Jewish theology requires the recovery of Jewish witness against idolatry, as testimony to life in its private and public dimensions, as the essential bond of Jews everywhere, and as the fundamental link to religious and humanist communities of good will around the globe.

Sixth, Jewish theology must, in its essence, be a call to *teshuvah*: commitment and solidarity in all their pain and possibility, as well as a critical understanding of the history we are creating and the courage it takes to change the course of that history.

Finally, Jewish theology must help Jews develop a discipline that can flourish in exile from mainstream Jewish life. Mainstream Jewish life has evolved into a new form of Judaism, one that seeks and maintains empire. It is a Constantinian Judaism, not unlike the Constantinian Christianity that formed when the Emperor Constantine elevated a marginal, and sometimes persecuted, Christianity to the religion of the empire in the fourth century. It is here that Christianity embarked on its global mission carried by the forces of colonialism and imperialism.

Blessing and using the power of the state, Christianity transformed itself and lost its witness in the world. Belatedly, and as many Christians seek to flee that form of Christianity, Jews have adopted its methods and outlook. Like Christians of today who say no to Constantinian Christianity and who learn to practice their Christianity outside its confines, so, too, dissenting Jews must learn how to practice their Judaism in the shadow of Constantinian Judaism.

Within an emerging Jewish theology of liberation, the revival of the prophetic and the pursuit of liberation is critical. Though these carry qualities found in the very origins of the Jewish community, our discussion demonstrates that their recovery must occur within the welter of our time: the prophetic and liberation themes confront the dialectic of Holocaust and empowerment, deepening the themes of renewal and solidarity already present.

Prophetic Jewish theology, or a Jewish theology of liberation, seeks to bring to light the hidden and sometimes censored movements of Jewish life. It seeks to express the dissent of those afraid or unable to speak. Ultimately, a Jewish theology of liberation seeks, in concert with others, to weave disparate hopes and aspirations into the very heart of Jewish life.

Because dissenting Jews are in exile from Constantinian Judaism, a Jewish theology of liberation will be developed in a community that includes Jews and others who are not Jewish. Jews in exile live among other exiles in an evolving community, what one might call the new Diaspora. The challenge of Jewish witness and particularity will be found here, in the new Diaspora, where people of different faiths and worldviews come together.

In the new Diaspora, no one faith or tradition will predominate. Rather, carrying the fragments and brokenness of different traditions and cultures, those in the new Diaspora will share experiences and hopes, disappointments and possibilities. From this sharing, a new overarching particularity will arise. The question remains as to what kind of individual particularities will survive, be transformed, and be spoken to the world.

Can a Jewish theology of liberation become the catalyst to break through the paralysis confronting the Jewish community today? Can it again ask the questions that are "resolved"? Can it challenge viewpoints inscribed in stone and the monuments now being erected and worshiped, often at the expense of our values and the life of others? And can this be done, not to disparage or despair of the Jewish community, but in the deepest solidarity with it and with our history and our future?[1]

The answer to these questions cannot be answered definitively in the affirmative. Perhaps that should not even be the goal. In the twenty-first century, the challenge seems to lie elsewhere, in a fidelity to a history that is being lost and to a community who has little or no interest in continuing the Jewish ethical tradition, except in a rhetorical and ritualistic way. It seems almost as if Jewish dissenters are embodying the ancient experiences of exile and remnant. Dissenting Jews are in exile to be sure; they may be a saving remnant.

To be sure, though a Jewish theology of liberation begins on the periphery of Jewish life, it carries a past and present with it. The voices of the Exodus movement and of the prophets, of the martyrs who went to their death with a prayer to God, and of those who refused prayer, of those who resisted with arms, and of those who resisted with the written word, are before us. The Holocaust theologians and the movements of dissent in America and in Israel are with us. And in the night, if we plumb the night's depths, the people of Guatemala, Nicaragua, and El Salvador, the people struggling to create a just post-apartheid South Africa, are with us, too.

Or so it could be, one day. Could it be that in our struggle we are not alone but are living rather in a broader tradition of faith and struggle, one that now seeks to galvanize the witness of each community and to share it with other struggling communities in a common struggle for liberation?[2]

Again we return to the diversity of exiles in the world and to the formation of the new Diaspora in the twenty-first century. But it is also true that while these exiles and the new Diaspora itself are contemporary in fact and attitude, there have been others in history that have faced similar challenges, which were to them as daunting and painful. Instead of looking at history as one of singular communities often pitted against one another—say Jews against Christians, Catholic Christians against Protestant Christians, Christians against Muslims, or Hindus against Muslims—perhaps dissenters from all these communities, their own struggles to be faithful—are part of our inheritance and, therefore, part of our community.

The broader tradition of faith and struggle identifies a new tradition that has evolved over the millennia in the embrace of community over empire. Don't these struggles inform our own? And, by informing our own struggle to be faithful, don't these other communities across the span of time become, in some way, our own?

And yet, we are reminded again and again that, although our own movement toward solidarity is flawed, there are many, even among those who struggle for justice, who fear and dislike Jews. The generation of Nazis is only now coming to an end; revelations of former United Nations Secretary General Kurt Waldheim's participation in the Nazi party and of his connection with atrocities is only one of many reminders for the Jewish people. Progressive Christians welcome Jews as individuals, but often ask that their Jewish particularity be left at the door.

One need not travel far to run into the young Catholic priest who would die for a peasant in El Salvador, but who admits to being anti-Semitic, or to hear a cocktail-hour discussion of conspiring atheistic Jews. Although Louis Farrakhan, the Black Muslim leader, rightly horrifies many with his anti-Semitic diatribes, it is the tone, rather than the substance, that is unique. The revival of anti-Semitism in Europe is also cautionary.

What if a Jewish critique of Israel, for example, uttered with integrity and concern, is used to reinforce ancient prejudices against one's own people? Or if the critique of Jewish affluence is used to substantiate the continuing allegations of Jewish control of the world economy? What do you say, as a Jew who seeks solidarity with suffering persons, when Christian liberationists ask you to explain (in a friendly, informative manner, as if you have the "inside scoop" because of your heritage) how it came to be that "Jews control the media"?

Surely the double standard continues unabated: for Palestinians, Yitzhak Rabin, Benjamin Netanyahu, and Ariel Sharon symbolize a fascist militarism and are identified as Jewish; but is Harry Truman, who ordered the atomic bombing on Hiroshima and Nagasaki, identified as a Christian or, for that matter, is Ronald Reagan or George W. Bush? More often, "American President" is the prefix, and when "Christian" is affixed, a denial of their authentic Christianity occurs. And yet, would not our analysis raise a similar question vis-à-vis Rabin's, Netanyahu's and Sharon's Jewishness? Would we be able to admit that such a perversion of our values—as represented by these prime ministers—arose in the Jewish community?

A Jewish theology of liberation must insist that the issue of anti-Semitism survives and must be confronted at every opportunity. At the same time, however, it must refuse to use anti-Semitism as an ideological weapon to instill fear and counter legitimate criticism. The slogan "Never Again" too often becomes the rationale for refusing to trust and to risk. It also blinds us to the fact that we have fostered a prejudice of our own by our treatment of the Palestinian and Arab peoples.

The use of September 11th as a galvanizing force against Arabs and Muslims must be analyzed in a critical way. And the alliance of the

United States and Israel, as joined in a fight against terrorism, must be questioned. Whatever the analysis of American foreign policy in Afghanistan and Iraq in relation to terrorism, the Palestinian struggle against occupation must be understood on its own ground. The September 11th hijackers committed suicide in a mission that they undertook as the will of God. The conceptual and religious framework, though to their mind Islamic, struck at symbolic targets in a country thousands of miles from their homeland.

Whatever one thinks of the Palestinian suicide bombings that began in earnest in 2001, the rationale and reality is quite different. Here, Palestinians are resisting an occupation of their land that continues on the ground and is increasingly consolidated. It is as if there is no future for which to fight and no ability to fight a military battle, just as a highly sophisticated Israeli military continues to invade Palestinian land, assassinate their leadership, demolish more and more homes, and build a wall that effectively ghettoizes an entire people.

It might just be that the real prejudice of the day is found neither in the United Nations nor in the Jewish critique of Israel, but in the Jewish community, where images of the unwashed, the ignorant and the terrorist are repeated *ad nauseam*. And if the Palestinian people's refusal to accept occupation on the West Bank and Gaza is somehow seen as anti-Semitic, could we also say that Israel's refusal to recognize the catastrophe that has befallen the Palestinian people is a form of prejudice against Arabs and Muslims unworthy of our people?[3]

This is also true with reference to African-Americans in the United States. Regardless of our history and how we interpret it, there is no question of who, in contemporary American life, is placed on the bottom of priority and opportunity. Although anti-Semitism assuredly exists in the African-American community, we cannot ignore the ugly fact that racism keeps many African-Americans on the margins of society. For too many Jews, a statement from a Black leader absolves us of our own social responsibilities and blinds us to the benefits we derive from a racist society. Anti-Semitism becomes a shield that deflects the difficult questions confronting us. A Jewish theology of liberation needs to turn the fact of anti-Semitism into a challenge for reflection and critical social analysis.

If anti-Semitism is seen as a challenge for the Jewish community, then the constructive efforts of Christians to overcome anti-Semitism become helpfully instructive. One thinks of many Christians in this regard, but feminist theologians are at the forefront. Both Rosemary Radford Ruether and Elisabeth Schussler-Fiorenza provide provocative analyses of the rise of anti-Semitism. They probe the annals of patriarchy to answer whether or not anti-Semitism is a function of patriarchal consciousness and structure, and they caution the contemporary women's movement that the division of Christian and Jew represents a patriarchal intrusion into the lives of women, who need unity to fight a common enemy.

Ruether is particularly instructive here, because she, almost alone among Christian theologians, has tackled the issue of anti-Semitism *and* Israel's destructive policies toward the Palestinians. For Ruether, both must be fought at the same time. The ecumenical dialogue between Christians and Jews has flourished over the years and a central point of that dialogue—deservedly central in Ruether's understanding—has been the need for Christians to repent for the sins of anti-Semitism. Yet over time, that repentance has given a blank check to Israel and to those Jews and Christians who argue for Israel.

Ruether believes that the sin of anti-Semitism should not lead to another sin, the refusal to condemn and fight against the sin of displacing and demeaning the Palestinian people. Israel is wrong in its policies; therefore, the policies of Israel must be struggled against. The use of unjust power by the state of Israel does not implicate the Jewish people as a whole to a point of discriminating against them. Rather, those Jews who support these unjust policies must be confronted, as any one should be confronted who participates in injustice.

Thus, Ruether calls for the continuation of the ecumenical dialogue, but the end of the ecumenical deal, where Israel becomes the sole vehicle for repentance of anti-Semitism. The ecumenical deal is a cover for a second crime, first, the crime against the Jewish people in Christian history, and now, a Jewish-Christian crime against the Palestinian people.

The ecumenical deal is crucial beyond the religious nature of the relationship between Christians and Jews and Ruether addresses this question as well. Over time, the ecumenical deal stifles dissent by Christians over the policies of Israel and has also worked to stifle Jewish dissent as well. Christian critics of Israeli policy are labeled as anti-Semites; Jewish dissenters are considered Jews motivated by self-hate. The stifling of dissent among Jews and Christians has resulted in a political deal, where, in the public realm, any criticism of Israel is seen as anti-Semitic. Therefore, the American political arena has either been strongly and uncritically pro-Israel, or silent in the face of Israel's unjust policies toward Palestinians. For a politician to speak out against these policies is to risk being labeled anti-Semitic, and therefore, unfit to hold public office.[4]

Ultimately, a Jewish theology of liberation must engage the Christian community and admit the possibility of a Christian witness that, mindful of its anti-Jewish past and of its complicity in many forms of domination, seeks to renew and even transform itself. First, however, we must speak to each other in the language of the heart and of the mind. There needs to be an honesty about the past and the present and the realization that, in many ways, both Christianity and Judaism have changed in the last decades. In general, that change represents a role reversal; as Christians have come to grips with the dark side of their own history, and sought to critique and abandon Constantinian Christianity, Jews and Judaism have embarked on a Constantinianism of our own. Where once Christians were oppressors, Jews have now assumed this role.

With this honesty, is it possible that, one day, we might embrace both our differences and our commonality? This may be the most radical solidarity of all, as well as the most healing, for the Jewish community gave birth to a Christian community that has not only forsaken its progenitor, but has also tried to destroy it. A great violence was done to our people in that tragic parting of ways, a violence extending to themes and persons within our tradition that today are still unspoken.

At the same time, the Jewish foundation of the followers of Jesus was torn away and the erratic, often tragic, history of Christianity suggests a need for Christians to reclaim their Hebraic heritage. Could the Holocaust become the catalyst for healing a brokenness that has plagued both communities for almost two thousand years? Perhaps. Yet, to dwell in the Holocaust without recognizing the recent history of the Jewish people in Israel and Palestine is to romanticize Jewish suffering as if Jews were only and everywhere victims. Today Jews come after the Holocaust *and* Israel, taking into account that Jews, when empowered, are liable to do the things that were done against us.

Recent books by Jewish authors point to such a possibility of reconciliation on the level of faith, but a Jewish theology of liberation needs to explore such a journey in the realm of social and political life as well. Though when the ecumenical dialogue began, the work of reconciliation was hard and seemingly endless—some thought impossible—today, another even more complex level of soul-searching is in order. For, paradoxically, the most difficult question of Jewish-Christian relations may not be the mutual recognition of dignity and difference, but the striking similarity of community behavior in certain contexts, and therefore, the daunting possibility that theological affirmation may obfuscate the deeper questions of fidelity.[5]

In the end, the question of empowerment is hardly difficult in and of itself; the form and manner of empowerment is the crux of the discussion. A Jewish theology of liberation affirms empowerment, with the proviso that one must affirm the empowerment of others as well. Israel, as an autonomous and powerful presence in the Middle East, is firmly established. What is needed, however, is a critical understanding of Israel's empowerment, an understanding that includes the injustices inflicted upon the Palestinian people, as well as their need for empowerment.

The counterpart to Israel is an autonomous presence, Palestine; and a Jewish theology of liberation begins to speak of Israel and Palestine together. That Israel is a state has less to do with religious principles than with national organization in the modern world. The Palestinian people, likewise, deserve a state, and Israel ought to participate in its rebirth through recognition and material help, if the Palestinians request it. But this state must be real, with control of its resources, borders, and land. A state that does not have continuity in geography and culture, or one that is surrounded on all sides by a foreign power, is a state in name only. To "concede" such a state and to pretend that it is a "generous offer" is to patronize and demean Palestinians; it also demeans Jewish history.

A Jewish theology of liberation is unequivocal in this regard: the Palestinian people have been deeply wronged in the creation of Israel and in the occupation of territories. As we celebrate our empowerment, we must repent of our transgressions and stop them immediately. If this is done today, perhaps a hundred years from now we can speak of a confederation of Israel and Palestine, and how, out of a tragic conflict, a healing took place which benefited both communities.

A Jewish theology of liberation must also question Jewish empowerment in the United States. As we have seen, the Jewish community looks to the United States to guarantee Israel's security. Rarely is the cost of this guarantee discussed. Too often the *quid pro quo* is unquestioning support of United States military build-up and intervention around the world. This was again seen clearly with the American invasion of Iraq in 2003. Both Elie Wiesel and Irving Greenberg wrote essays supporting the war as important for America and for Israel.

Our ethics propel us toward solidarity; our *realpolitik* sees the poor, here and in the Third World, as threats to a system that is working in our favor. But what if United States militarism and intervention continues and deepens a cycle of poverty for a majority of the world's population? Even liberal statements that emerge from Jewish organizations carry little realistic analysis of the situation. Increasingly vague and rhetorical, the liberal agenda, while important for its time, carries little other than a hope that we will remain undisturbed.

The vague liberal dialogue that now passes for ethical concern continues, despite the unethical actions by the state of Israel. We engage in such dialogue in order to protect our own affluence. There is little dispute that Jews have made it in America, though there are poor Jews about whom neither Jews nor non-Jews want to speak. Impoverished Jews are a part of our past that we want to bury, for they remind us of the ghetto we have now escaped. Could we say that, although numerous museum and theatrical celebrations of our recent past abound, we are actually ashamed of our lives lived on the periphery, unnoticed by the general society and unrewarded with money and status?

Norman Podhoretz, a leading Jewish neoconservative, woke up one morning and realized it was better to be rich than poor, better to be powerful than weak. In some ways this has been a collective awakening, rather than an individual's inspiration. Few would argue with his general theme (unless an alternative was presented): that it is better for all to have access to the goods of life and to be empowered to participate equally in the decision-making process in society. However, to reach this goal is to understand how affluence is created and how, in its creation, others are denied.

As defined in our society, power too often demands the weakness of others and feeds on that weakness. Democracy may be the watchword; oligarchy is the reality. Capitalism, as practiced, may represent affluence for the few; it means unemployment and poverty for many. Most often, as Jews, we are aware of this only dimly, through newspapers and television. But those below us know we are riding the crest of a tidal wave. A Jewish theology of liberation asks that the liberal analysis that supports our affluence be deepened with a liberationist economic and political critique, which, paradoxically, has often been pioneered, nurtured, and expanded by secular Jews on the Left.

Practicing Justice and Compassion in a Post-Holocaust/Post-September 11th World

A Jewish theology of liberation is also a call to those Jews who have ceased to identify with the Jewish community. In the nineteenth and twentieth centuries, "secular" Jews abandoned or were forced out of the community because of their ideals and activism. Their critique of economic and political power carries forth the Jewish ethical ideal without religious language. Though progressive religious Jews did exist, the critique of religion and capitalism left many with little choice but to break out on their own.

Many Jews on the Left became a-theistic toward the religion and economy of their day, and it is only now that we can recognize the peculiar paradox they represented: many of those who refused the God of the status quo carried forth in various ways the essential witness of Jewish life, and many of those who prayed fervently adopted the idols of modern life. However, while it is true that some religious Jews actively pursued justice, it is also true that some who broke away adopted new idols, a monolithic secularism, and, too often, a Stalinist Marxism.

This split, perhaps inevitable for its time, serves little purpose today. The religious Jew needs the secular political critique in order to be more fully Jewish, and the secular Jew benefits from ideals and symbols spoken in a language that has languished. For what is a religious Jew, if not one who transforms the world because of his or her faith? And what is a progressive secular Jew, if not a practicing Jew without portfolio? And the division between religious and secular, as well as the possible dialogue, raises an important question that a Jewish theology of liberation cannot shirk: in the midst of Holocaust and empowerment, who indeed is a practicing Jew?

The Holocaust theologians portray a Jew today as one who remembers the Holocaust and participates in the survival and empowerment of the Jewish people. A secondary, although important, theme is the pursuit of the ethical. As we have seen, a Jewish theology of liberation raises the ethical again to a primary status, with the additional dynamic of solidarity and remembrance of paths untaken. Holocaust theologians thus have redefined the notion of practicing Jew from one who engages in ritual and observance of the Law to one who cherishes memory, survival, and empowerment, and a Jewish theology of liberation adds to that definition a critical and efficacious pursuit of justice and peace.

Yet most Jews, whether denominationally Orthodox or confirmed secularists, continue to accept the definitions established in a different era. How often do we meet a secular Jew giving his or her life to justice and feeling estranged from "religiosity," and an Orthodox Jew who contributes to injustice and feels self-righteous about his or her religiosity? Today, we must reevaluate the notion of a practicing Jew if the term itself is to retain any value at all.

We must also assert quite clearly that identification with the Israel is not, in and of itself, a religious act. The contrary is also true: the refusal to see Israel as central to Jewish spirituality is not, in and of itself, an offense warranting excommunication. A practicing Jew within the liberationist perspective sees Israel as neither central nor peripheral, but rather, as a necessary and flawed attempt to create an autonomous Jewish presence within the Middle East. The Jewish people have had a continuous presence in the area for more than five thousand years, and recent history has sparked a return. However, a Jewish liberationist perspective denies that Jewish history revolves around a return to the land and that Israel is *the* important Jewish community. Jewish people live in Israel, and thus deserve solidarity with Jews in America and elsewhere; the reverse is true as well.

Yet that solidarity cannot be uncritical. Today, solidarity with the Jews of Israel is not authentic without a solidarity with the Palestinian people. This double solidarity has its own dynamic and must guard against equivocation and false symmetries.

The struggle between Jews and Palestinians is not an equal one in terms of power or even morality. It is not that both are right, that both have suffered, and that both are wrong. In this case, Palestinians have suffered at the hands of Israel for no fault of their own, and even the argument of the Jews needing a place of refuge after the Holocaust is more and more difficult to sustain because of continuing Israeli aggression and expansion, well after the emergency years have faded into history.

The equation of Zionism with Judaism is clearly inappropriate. Zionists are those who have settled in Israel, and even in Israel, non-Zionist Jews appear. Those outside of Israel who claim Israel as the center of their Jewish identity are "Israelists" or "Israel-identified," Jews rather than Zionists. In the twenty-first century, Israelis are leaving Israel at a higher rate than Diaspora Jews are emigrating to Israel. Israelis who leave Israel are Israeli-born Jews who live elsewhere; they are no longer Zionists. The great majority of the Jewish people may be Israel-identified, but, by definition, they are something other than Zionists.

Solidarity with one's own people is hardly exhausted by one's position on the issue of Zionism and Israel, though the framers of the discussion would have us believe this to be the case. So much energy and emotion have been spent on equating Zionism and Judaism that an understandable fear exists when even an adjustment is suggested. But, what if Israel as a nation-state ceased to exist, or joined a confederation with the Palestinians and perhaps with Jordan and Syria? Would Judaism and the Jewish people cease to exist, or would the energies of Jewish resistance and hope be re-channeled? The Jewish people existed before the state of Israel and will exist long after the nation-state system ceases to be the building block of the international system.

Necessarily involved with the Jewish people, a practicing Jew is also called to enter into the broader tradition of faith and struggle. As we have seen, the ecumenical dialogue, as defined over the last quarter century, has its importance and its limitations. Today, we have to understand the limitations of ecumenical dialogue and where that dialogue is leading. The broader tradition of faith and struggle is occurring within a context wholly different from traditional Jewish and Christian institutions. Too often these power brokers retain power by maintaining the status quo, and this, in return, means maintaining domination and oppression.

There is no doubt, also, that the implicit or explicit theology brought to these dialogues from the Jewish side is a Holocaust theology that centers on empowerment and support of Israel. Yet, where can this dialogue lead, if its main focus is shifted simply from the Christian propensity to seek conversion of the Jews to the Jewish effort to demand the conversion of Christians to Zionism?

What each community needs, instead, is a critical partner who repents for past transgressions and is also allowed to think critically. As painful and as paradoxical as it might seem to many, the Jewish community cannot address the question of Israel alone for any length of time: yes-men and women for partners render little assistance to a community that needs assurance and critique.

A Jewish theology of liberation encourages a dialogue with other liberationist theologies and communities in a gesture of humility and solidarity. At this point, the few contacts that have been made are by Jews on the Left without Jewish identification, or by Jewish institutional leaders and academics who often seek to lecture Christian theologians on their faulty exegetical methods and their revival of Christian triumphalism.

The main point seems to be that the Jewish community fears the theological and political change such liberationist perspectives engender. But are we not missing the essential point of their struggle? The point is that we should be speaking for those who are suffering. And this should open the way to solidarity between our Jewish community and liberation theologians. Our fear for survival seems to cover over a deeper fear: the discovery that we are less and less in touch with our own witness.

Instead of the affluent and relatively empowered lecturing powerless people on the importance of uncritical support for Israel, perhaps it is time for us to be silent and to listen to the painful, moving, and sometimes contradictory stories that emerge from the underside. By listening, instead of lecturing, we might find that we are increasingly complicit in their suffering and, at the same time, we might begin to discover paths to solidarity important to them and to us.

After September 11th, this dialogue needs to be expanded beyond Christians and Jews. Islam is the most obvious religion that needs to be engaged, but it is important that this engagement also be self-critical. The desire to define Islam as a religion of peace, and the September 11th hijackers as deviants from the true teachings of Islam, is to romanticize Islam. It is to repeat the cycle of demonization and romanticization that so plagues the Jewish-Christian encounter.

For, if we have learned anything over the years about monotheistic religions, it is that they contain within them a wide range of potentialities. In certain contexts, each religion can be peaceful or violent, emphasizing justice or injustice, resting easy with other religions or persecuting them. The struggle for community or empire can be found in every religion, and in each generation the direction toward or away from either must be wrestled.

Constantinian Christianity has now been joined by Constantinian Judaism. Constantinian Islam is also a reality. Yet there are Christians, Jews, and Muslims who also oppose and suffer under Constantinianism. Could it be that those who participate in Constantinian religiosity—whether Christian, Jew or Muslim—are, in effect, practicing the same religion, albeit with different symbol structures and rituals? And that those who seek community are also practicing the same religion?

After September 11th, the challenge is to move beyond an ecumenism defined by difference or even the recognition of pluralism. Movements of justice and compassion across community and religious boundaries may be the vehicles for a better understanding of commonalities in religiosity that can no longer be defined by traditional religious labels.

A Jewish theology of liberation encourages a dialogue with other liberationist theologies and communities in a gesture of humility and solidarity. At this point, the few contacts that have been made are by Jews on the Left without Jewish identification, or by Jewish institutional leaders and academics who often seek to lecture Christian theologians on their faulty exegetical methods and their revival of Christian triumphalism.

As Walter Benjamin correctly points out, the memory of our enslaved ancestors can either enslave us or set us free. Paradoxically, the Exodus paradigm may be enlightening here. For the memories of past slavery may encourage a return to bondage in the guise of freedom, as if a known reality is better than the unknown. Those who sought a return to Egypt were refusing the risk of the wilderness, certainly an understandable position. Yet, freedom lay elsewhere, beyond the known, and new patterns of life and worship were to be developed in the pain and struggle of liberation.

As risky and problematic as it is, we are called today to the wilderness; but that call is a promise of liberation. Chastened by history, we can no longer see liberation as the omnipotent preserve of God hovering over us by day and leading us by night, or simply as the search for the empowerment of our own people in America and Israel. We can ill afford such innocence in the presence of burning children, whether they be in Poland or in Palestine.

As people in perpetual exile from Jerusalem, a status that formed the heart of our prayerful lamentations, we return today to form our prayers for a new generation of exiles that we have created. The celebration of our Exodus from Egypt, the Passover, again contains lessons: we mourn the loss of Egyptian blood shed for our liberation and are cautioned on our most festive holiday to recall the strangers in our own midst, for we were once strangers in a strange land.

The Haggadah also asks us to go one step further, to imagine ourselves in slavery. The celebration of freedom is thus disturbed by our own bondage. The warning is twofold: empowerment is covered with blood, and even the oppressors' blood is lamented; and empowerment, with its rationale and justification, is always confronted with forms of bondage into which we are tempted to enter.

Empowerment is neither final nor univocal: it is a stage toward a solidarity with self and others and contains its own critique, fashioned not by the victors but by the slaves of history and slaves of today. It is understandable that we often confuse empowerment with liberation because empowerment is convenient and self-serving. As we have also seen, however, empowerment of one people can force others into exile.

The voices of critique and renewal within empowerment—those willing to enter the night and create bonds of solidarity—walk the path of liberation within the Jewish community today, though they are often uncelebrated and unrecognized. As in other communities, the path of liberation is lightly traveled, and the great majority carry on as if the victors have the final word.

That the victims, once empowered, behave like the victors against whom they once rebelled, is a sad, but not unique, fact of history. That the security of the victors is one step from the anguish of the victims is rarely understood, even when the victors have recently emerged from the fires. There is cynicism in both power and despair, and perhaps the two are linked in a cycle from which it is impossible to escape. The exilic voices, then, represent an idealism that many feel is best left on the periphery.

The hope of liberation, however, remains always before us, and five thousand years of history, with its chapters of Holocaust and empowerment, provide a unique foundation upon which to build a future. The prophetic, like faith itself, ebbs and flows, waiting to be rediscovered by the people who bequeathed it to the world. The new urgency, represented by the "burning children" of all peoples, calls us to this rediscovery with a bewildering urgency. As much as at any time in history, the world needs this witness, and at the crossroads of our own history, so do we. A Jewish theology of liberation seeks to join with others in rediscovering the prophetic voice, with the hope that we can become what we are called to be.

Is Peace Possible in the Middle East in the 21st Century? Some Guidelines

Yet, we also know that the prophetic is not enough. The prophetic must be spoken; it is a guiding vision that moves beyond the superficial and the immediate. However, the prophetic is always compromised and on the verge of being lost. When the prophetic insists on its vision as the only possible way, then it may itself become a form of violence. A Jewish theology of liberation must be insistent on the need for confession and action on behalf of justice. At the same time, reality as it is cannot be ignored. It is in the intersection of the prophetic and the real that compassion and possibility is found. If it is impossible to implement the prophetic as if injustice is banished by the very word of the prophet, it is also impossible to accept injustice as if the prophetic is only a utopian ideal.

In the case of Israel and Palestine, the prophetic word must be spoken. At the same time there must be a search for a middle ground. The middle ground, like the broken middle of Jerusalem, is less and more than justice; it provides a possibility of beginning again and moving toward a reconciliation that ends the cycle of violence and atrocity.

When we come to the discussion of the future of Israel and Palestine, it is always difficult to know whether a committed and emotional rationality or an irrational rationality will predominate. In my experience of lecturing on this subject, I sense that the audience brings both of these understandings to the discussion, and I do as well. For as a Jew, could I pretend to a disinterested objectivity, to a commitment that is only rational? If this were so, the Middle East would be one among other issues in the world, no more or less important to me than any other political issue. This is clearly not the case.

Those of Christian background are drawn to the conundrum as well. The Holy Land looms large in Christian history, as well as in the Christian imagination. Jerusalem, especially, is vital here, for it is in this city that the man whom Christians worship as the messiah and God held forth, was arrested and was executed. The biblical narrative of Jesus' ministry is read daily by millions of Christians around the world; Jerusalem is the center of that narrative, as are the Jews. It is difficult for Christians to read the New Testament, or for that matter the Hebrew Bible, the Christian Old Testament, without being drawn to or repulsed by the Jews. Whatever the evolving Christian interpretations of Judaism and Jews—whether Jews are consigned to hell for the rejection of the messiah or embraced as the chosen people whom God has never forsaken —there can be no neutrality toward Jews. The contemporary drama in the Middle East—as well as the tragic reality of the Holocaust almost always figuring into this drama—only accentuates what is a perennial theme in Christian history: how the new Israel relates to the old Israel.

The involvement of the United States in the region again accentuates the centrality of Israel and Palestine for Americans of Jewish, Christian and Islamic backgrounds. There are few examples in world history of a superpower like the United States expending so much material and moral energy, with so little to show for that effort. Or perhaps, more accurately stated, the Middle East, at least since the demise of the Soviet Union, has largely become an American playing field, where difficulties abound, but where temporary solutions allow the smooth flow of oil and the backing of governments beholden to American military and economic support.

The most disrupting factor in the region has been the Israeli-Palestinian conflict. Though to a large extent shaped by the politics of America and the Arab world, the conflict has been difficult to resolve.

The very unpredictability of the conflict has led to other unpredictable factors, not the least being the issue of terrorism, so painfully evidenced in the attacks of September 11th, the subsequent war in Afghanistan, and the war in Iraq.

The stakes are high on many levels, and this is to leave unmentioned other issues, such as the historic confrontation between Christianity and Islam, the seemingly intractable Palestinian refugee crisis in the Arab world, the pro-Israeli lobby in the United States that features the fascinating alliance between the Jewish establishment and evangelical Christians, and the current leadership of both Israel and the Palestinians. In this season of war, a continuing and escalating war between Israel and the Palestinians is in evidence.

So, without pretense of objectivity and without being able to separate completely the rational and irrational, the question needs to be asked: Is there a middle ground? Can we come to a sensibility of a middle position, where Israel and Palestine can, for the moment, survive each other and, over time, flourish together? Is there a midpoint between those Jews in Israel and America who want all of Palestine and those Palestinians who want all of Israel?

For some years that midpoint has been seen within the context of a two-state solution: Israel within the borders of the state, as it was before the 1967 war, alongside a Palestinian state comprising East Jerusalem, the West Bank and Gaza. It is important to point out that this midpoint is actually more and less than that: it neither grants Palestinians a full equality of land within historic Palestine, nor envisions a state of Palestine with the sovereign rights of any other nation-state.

In most understandings of this two-state solution, Palestine is without a military and their borders are to be controlled by international and Israeli forces. Refugees outside of Palestine are restricted in their aspirations to return to their homes within what became Israel, and it is widely understood that East Jerusalem will only have symbolic Palestinian control. It is also understood that the Jewish settlements that ring Jerusalem and effectively make Jerusalem a Jewish city will remain and even grow.

So the midpoint settlement is one where Israel, though constrained from a complete victory, is dominant and where Palestine, though short of a complete surrender, accepts a historic and final loss of its continuity and completeness. Of course, this settlement, which has been a matter of international consensus for over three decades and remains central to the stated foreign policy of the United States, contains possibilities of further movement between the two nations as trust is built and the complex details of geography and demography are worked out. This was the hope of Oslo and the handshake on the White House lawn in 1993. But that agreement and handshake seem so ancient today, almost unreal. If Oslo represents the midpoint as described above, with its limitations and possibilities, it also seems that its implementation today would be little short of a miracle.

If the midpoint is no longer in view, then the task is either to devise a path where the parties can be brought back to the midpoint, or to abandon the previous consensus and move toward a new one. The former seems, at this point at least, almost impossible. If we leave aside the moral and ethical questions, what politics or military power can bring the situation back?

Though Israel has a contentious political debate within its borders about domestic and foreign policy, recent Israeli administrations have been bent on establishing a new understanding of the final settlement between Israel and the Palestinians.

Exactly what the contours of that settlement are, in the mind of the Israeli government, is difficult to know exactly. But, if his past understandings and present policies are an indication, then the extent of Palestinian hope for a real state in the West Bank and Gaza, with even a foothold in Jerusalem, is negligible to non-existent. According to the maps outlining positions on the final settlement that have surfaced over the last years, the most the Palestinians will receive is a non-contiguous and unempowered autonomy in Palestinian population centers on the West Bank and Gaza, surrounded on both sides by the Israeli army and fragmented by Jewish settlements. Nothing is envisioned for Palestinians in Jerusalem.

Though it is easy to blame the more conservative parties and prime ministers of Israel for this situation or to label them as extremist, liberal parties and prime ministers also had similar, though less drastic, maps of the final settlement with the Palestinians. The Oslo agreements signed by Prime Minister Rabin designated areas in the West Bank to be controlled by Palestinians, areas to be jointly controlled by Israel and the Palestinians, and areas to remain under the control of Israel. It seems that the final settlement envisioned by Rabin under Oslo would combine the Palestinian autonomous areas and the jointly-held Israeli and Palestinian areas to form the Palestinian state. But the third area would be part of an expanded Israel: this area included Jerusalem, most large Jewish settlements in the West Bank, security corridors and bypass roads connecting the settlements, and security buffer zones on the West Bank of the Jordan River and outside the 1967 borders of Israel.

As we know now, Rabin's ultimate successor, Prime Minister Netanyahu, was closer to Sharon than to Rabin, and Netanyahu's successor, Prime Minister Barak, was closer to Rabin than to Sharon. However, if the maps that each proposed are examined, rather than the rhetorical differences between Labor and Likud, the similarities should be emphasized.

The Arab world certainly cannot challenge Israeli power over the Palestinians and, in some ways, they simply compound the weakness of the Palestinians themselves. The Palestinians are divided into many factions, and their own inability to create civil and democratic institutions, after the establishment of the Palestinian Authority under Oslo, and to transform their society into one that can develop a politics of engagement and compromise with Israel, is the subject of scholarly and popular discussion within Palestinian circles and indeed around the world. The Arab world is not only weak; it lacks, aside from rhetoric, a desire for a real, empowered and democratic state of Palestine. That kind of Palestine might be an example to their own citizenry and, thus, challenge their own legitimacy as autocratic and often dictatorial regimes.

The United States has interests in the region well beyond Israel and the Palestinians. For the most part, oil and the proximity to the Soviet Union guided America's support of Israel during the Cold War era. The new relationship with Russia contains elements of the old, but without the high stakes of nuclear war. The collapse of the Soviet Union has had profound effects on the Arab countries, forcing them under the umbrella of the United States. Moral considerations of Jewish suffering in the West and Christian biblical understandings of the return of Jews to their homeland also play their part, so America's support for Israel is not only geo-political. Coupled with the domestic concerns of Jews and other supporters of Israel, United States foreign policy has tilted against Palestinians for these reasons and others. The post-September 11th invasions of Afghanistan and Iraq have only verified these understandings.

It seems that the consensus among the actors in the Middle East policy world, in the United States and abroad, is to develop and implement a policy of containment vis-à-vis the Palestinians. None has a desire to grant the Palestinians a real state, but all are wary of the ability of Palestinians to destabilize the region. Therefore, attention needs to be given to Palestinians, but primarily for the support of other interested parties—Jewish, Israeli, Arab, and American.

Is there a way forward? Here are some guidelines. In the following points, I outline some places from which the discussion of a future should begin.

Surely the existence of Israel can be argued from the exigencies of Jewish history. Zionism arises within a European context that will soon empty itself of its Jewish population, and, though most Jews who had a choice came to America during and after the Holocaust, the need for a secure place and refuge gathering point for other Jews after such a tragic event hardly needs arguing.

At the same time, the expectation that Palestinian Arabs, or the Arab world for that matter, should welcome an organized Jewish polity as part of its own obligation or on behalf of the world is an expectation that few people or other areas of the world, including ourselves and our nation, respond to in the affirmative.

That the Arab world had its own concerns and rivalries as well as its own limitations cannot be used as an argument for the creation of Israel or for its lack of acceptance in the Arab world. Those who suffer are innocent as a people, regardless of their background, societal structure, and political intrigue. No one today would argue that the Jews of Europe should have been oppressed for any failing that they might have had, and no one, then or now, should argue that the rescue of the Jews should have been dependent on any aspect of Jewish qualities or lack thereof.

The claims of the Palestinians that they were displaced by the hundreds of thousands are not disputed in the scholarly communities of Palestine, the United States, or Israel. While the necessity of the creation of a state for Jews, after the history of Jews in Europe culminated in the Holocaust, can be debated by Jews, Palestinians or other Arabs, the claim of displacement and the wrong of that displacement for the people involved cannot be circumvented. Jews have been refugees in the world; Jews, in what later became Israel, have created a Palestinian refugee population.

What the Arab world did and did not do vis-à-vis this refugee population, indeed, what it could and should have done, as well as what the Palestinians could have and should have done over the years can be debated on all sides. The reality remains on the ground that millions of Palestinians within Jerusalem, the West Bank, and Gaza are either under or profoundly affected by Israeli occupation, and a substantial Palestinian refugee population exists uneasily and, mostly, in a precarious situation in the Arab world

Israel is recognized within the international community and by the United Nations as a nation-state, with all the rights and responsibilities of such an entity. There can no longer be an argument about Israel's status in this regard. However, there can be a debate about the shape of Israeli society and nationality, and Israel must be held, as are other nations, to standards of behavior and responsibility within and outside its borders. Criticism can be made and a fundamental transformation of Israeli society can be discussed, even the transformation of a Jewish state into a secular democratic state of Palestinians and Jews, but that transformation would have to come through the evolution of a consensus within Israel and between Jews and Palestinians. It would have to happen democratically.

Obeying international law is always selective. International law is created by the powerful in dialogue with the less powerful. The powerful and less powerful invoke that law when it is supportive of their goals and neglect or violate that law when it is injurious to their self-interest. International law can enhance justice as well as impede it. Thus, the argument from international law or United Nations resolutions should be listened to and taken seriously, while being neither definitive nor univocal. Israel, like the United States, and like the Palestinian Authority, upholds *and* violates aspects of international law and United Nations resolutions.

The Palestinian refugees have the right, under international law, to return to the land that was taken from them in the creation and expansion of Israel. Israel does not have a right to the annexation of Jerusalem or to the expansion of Israel in the West Bank. However, the power of Israel, and the recognition of Israel's pre-1967 borders by the international community, make a Palestinian return and a complete withdrawal from East Jerusalem and significant parts of the West Bank almost impossible to imagine. The sloganeering by Palestinian activists, about the right to return and by Jewish and Israeli activists about the complete end of the occupation, are, therefore, counterproductive, mouthing words that inflame the situation and present unrealistic hopes for an embattled population.

The idea that the only "Jewish" response among Jews, in Israel and beyond, should be silence or unity or a further militarization is also counterproductive. The litmus test for being Jewish is far too narrow and self-defeating. Those Jews who identify conscience and justice as central to Judaism and Jewish life have every right, indeed a moral obligation, to speak on behalf of Palestinians and, therefore, on behalf of what they see as the essence of Judaism. The attempt to censor this speech and the speech of others on college campuses—college campuses playing a historically vigorous role in promoting free and open debate—as anti-Semitic is wrong and should be opposed.

Israel functions as a nation-state, but it also claims to be a representative state, indeed, a beacon of hope, to and for the Jewish people historically and in the present. Jews around the world support Israel in this dual role. Navigating statehood and Jewishness is difficult, perhaps impossible, but support for the state as a home for a displaced people, and as a hope for the survival and flourishing of the Jewish people among Jews and non-Jews around the world, was crucial for the establishment and survival of Israel. Without this special status among Jews and the world, Israel could only have been seen as one of the last colonial ventures of the Western powers in the Third World.

Israel's legitimacy and long term support is dependent on retaining the claims that Israel itself made at its founding and continues to make today. The moral dimension of statehood cannot be lived perfectly and the amount of divergence illustrated by the occupation of the West Bank ultimately undermines the *raison d'etre* of Israel. This does not mean that only Israel is wrong or worse than other nation-states in its exercise of power; it means that the peculiar circumstances of Israel's founding and support demand a reflection on issues that most political entities are free to ignore.

The Palestinians are not free of blame in this situation. Their leadership, a leadership that was sponsored by Israel in their return to the Palestinian territories under the Oslo accords, is often lacking in ability and ethics. Like Israeli leaders, especially Ariel Sharon, Palestinian leaders have not shied from using violence as a form of political resistance and engagement. In a war for dominance and survival, ethical conduct is difficult to enshrine as a principle of combat. Palestinians have a responsibility to control military resistance against Israel and its population when, and only when, a path toward real statehood is agreed upon and the timetable for reaching that state is announced, confirmed, monitored and followed. The use of the word "terrorism" and its association with September 11th is false. If we employ the term terrorism, than we engage in a cycle of discussions on state terror as well. Without the terror of occupation, the terror of resistance is delegitimized. Then, terror can be judged unacceptable and liable for punishment.

The United States has not been an honest broker, first and foremost, because it has perceived its interests in the region to be tied to Israel and to Arab governments that provide access to the resources that the United States desires. As a global power, the United States can act this way, but other claims that it makes about these policies should be jettisoned. The United States has also tilted toward Israel for reasons of domestic politics, which includes Jewish voters and campaign contribution support and the negative view that many Americans of non-Jewish background have about Arabs and Islam. We can have those views and create foreign policy to serve those understandings, but we cannot have it both ways: if Jews and Arabs in the Middle East are equally worthy of our concern, as recent political and public rhetoric would have us to believe, then Israel must be forced back to its borders and a real Palestinian state must be created with American support.

Because of the history of the region, including the weakness of the Palestinians and the Arab world, America would have to back this up with policies that reward and penalize both parties, as the goal of a two-state solution is pursued. That means the use of aid monies to Israel and the Arab world as a penalty/reward arena and, ultimately, the decision to either abandon the parties to themselves or to introduce American troops along the borders of these two states in the making. Without this explicit possibility of American military intervention, the honest broker image will be judged by the world, correctly in my view, to be an illusion, a cover for other designs in the Middle East.

The Coming of Constantinian and Evangelical Judaism

In its most obvious sense, the future of Israel and Palestine is in doubt. The forces against the two-state solution are enormous. To compel a complete Israeli withdrawal from the West Bank and East Jerusalem requires a stronger power than exists. A state of Palestine will be created in the next decades, but it will be a state in name only, its contours limited by a mapping of boundaries that are more or less similar to those proposed by the previous Israeli prime ministers of either party. In this way, the Israeli occupation of East Jerusalem and the West Bank will be redrawn to comport with those boundaries, while at the same time becoming permanent. Israeli control of Jerusalem will likewise become permanent and the settlements will continue to thicken, until the cities and villages of Palestine, surrounded by an ever-expanding Israel, become holding sites for cheap labor and underdevelopment.

On the Palestinian side, the question is no longer nationality or slogans, but survival. On the Israeli side, the question is not about victory, but its costs. On the one hand, victory brings expansion in land and economy to Israel and even a sense of increased security. The enemy defeated and in disarray is certainly preferable to one that is strong and self-assured. Yet, the victory of Israel, like all victories, has other consequences, mostly unforeseen.

The struggle for survival releases a traditional culture from its own mores and from the inhibitions that characterize the majority of any society, thus, the appearance of suicide bombers. The desperation of the situation also allows a slow acceptance of defeat, which may lead to quiescence and a normalization where populations begin to interact and comingle in more natural and ordinary ways. Victory for Israel may, therefore, erase the strict division of Jew and Palestinian, both within and beyond the 1967 borders of Israel. Over time, assimilation of populations in close proximity is the norm. Will it be any different between Jews and Palestinians?

So a future comes into view that may baffle the experts and the contemporary trajectory and power relations within which we live. Here are possible aspects of that future.

1   Israel's territorial consolidation is essentially completed. The expansion of Israel into East Jerusalem and the West Bank continues. A limited Palestinian autonomy is allowed, mostly in Palestinian population centers. The thickening of the settlements continually decreases the areas into which a growing Palestinian population would naturally expand. The decrease in territory and the inability to struggle successfully against Israeli power eventually deprives Palestinians of their will to resist. The Arab world is torn between the rhetoric of support for Palestinians and Palestine, and the desire to get on with their own development and flourishing. Thus, the acceptance of "autonomy" is forced upon the Palestinians by their own situation itself and by the apathy of the Arab world. The United States helps to broker this deal as the "best" for the region and, of course, for American interests. The steady depletion of world oil reserves, coupled with their concentration in the Middle East, makes this solution appear to be in the world's interest as well.

2   A triumphant Israel leads to a normalization of life in the Middle East. With an ordinary pattern of life, a majority of Jews in Israel become more and more cosmopolitan in their interests and identity. A distinct minority of Jews become more and more parochial in their sensibilities and insist on a Jewish religious state. The divide in Israel between secular and religious Jews accelerates until an uneasy truce between the two communities becomes a dividing line which citizenship can no longer bridge. In the meantime, the Palestinian minority within Israel continues to grow, becoming 30% or more of the Israeli population. Their struggle is for an equality that their citizenship promises, but that the Jewishness of the state does not allow. The Palestinian civil rights struggle within Israel becomes more active and successful, arguing alongside more and more secular Jews, and over against the religious Jewish commu-

nity, that citizenship is open to all and defined in terms of responsibilities and privileges. Within Israel proper, the trend toward citizenship increases, but, in East Jerusalem and the West Bank, Jewish exclusivity is emphasized. Thus, the division between Jews and Palestinians, once clear and irrevocable, becomes only one of multiple divisions in Israeli society, and, at least on some issues, the least important. Within Israel proper, an expanded sense of Israeli identity—which will include the Palestinian citizens of Israel—is developed as the expanded parts of Israel become more militant vis-à-vis secular Jews and the Palestinians in the West Bank. Conflicts regarding ideology, land, and resources will, on the one hand drive militancy, and on the other, accentuate the process of accommodation and assimilation.

3   American Jews are busy at home continuing to expand their success in the American free enterprise system. Jewish institutions continue to function and flourish, at least in the economic sense and in the public realm. An intellectual elite is educated Jewishly, but the mainstream of American Jews, recently mobilized by the Holocaust and Israel, drift. The questions of God and Jewish particularity, once bracketed and overwhelmed by the Holocaust and Israel, become non-questions. There is no way to pick up where the Jewish world left off, and besides, that history belongs to a different era. The need for Jewish pride and assertiveness remains, but the fuel of anti-Semitism and empowerment are spent. The drama of Jewish life is no longer felt as an existential reality. What takes shape is a new kind of Jewish religiosity, a hybrid of the Hebrew Bible and a renewed Christianity, containing elements of progressive and evangelical Christianity. The Vice-Presidential candidacy of Joseph Lieberman in 2000 represents the expansion and development of this new kind of Judaism, an evangelical Judaism peculiar to the American spirit.

4   The future of Jews and Judaism is, thus, tripartite: 1) within the 1967 borders of Israel, the creation of an ordinary life, primarily secular, within an expanding sense of citizenship, which over time includes Palestinians; 2) Jerusalem and the West Bank overwhelmingly become militantly and religiously Jewish, with an expanding and subservient Palestinian population; and 3) an evolving and increasingly

evangelical Judaism in America. Thus, the understanding that Jews are dividing into two distinct communities— American and Israeli—is actually more complicated. Obfuscating the picture further are the minority communities within this tripartite division: religious Jews and Jews of conscience within the pre-1967 borders of Israel; secular Jews in East Jerusalem and the West Bank; Jews traditionally religious in America, as well as Jews of conscience, who dissent on domestic and foreign policies embraced by evangelical Jews.

5   Jews of conscience are particularly important here, though their numbers are few and their future bleak. These are Jews in Israel and America who dissent from the accommodations that Jews and Judaism are making in Israel and America. Though mostly secular, they combine a secularity and a Jewishness that is peculiar in Jewish history and that has been the fuel of social justice movements in the West for almost a century. In some ways they are already a spent force, birthed in Europe and the earlier immigration of Eastern European Jews to the United States, spawned and defined by traditions within Judaism that no longer exist. Yet, in another way, they may be a bridge to a Jewishness and Judaism that moves beyond the future divisions, or at least provides a subversive element to each.

Predicting the future is always risky. There could be breakthroughs on a variety of fronts. Though the Israeli occupation will continue indefinitely, it is possible that it will be more limited than in the scenario above. The cost of occupation in lives, economy and political capital may become too great for Israel to bear. Arab governments could reform and, with that reform, speak more credibly to the world community about the plight of the Palestinians. The Palestinians themselves could, in the context of a general surrender, regroup, reform and develop an internal strength that forces Israel to take notice of a possible alternative relationship with them as a people.

The United States could change the direction of its foreign policy. Practical matters such as stability and oil might suggest that, without some justice, the Middle East will remain unstable and may even become hostile to American initiatives. Moral considerations may play a role if Israel moves beyond its occupation to another expulsion of Palestinians into Lebanon and Jordan. Israel itself might wake up to the international consensus that Palestinians have a right to be free in their own homeland.

Jews and Palestinians within Israel might link together, as some do even now, to support Palestinian aspirations in the West Bank. This connection within Israel might also reach out to a new coalition of Diaspora Jews and Palestinians in America, thus pressuring Israel, the Palestinians, the Arab world and American foreign policy to change its direction.

While various scenarios are possible, the needed changes in all directions make an alternative future highly unlikely. Political rallies and sloganeering will continue, but the bottom has dropped out. They are being shouted into a void.

The idea that, because of its policies and divisions Israel will self-destruct, is fanciful. So, too, the warnings about anti-Semitism. Though anti-Semitism is alive and well in the world, this ideology will be confined to the sidelines and to a small segment of those who are losing the struggle for Palestine. Terrorism will remain in the world; after all in its state and freelance forms, it is a constant feature of human history. But the idea that terror on behalf of the Palestinians, whether solicited, approved of or not, will reverse the Israeli-Palestinian situation, is an illusion.

In many ways, the Palestinian people are fated, at least for the foreseeable future, to exist in an apartheid-like situation in the West Bank, as refugees in the Arab world, with a virtual home in Jordan, though without Palestinian nationality, and as successful citizens in Australia, Europe, Canada and the United States.

Gaza is a symbol of that fate, the uncontested place where Palestinians congregate and where the world has little interest. There, Palestinians will be free, but under the constraints of geography and resources, surrounded by Israel and Egypt and the sea. America is also a symbol of the fate of Palestinians, an open society to refugees, as long as they assimilate to America and eventually leave behind their homeland in identity and politics.

The transition of Jews to evangelical Judaism is instructive here. As part and parcel of Jewish assimilation to the American Christian view of the world, Palestinian Muslims and Christians in America must embark on that journey as well. To assimilate to American values and hope is to distance oneself and the community from the old world and its decadence, in this case, from Arab, Eastern Christianity and "fanatical" Islam.

What is amazing about the Jewish shift to evangelical Judaism is that Jews in America have brought Israel and its Jews into the American mainstream. If it is true that the Holocaust has been Americanized—hence, the prominent United States Holocaust Memorial Museum on the Mall in Washington, D.C., commemorating an event in Europe that happened to European Jews—so, too, Israel. Though reference to Israel as the fifty-first state of the union is too strong, its prominence in American foreign policy, and the rhetoric that speaks about the glory and importance of Israel to America, signal a transition that is significant in American history. With Arab Jewry safely assimilated into Israeli society and with the descendants of remnant European Jewry prospering in the United States, and the more derogatory imagery of Jews has been removed. Jews in America are to be celebrated, and all Jews everywhere are, in a sense, honorary Americans.

Few Jews will pause and ask about the cost of this transition. For, before this transition, the toll in Jewish life was too high. Should Jews now think about the cost to others, the Palestinians, as also a cost to Jews? In the realm of ethics and morality, it is difficult to argue that Jews, in fact, are different than others; in the future, such assertion will become impossible. The celebration of empowerment is long overdue in Jewish history, but it is doubtful that the center of Jewish history, the covenant and the prophetic, can survive this transition.

America is a country *and* a state of mind, where history drops from the equation and the dawn of the new morning, empire, praised in the name of innocence, is defining. So it is with evangelical Judaism, the future of Jews, the fate of Palestine.

Irving Greenberg wrote about the three eras of Jewish history: the historical ones, the biblical and Rabbinic eras, and, after 1967, the era characterized by the centrality of Holocaust and Israel. Though the duration of the first two eras was several thousands of years each, the Third era has lasted mere decades. In the twenty-first century, we have already entered a new era of Jewish life. Here, remnants of the first three eras remain and are now transformed in a new configuration.

Hence, the Fourth era of Jewish life is characterized by its evangelical and Constantinian qualities: the normalization of Jewish life in Israel and America; the continued and expanded empowerment of Jews in both societies; the conquering of Palestine and with that, and for all practical purposes, the quieting of Jewish dissent. Violence will rest at the heart of the covenant, much as it has rested at the heart of Christianity. As in Christianity, there will be Jews who struggle against this violence, a struggle that will, as in Christianity, be a testimony and a witness. Yet, in the end, the quest for Judaism and Jewishness to be different will fail. The argument for Jewish difference will become more and more untenable.

Perhaps we have never really been different and the argument of chosenness, secularized and empowered as innocence, needs to be demystified. Yet, what lies beyond a deconstruction that strikes at the heart of a tradition, which stretches through recorded time? In the twenty-first century the synagogues are plush and inviting; the Holocaust memorials are part of the landscape of America; Israel flourishes in economy and technology. But, whither the prophetic voice in Jewish life and beyond? Can we, as Jews, speak for others in the name of justice, when the people we can free have been denied their freedom in its fullness?

It could be that the Fourth era of Evangelical and Constantinian Judaism will soon pass. It may one day be enfolded into the Third era, as a quartet joining Holocaust and Israel as the defining elements of our time. Perhaps all four are tied together, fated within history, and now, as much a part of Jewish destiny as previous eras. Thus, the Jewish conversation continues, the plot thickens, and new material is added with which future generations will struggle.

Surely it is too late for the Jewish struggle to be faithful to pass into history as an artifact. If this struggle was only historical and contextual, that passing would have occurred long ago. For battling against the norms of life and society only as a strategy for success and power is limited in time and scope; it ends when victory is achieved, when a new political and religious orthodoxy is established, and when a new and everlasting power paradigm—empire—is configured.

Yet, it is so that there have always been Jews who have struggled within and against empire for a more just future. And that struggle has been linked so intimately with history and with God that the world has experienced a deep calling, previously unknown in history, to worship a God and to embrace a covenant that has justice at its center. A Jewish theology of liberation affirms this calling in the present, and holds out the possibility that one day, perhaps soon, that voice will be heard again in Jewish life, and that this hearing—and response—is the only future worth bequeathing to our children.

Faith tells us that history is open; that empire does not have the final word; that community is possible. In the times when this hope seems impossible, the unexpected happens, and what previously was impossible becomes a possibility. What was seen as a utopian path is now seen as bare reality. Preparing the path is our task. But the hour is late, and the normalization of injustice makes the prophetic argument ever more difficult to sustain.

If we throw strategy to the wind and end our hope for victory, then we are free to be faithful. It is this fidelity that defines us in every Jewish era, no less the fourth, our time, that surrounds us and provides the context for our struggle and our embrace.

Notes

1. The Attorney-General of the government of Israel v. Adolph Eichmann, District Court of Jerusalem, criminal case No. 40/61, minutes of session no. 30, pp. L1, M1, M2, N1.

2. Richard L. Rubenstein, *The Cunning of History: Mass Death and the American Future* (New York: Harper & Row, 1975) 4–5. Although the long and distressing history of Christian anti-Semitism has been well documented, a brief examination of some of its manifestations, as outlined by Jewish Holocaust historian Raul Hilberg, is illuminating. See his monumental work *The Destruction of the European Jews* (New York: Harper and Row, 1961) 5–6. Anti-Semitism, of course, was not restricted to the Roman Catholic church during this period; it also permeated the thoughts and teachings of the Protestant Reformers. This is most clearly evident in the writings of Martin Luther. In his book, *About the Jews and Their Lies*, Luther sketched the main outlines of what later became the Nazi portrait of the Jewish people. "Herewith you can readily see how they understand and obey the fifth commandment of God, namely, that they are thirsty bloodhounds and murderers of all Christendom, with full intent, now for more than fourteen hundred years, and indeed they were often burned to death upon the accusation that they had poisoned water and wells, stolen children, and torn and hacked them apart, in order to cool their temper secretly with Christian blood. . . . Now see what a fine, thick, fat lie that is when they complain that they are held captive by us. It is more than fourteen hundred years

since Jerusalem was destroyed, and at this time it is almost three hundred years since we Christians have been tortured and persecuted by the Jews all over the world (as pointed out above), so that we might well complain that they had now captured us and killed us—which is the open truth. Moreover, we do not know to this day which devil has brought them here into our country; we did not look for them in Jerusalem" (quoted by Hilberg, 9). Luther's portrait of the Jews as wanting to rule the world, as arch-criminals, killers of Christ and of all Christendom, and as plague, pestilence, and pure misfortune was inherited by the Nazis. Thus, for Hilberg, the Nazi persecution of the Jews should be seen in continuity with Christian persecution, a continuity the Nazis brought to logical conclusion. According to Hilberg, there have been three anti Jewish policies since the fourth century of the Common Era: conversion, expulsion, and annihilation. "The missionaries of Christianity," Hilberg writes, "had said in effect: You have no right to live among us as Jews. The secular rulers who followed had proclaimed: You have no right to live among us. The German Nazis at last decreed: You have no right to live" (3–4). Hilberg continues, "The process began with the attempt to drive Jews into Christianity. The development was continued in order to force the victims into exile. It was finished when the Jews were driven to their deaths. The German Nazis, then, did not discard the past; they built upon it. They did not begin a development; they completed it" (4).

3. Irving Abella and Harold Troper, *None Is Too Many* (Toronto: Lester and Orpen Dennys, 1983) v. After discussing the terrible record of England, Argentina, Brazil, Australia, and the United States, with regard to Jewish refugees, the authors relate, "As for Canada: between 1933 and 1945 Canada found room within her borders for fewer than 5,000 Jews; after the war, until the founding of Israel in 1948, she admitted but 8,000 more. That record is arguably the worst of all refugee-receiving states" (vi). For the response of the United States, see David S. Wyman, *The Abandonment of the Jews: America and the Holocaust 1941–1945* (New York: Pantheon, 1984).

4. Alexander Donat, *The Holocaust Kingdom: A Memoir* (New York: Rinehart, 1965), 9.

5. Elie Wiesel, *A Jew Today* (New York: Random House, 1978), 11.

6. Ibid., 18.

7. Elie Wiesel, *Night*, trans. Stella Rodway (New York: Avon, 1969), 44.

8. Robert McAfee Brown, *Elie Wiesel: Messenger to All Humanity* (Notre Dame: University of Notre Dame Press, 1983), 54. Wiesel, *Night*, 78.

9. Wiesel, *Night*, 76.

10. Elie Wiesel, *Dimensions of the Holocaust* (Evanston: Northwestern University Press, 1977), 16.
11. Elie Wiesel, *The Gates of the Forest* (New York: Avon, 1967) 69.
12. Rubenstein, *Cunning of History*, 68–77. Also see Rubenstein's *After Auschwitz: Radical Theology and Contemporary Judaism* (New York: Bobbs-Merrill, 1966). For a detailed study of Jewish leadership during this difficult time, see Isaiah Trunk, *Judenrat: The Jewish Councils in Eastern Europe Under Nazi Occupation* (New York: Stein & Day, 1977).
13. Rubenstein, *Cunning of History*, 2, 92–94.
14. Ibid., 91. Rubenstein writes: "Does not the Holocaust demonstrate that there are absolutely no limits to the degradation and assault the managers and technicians of violence can inflict upon men and women who lack the power of effective resistance? If there is a law that is devoid of all penalty when violated, does it have any functional significance in terms of human behavior? . . . We are sadly forced to conclude that we live in a world that is functionally godless and that human rights and dignity depend upon the power of one's community to grant or withhold them from its members" (90, 91).
15. Emil Fackenheim, *God's Presence in History: Jewish Affirmations and Philosophical Reflections* (New York: New York University Press, 1970), 81.
16. Ibid., 84. Also see 87. Fackenheim continues: "A Jew is commanded to descend from the cross and, in so doing, not only to reiterate his ancient rejection of an ancient Christian view but also to suspend the time-honored Jewish exaltation of martyrdom. For after Auschwitz, Jewish life is more sacred than Jewish death, were it even for the sanctification of the divine name. The left-wing secularist Israeli journalist Amos Kenan writes: 'After the death camps, we are left only one supreme value: Existence'" (87).
17. Emil Fackenheim, *To Mend the World: Foundations of Future Jewish Thought* (New York: Schocken Books, 1982), 25; Pelagia Lewinska, cited there, 25, 26. For a more detailed sense of the struggle to be faithful within the Holocaust world, see Marc H. Ellis, *Faithfulness in an Age of Holocaust* (Amity, NY: Amity House, 1986).
18. Irving Greenberg, "Cloud of Smoke, Pillar of Fire: Judaism, Christianity and Modernity After the Holocaust," in *Auschwitz: Beginning of a New Era?*, ed. Eva Fleischner (New York: KTAV, 1977), 9–19, 28, 29. Greenberg continues: "Modernity fostered the excessive rationalism and utilitarian relations which created the need for and susceptibility to totalitarian mass movements and the surrender of moral judgement. The secular city sustained the emphasis on value-free sciences and objectivity, which created unparalleled power

but weakened its moral limits. . . . In the light of Auschwitz, secular twentieth-century civilization is not worthy of this transfer of our ultimate loyalty" (28).

19. Ibid., 32.

20. Ibid., 22.

21. One beautiful example of Christians providing refuge for Jews is found in Philip Hallie, *Lest Innocent Blood Be Shed: The Story of the Village of Chambon and How Goodness Happened There* (New York: Harper & Row, 1979). Also, see Nechama Tec, *When Light Pierced the Darkness: Christian Rescue of Jews in Nazi-Occupied Poland* (New York: Oxford University Press, 1986). The history of those who were not willing to do all that was needed to be done is recorded in John E. Morley, *Vatican Diplomacy and the Jews During the Holocaust 1939–1943* (New York: KTAV, 1980). Rev. Morley writes, "It must be concluded that Vatican diplomacy failed the Jews during the Holocaust by not doing all that it was possible for it to do on their behalf. It also failed itself because in neglecting the needs of the Jews, and pursuing a goal of reserve rather than humanitarian concern, it betrayed the ideals that it had set for itself. The Nuncios, the Secretary of State, and most of all, the Pope share the responsibility for this dual failure" (209).

22. Johann Baptist Metz, *The Emergent Church: The Future of Christianity in a Postbourgeois World*, trans. Peter Mann (New York: Crossroad, 1981), 19. As we shall see, this dictum, when applied to Christians and Jews, may provide the path to a new form of solidarity.

CHAPTER 2

1. Irving Greenberg, "The Third Great Cycle in Jewish History," *Perspectives* (September 1981; originally an occasional publication [in the form of a pamphlet] of the National Jewish Resource Center).

2. Ibid., 3–6.

3. Ibid., 8.

4. Ibid., 9.

5. Ibid., 15, 18

6. Ibid., 21, 22, 23.

7. Ibid., 25, 26. As to the use of immoral strategies to achieve moral ends, Greenberg writes, "The acceptance of the guilt inherent in such actions calls for people of exceptional emotional range and strong orientation both to absolute norms and relative claims, both to judgement and to mercy." At the same time, Greenberg fears a "morally deadening rearmament" and the possibility of idolatry, if Judaism fails to critique even as it affirms the state of Israel (25).

8. Ibid., 24, 27, 28.
9. Ibid., 28. Also, see Irving Greenberg, "On the Third Era in Jewish History: Power and Politics," *Perspectives* (December 1980), 18, 19.
10. Greenberg, "Third Era," 6.
11. Irving Greenberg, "Power and Peace," *Perspectives* 1/3 (1985): 3, 5; Greenberg, "Third Cycle," 28.
12. Greenberg, "Third Cycle," 32, 33.
13. Ibid., 40.
14. Nathan Perlmutter and Ruth Ann Perlmutter, *The Real Anti-Semitism in America* (New York: Arbor House, 1982) 107. For a similar view of the world, see Irving Kristol, "The Political Dilemma of American Jews," *Commentary* 67 (1984): 23–29.
15. Perlmutter, *Real Anti-Semitism*, 156, 157, 170–71. The Holyland Fellowship of Christians and Jews, founded by Rabbi Yechiel Eckstein, seeks to solidify the bond between Fundamentalist Christians and the Jewish community, primarily in relation to Christian support for the state of Israel. Among their endorsers are Ronald Reagan, Jack Kemp, conservative Congressman from New York, Pat Robertson of the Christian Broadcasting Network, and Thomas Dine, Executive Director of AIPAC. See *Holyland Fellowship Bulletin* 1 (1986): 1–5.
16. Earl Shorris, *Jews Without Mercy: A Lament* (Garden City: Doubleday, 1982), 57–59.
17. Ibid., 12–15.
18. Ibid., 60.
19. Roberta Strauss Feuerlicht, *The Fate of the Jews: A People Torn Between Israeli Power and Jewish Ethics* (New York: Times Books, 1983) 5, 185–87. Feuerlicht writes: "Historically, the relationship between Jew and black in America has not been one of equality. Jews were traders and masters; blacks were merchandise and slaves and servants. In America there is no record of a black who traded in Jews or of a black who owned Jews; I doubt that there are any black housewives who have a Jewish 'girl' come in one day a week to clean. Where blacks were available, neither Jews nor any other whites touched bottom" (186–87).
20. Ibid., 203–5.
21. Ibid., 220, 245.
22. Ibid., 260. Rabbi Balfour Brickner echoes some of these sentiments in relation to the occupation of the West Bank when he writes that "many of us experience a concern that borders on anguish." See Brickner, "The West Bank: Right, Rights and Wrongs," *The Jewish Spectator* 48 (1983): 22–24.
23. Feuerlicht, *Fate of the Jews*, 251. For an Israeli—Palestinian dialogue that seeks to undo this new equation, see Uri Avnery and Hanna

Siniora, "A Middle East Peace Is Possible," *The Nation*, April 5, 1986: 473, 487–89.

24. Feuerlicht, *Fate of the Jews*, 258, 259, 287. The casualty figures in the Lebanese War were enormous. Alexander Cockburn writes: "Beginning in the early 1970s Israel systematically bombed Palestinian refugee camps in south Lebanon and Beirut and as far north as Tripoli, killing many thousands. And during the summer of 1982, the Israeli army, conservatively, killed about 19,000 people in Lebanon, mostly Palestinians." See Cockburn "More Swill From Marty," *The Nation*, March 15, 1986, 295.

CHAPTER 3

1. Phillip Lopate, "Resistance to the Holocaust," *Tikkun* 4 (1989): 56.
2. Ibid. Lopate adds: "A good deal of suspicion and touchiness resides around the issue of maintaining the Holocaust's privileged status in the pantheon of genocides. It is not enough that the Holocaust was dreadful; it must be seen as uniquely dreadful" (57).
3. Avishai Margalit, "The Kitsch of Israel," *New York Review of Books* 35 (November 24, 1988): 23.
4. Ibid., 24. All of this is also crucial for the marketing of Israel to the American Jewish community. See ibid., 22. For Elie Wiesel's response to the trivialization of the Holocaust, see his "Art and the Holocaust: Trivializing Memory," *The New York Times*, June 11, 1989. To the question of how one transmits the message without trivializing it, Wiesel responds, "Listen to the survivors and respect their wounded sensibility. Open yourselves to their scarred memory, and mingle your tears with theirs. And stop insulting the dead" (38).
5. Boas Evron, "The Holocaust: Learning the Wrong Lessons," *Journal of Palestine Studies* 10 (1981): 16, 17, 18. For an illustration of the need for common struggle within the Holocaust, see Helen Fein, *Accounting for Genocide: National Responses and Jewish Victimization During the Holocaust* (Chicago: University of Chicago Press, 1979).
6. Evron, "Holocaust," 23, 21, 17–20.
7. Ibid., 26.
8. Rubenstein, *Cunning of History*, 69.
9. Ibid., 74, 76. For a detailed study of the Jewish Councils, see Trunk, *Judenrat*.
10. Richard L. Rubenstein, *The Age of Triage: Fear and Hope in an Overcrowded World* (Boston: Beacon Press, 1982), 135.
11. Rubenstein, *Cunning of History*, 11.
12. Ibid., 6, 94–95. Despite his differences with Wiesel, Fackenheim, and Greenberg, Rubenstein's radical analysis of the twentieth cen-

tury leads him, as it does all Holocaust theologians, to a neoconservative political stance. However, his analysis of the Holocaust as a paradigmatic event also leads him to place less emphasis on the state of Israel. Of all the Holocaust theologians, he has written the least on Israel and not at any length since the 1960s. Even so, there is a similarity with Wiesel and Fackenheim: the central event is the Holocaust. For his conservative positions, see ibid., 96–97. For his fascinating piece on Israel, see *After Auschwitz*, 131–44.

13. Shlomo Avineri, *The Making of Modern Zionism: The Intellectual Origin of the Jewish State* (New York: Basic Books, 1981), 3–13. On the origins of Zionism, also see Arthur Hertzberg, *The Zionist Idea* (Philadelphia: Jewish Publication Society of America, 1959); Walter Laquer, *A History of Zionism* (New York: Schocken, 1976); and Ben Halpern, *The Idea of the Jewish State* (Cambridge: Harvard University Press, 1969).

14. Ahad Ha'am, *Nationalism and the Jewish Ethic*, ed. Hans Kohn (New York: Herzl Press, 1962), 74–75.

15. Ibid., 67.

16. Ibid., 203.

17. Ibid., 122–23.

18. Quoted in Gary Smith, *Zionism: The Dream and the Reality* (New York: Harper & Row, 1974), 31.

19. Ibid., 36, 37. For an extended discussion of Ahad Ha'am's philosophy, see Bernard Avishai, *The Tragedy of Zionism: Revolution and Democracy in the Land of Israel* (New York: Farrar Straus Giroux, 1985), 45–66.

20. See Arthur A. Goren, ed., *Dissenter in Zion: From the Writings of Judah L. Magnes* (Cambridge: Harvard University Press, 1982), 226. For a discussion of Magnes's life, see ibid., 1–57. Also see Norman Bentwich, *For Zion's Sake: A Biography of Judah L. Magnes* (Philadelphia: Jewish Publication Society of America, 1954).

21. Goren, *Dissenter in Zion*, 227.

22. Ibid.

23. Ibid., 276.

24. Ibid., 279, 277.

25. Judah Magnes, *Like All the Nations?* (Jerusalem: Herod's Gate, 1930) 22, 27. Magnes wrote: "Whether through temperament or other circumstances I do not at all believe, and I think the facts are all against believing, that without Palestine the Jewish people is dying out or doomed to destruction. On the contrary it is growing stronger, for Palestine without communities in the Dispersion would be bereft of much of its significance as a spiritual center for the Judaism of the world" (22).

26. Ibid., "Toward Peace in Palestine," *Foreign Affairs* 21 (1943): 239, 240–41. Magnes felt America's "moral and political authority" to be crucial to solving a crisis that the parties to the crisis could not: "In view of the intransigence of many responsible leaders on both sides the adjustment may have to be imposed over their opposition" (241).
27. Hannah Arendt, "To Save the Jewish Homeland: There Is Still Time," in *The Jew as Pariah*, ed. Ron H. Feldman (New York: Grove Press, 1978), 181.
28. Ibid., 187.
29. Ibid., 182, 184, 186, 188, 189.
30. Ibid., 192.
31. Ibid., 221–22.

CHAPTER 4

1. Howard Greenstein, *Turning Point: Zionism and Reform Judaism* (Chico: Scholars Press, 1981), 1.
2. Ibid., 129.
3. Ibid., 128.
4. Ibid., 29.
5. Ibid., 56.
6. William Zukerman, *Voice of Dissent: Jewish Problems, 1948–1961* (New York: Bookman Associates, 1962), 141. I am grateful to Wes Avram, who introduced me to Zukerman and his dissent.
7. Ibid., 151, 154.
8. Ibid., 158.
9. Ibid., 35.
10. Ibid., 296–97.
11. See I. F. Stone, "The Harder Battle and the Nobler Victory" in *I. F. Stone, In a Time of Torment: 1961–1967* (Boston: Little, Brown, 1989), 441–45; Michael Selzer, ed., *Zionism Reconsidered: The Rejection of Jewish Normalcy* (New York: Macmillan, 1970); Noam Chomsky, *Peace in the Middle East: Reflections on Justice and Nationhood* (New York: Vintage, 1974).
12. Chomsky, *Peace*, 57–58, 75, 34. For the heavy attacks on Chomsky and other dissenters, see Chomsky, *Peace*, 153–98.
13. Noam Chomsky, *The Fateful Triangle: The United States, Israel and the Palestinians* (Boston: South End Press, 1983), 43, 45.
14. Ibid., 48, 49.
15. Ibid., 202–4; 334–35. As Chomsky points out, the invasion of Lebanon was linked to further repression in the occupied territories. See 205–9.

16. Ibid., 404. Also see Zetev Schiff and Ehud Ya'ari, *Israel's Lebanon War*, trans. Ina Friedman (New York: Simon & Schuster, 1984), 250–85. For the Kahan Commission Report, see *The Beirut Massacre*, intro. Abba Eban (New York: Karz-Cohl, 1983).

17. Jacobo Timerman, *The Longest War: Israel in Lebanon, trans. Miguel Acoca* (New York: Vintage, 1982), 158, 159. Timerman writes: "Today in Beirut Arab children have their legs and arms amputated by candlelight in the basements of hospitals destroyed by bombs, without anesthetics, without sterilization. It is eleven days since proud veteran Israeli troops cut the electricity and water, and food and fuel supplies" (162). The war precipitated a new level of dissent within Israel. See *The Other Israel*, no. 2 (1983): 1–4 and ibid., no. 3 (September–October 1983): 1-6.

18. Jacob Neusner, "The Real Promised Land Is America," *International Herald Tribune*, March 10, 1987.

19. Jacob Neusner, "It Isn't 'Light to the Gentiles' or Even Bright for Most Jews," *International Herald Tribune*, March 11, 1987. For two longer treatments of the subject, see his *Stranger at Home: The Holocaust, Zionism, and American Judaism* (Chicago: University of Chicago Press, 1981), and *The Jewish War Against the Jews: Reflections on Golah, Shoah and Torah* (New York: KTAV, 1984).

20. The tradition of dissent is almost endless and thus deserves a book-length treatment of its own. Still, a mention must be made of Israel's influence on American foreign policy and the pioneering work done by Alfred M. Lilienthal, begun in the 1950s and culminating in his massive volume, *The Zionist Connection II: What Price Peace* (New Brunswick: North American, 1978). This work has been carried forward by Cheryl A. Rubenberg in her book, *Israel and the American National Interest* (Chicago: University of Illinois Press, 1986). For Israel's foreign policy, see Jane Hunter's journal *Israeli Foreign Affairs*, which began publication in 1987, and Benjamin Brit-Hallahmi, *The Israeli Connection: Who Israel Arms and Why* (New York: Pantheon, 1987). Also see Aaron S. Klieman, *Israel's Global Reach: Arms Sales as Diplomacy* (Washington: Pergamon Brassey's, 1985).

21. Alexander Schindler, "To the President of Israel," in *AS Briefings: Commission on Social Action of Reform Judaism*, March 1988: Appendix A; Albert Vorspan, "Soul Searching," *New York Times Magazine*, May 8, 1988: 40. Two days after Schindler's telegram Irena Klepfisz, a feminist poet, spoke critically at the Israeli Consulate in New York. See Irena Klepfisz, "Hurling Words at the Consulate," *Genesis 2* (1988): 18–20.

22. Yehuda Amichai, Amos Elon, Amos Oz, A. B. Yehoshua, "Silence of American Jews Supports Wrong Side," *The New York Times*, February 21, 1988; "Israel Must End the Occupation," *The New York Times*, February 21, 1988. For three other interesting positions publicized at the same time, see "Remember When It Was a Symbol of Hope?" *The New York Times*, April 27, 1988; "Why Must Jewish and Arab Blood Be Shed: It's Time to Call It Quits," *The New York Times*, February 15, 1988; "Time to Dissociate from Israeli Policies," *The Nation*, February 13, 1988, 193.

23. Arthur Hertzberg, "The Uprising," *New York Review of Books* 35 (February 1988): 32; idem., "The Turning Point," *New York Review of Books* 35 (October 1988): 60. Also see his essay "The Illusion of Jewish Unity," *New York Review of Books* 35 (June 1988).

24. Elie Wiesel, "Let Us Remember, Let Us Remember," *The New York Times*, April 1, 1988; idem., "A Mideast Peace—Is It Possible?" *The New York Times*, June 23, 1988.

25. Wiesel, "Mideast Peace."

26. Arthur Hertzberg, "An Open Letter to Elie Wiesel," *New York Review of Books* 35 (August 1988): 13.

27. Ibid.

28. Ibid., 14.

29. Michael Lerner, "The Occupation: Immoral and Stupid," *Tikkun* 3 (1988): 7.

30. Ibid.

31. Ibid., 9.

32. Ibid.

33. Ibid., 10, 12.

34. "The Twenty-first Year: Covenant for the Struggle Against Occupation," *Tikkun* 3 (1988): 68–69. The covenant concludes: "Refusal is the only morally and politically sound form of participation in Israeli society during the Age of Occupation. Refusal is a way out, a source of hope for our moral integrity as Israelis" (69). For a chronicle of Israeli protests that emerged with the uprising, see *The Other Israel* 30 (1988): 5–6 and *Israel and Palestine Report* 139 (1988): 17.

35. As quoted in the *The New York Times*, September 14, 1993.

36. Michael Lerner, "Settler Violence and the Rape of Judaism," *Tikkun* 9 (1994): 27–28.

37. Avishai Margalit, "Settling Scores," *New York Review of Books* 48 (September 2001): 20–25.

38. Roy's analysis can be found in Sara Roy, "The Palestinian-Israeli Crisis: An Analysis," presented at the United States in the Middle East: Politics, Religion and Violence Conference, University of

Delaware, February 2001, or in Sara Roy, "Why Peace Failed: An Oslo Autopsy," *Current History* (January 2002): 8–16.

39. Ibid.

40. James Bennet, "Hopes Are Modest as Israelis and Palestinians Await the Bush Plan," *The New York Times*, October 12, 2001.

41. Ibid.

42. "Be Heard," *The New York Times*, August 29, 2001.

43. Elie Wiesel, transcript of speech, New York Israel Solidarity Rally (October 12, 2000), September 15, 2003, http://www.aish.com/Israel/articles/Elie_Wiesel_Speaks_Out.asp.

44. Gideon Levy, "As Ramon Was Launched Into Space," *Ha'aretz*, January 19, 2003.

CHAPTER 5

1. Israel Shahak, "Collection: Atrocities as a Method," n.d., 1. These monthly translations and commentaries from Israel were published by the American Educational Trust in Washington, D.C.

2. Israel Shahak, "The Givati Brigade: Its Misdeeds and the Politics Behind Them," from the *Hebrew Press* 1 (1989): 2.

3. Ibid. As Shahak comments, "The Arabs understand 'nothing but force' is a very common racist stereotype in Israel, as is the belief that public humiliation is the 'right' way of 'dealing with the Arabs'" (2).

4. Tikvah Parnass-Honig, director of the Alternative Information Center in Jerusalem, detailed this solidarity of Palestinians and Israelis in her unpublished paper delivered at the United Nations in June 1988, "Another Aspect of the Intifada: Stepping up the Occupation Policy—Repression of Any Public Activity of Palestinians and of the Inevitable Cooperation Between Them and Israelis."

5. David G. Roskies, *Against the Apocalypse: Responses to Catastrophe in Modern Jewish Culture* (Cambridge: Harvard University Press, 1984), 198, 197.

6. Ibid., 212.

7. Ibid., 202.

8. Irving Greenberg, "Some Lessons from Bitburg," *Perspectives* (May 1985): 1. Not content with protest, Greenberg offered, in a following essay, a speech that Reagan should have given at Bitburg recognizing that this had become a public liturgy. Greenberg addressed five audiences: the German people, German youth born after 1945, the veterans and families of the Allied armies, the Jewish survivors, and the world. See his "The Speech Ronald Reagan Should Have Given at Bitburg," *Perspectives* (Spring 1985): 5. For the international

scope of the Bitburg affair see Ilya Levkov, ed., *Bitburg and Beyond: Encounters in American, German and Jewish History* (New York: Shapolsky, 1987).

9. Elie Wiesel, "'Your Place Is With The Victims,' Wiesel Tells Reagan," in Levkov, *Bitburg and Beyond*, 43, 44. Not everyone agreed with the substance or tone of Wiesel's speech. For a vigorous criticism, see Jacob Neusner, "Reagan Did Better Than Wiesel," in Levkov, *Bitburg and Beyond*, 386–87. Neusner starts his essay with these words: "If Elie Wiesel had asked my advice about what to say to President Reagan and how to say it, I would have told him this: Remember, not everyone in the world is Jewish."

10. See Janet Aviad, *Return to Judaism: Religious Renewal in Israel* (Chicago: University of Chicago Press, 1983). For an example of such conversion literature and its limitations in the United States, see Arthur Waskow, *Godwrestling* (New York: Schocken, 1978).

11. Ian Lustick, *For the Land and the Lord: Jewish Fundamentalism in Israel* (New York: Council on Foreign Relations, 1988), 2.

12. Ibid., 126. For a discussion of how religious and secular ultranationalists work together see Ehud Sprinzak, "The Emergence of the Radical Right" *Comparative Politics* 21 (1989): 171–92.

13. Benny Morris, *The Birth of the Palestinian Refugee Problem, 1947–1949* (Cambridge: Cambridge University Press, 1987), 210.

14. Ibid.

15. Ibid., 211.

16. Ibid., 222–23.

17. Ibid., 231.

18. Ibid., 233.

19. Amos Kenan, "The Legacy of Lydda: Four Decades of Blood Vengeance," *The Nation*, February 6, 1989, 155–56.

20. Ibid., 156.

21. Yossi Sarid, "The Night of the Broken Clubs," *Ha'aretz*, May 4, 1989.

22. Gideon Spiro, "You Will Get Used to Being a Mengele," *Al Hamishar*, September 19, 1988.

23. Greenberg, "Third Great Cycle," 25, 26. See also Emil Fackenheim, *What Is Judaism: An Interpretation for the Present Age* (New York: Summit Books, 1987); Arthur A. Cohen and Paul Mendes-Flohr, eds., *Contemporary Jewish Religious Thought* (New York: Free Press, 1987).

24. Wiesel, *Jew Today*, 121, 122, 126–27. Also, see Wiesel's letter "To a Brother in Israel" in ibid., 129–37. The letter revolves almost completely around the question of why a Diaspora continues when there

is a Jewish state. Unfortunately, Palestinian Arabs are mentioned only once and in passing.

25. Elie Wiesel and Albert Friedlander, *The Six Days of Destruction: Meditations Toward Hope* (Oxford: Pergamon Press, 1988); Greenberg, *The Jewish Way* (New York: Summit Books, 1988). A major theme of Wiesel and Friedlander's book is that Christians need to integrate the Jewish experience into liturgical acts, and, therefore, they provide a set of guidelines for such liturgy and a sample liturgy. At the same time, even the most recent public articulation of Holocaust liturgy, revolving around the placing of a Catholic convent at Auschwitz and the removal of the Berlin Wall, elicits no discussion of the Palestinian people. See "Elie Wiesel Speaks Out on Auschwitz," *National Catholic Reporter*, September 15, 1989, and Elie Wiesel, "I Fear What Lies Beyond the Wall," *The New York Times*, November 17, 1989.

26. Simha Flapan, *The Birth of Israel: Myths and Realities* (New York: Random House, 1987), 5.

27. Ibid., 7–9; 235–36.

28. See Avi Shalim, *Collusion Across the Jordan* (New York: Columbia University Press, 1988); Ilan Pappe, *Britain and the Arab-Israeli Conflict, 1948–1951* (New York: Macmillan/St. Anthony's Press, 1988); Tom Segev, *1949: The First Israelis* (New York: Free Press, 1986); Benny Morris, *Palestinian Refugee*. See also Benny Morris, "The New Historiography: Israel Confronts Its Past," *Tikkun* 3 (1988): 19–23, 99–102.

29. Morris, *Palestinian Refugee*, 288–89, 292, 293–94.

30. Segev, *1949*, 26–27.

31. "Territory for Peace—Bad Deal: International Conference—A Trap," *The New York Times*, March 14, 1988. With Shamir's visit to the United States in November 1989 a similar message was published. See "An Open Letter to Prime Minister Shamir of Israel," *The New York Times*, November 15, 1989.

32. Jack Mondlak, "To the Jews of America and Jewish Youth the World Over!" *The New York Times*, May 12, 1988. Cynthia Ozick, the novelist, has also been part of this conservative movement. See "To Mr. Arafat: Stones Are Not Jewels," *The New York Times*, February 29, 1988. For Ozick's attempt to address the politics of "anti-Zionism," see Jonathan Mark, "Peace Group to Refute Mideast 'Myths'," *The Jewish Week*, December 1, 1989. Nonetheless there are those within the Jewish community who press forward. For an attempt to circle the old city of Jerusalem with a human chain for peace see "Jews Join in Rally with Palestinians," *The New York Times*, December 31, 1989.

33. Sarah Roy, "Living with the Holocaust: The Journey of a Child of Holocaust Survivors," *Journal of Palestine Studies* 32:1 (2002): 5–12.
34. Amira Hass, *Drinking the Sea at Gaza: Days and Nights in a Land Under Siege*, trans. Elana Wesley and Maxine Kaufman-Lacusta (New York: Metropolitan Books, 1999).

CHAPTER 6

1. Michael Walzer, *Exodus and Revolution* (New York: Basic Books, 1985), 6.
2. James H. Cone, *Black Theology and Black Power* (New York: Seabury, 1969), 6, 43, 44.
3. Quoted by James H. Cone, *The Spirituals and the Blues* (New York: Seabury, 1972), 44.
4. Cone, *Black Theology*, 39, 40. For Cone's later works see his *God of the Oppressed* (New York: Seabury, 1975) and *For My People: Black Theology of the Black Church* (Maryknoll, NY: Orbis, 1984). See also James H. Cone, *Risks of Faith: The Emergence of a Black Theology of Liberation, 1968–1998* (Boston: Beacon Press, 1999).
5. *Second General Conference of Latin American Bishops, The Church in the Present-Day Transformation of Latin America in Light of the Council* (Washington, D.C.: National Conference of Catholic Bishops, 1979), 28.
6. Gustavo Gutiérrez, *A Theology of Liberation: History, Politics and Salvation*, trans. Cardidad Inda and John Eagleson (Maryknoll, NY: Orbis, 1973), 155, 156, 157, 159.
7. Ibid., 177. Also see Gustavo Gutierrez, *The Power of the Poor in History*, trans. Robert R. Barr (Maryknoll, NY: Orbis, 1983). More recent works include *The God of Life*, trans. Matthew J. O'Connell (Maryknoll, NY: Orbis, 1991), *The Density of the Present: Selected Writings* (Maryknoll, NY: Orbis, 1999), and *We Drink From Our Own Wells: The Spiritual Journey of a People*, trans. Matthew J. O'Connell (Maryknoll, NY: Orbis, 2003).
8. *The Kairos Theologians, The Kairos Document: Challenge to the Church* (Stony Point, NY: Theology Global Context, 1985), i, 16.
9. Suh Kwang-Sun David, "A Biographical Sketch of an Asian Theological Consultation" in *Minjung Theology: People as the Subjects of History*, ed. Commission on Theological Concerns of the Christian Conference of Asia (Maryknoll, NY: Orbis, 1983), 16.
10. Moon Hee-Suk Cyris, "An Old Testament Understanding of Minjung," in *Minjung Theology*, 136, 137. For a more detailed discussion see Cyris, *A Korean Minjung Theology: An Old Testament Perspective* (Maryknoll, NY: Orbis, 1986).

11. Jean Corbon, George Khodr, Samir Kafity, and Albert Lahham, "What Is Required of the Christian Faith Concerning the Palestine Problem," *Biblical and Theological Concerns* (Limasol, Cyrus: Middle East Council of Churches, n.d.), 11–13. Also, see Jean Corbon, "Western Public Opinion and the Palestine Conflict" in *Christians, Zionism and Palestine* (Beirut: Institute for Palestine Studies, n.d.). Corbon's lecture was presented in February 1969. This understanding of Zionism as a form of racism was adopted by the United Nations on November 10, 1975. For an interesting discussion of this theme, see *Zionism and Racism: Proceedings of an International Symposium* (Tripoli, Libya: International Organization for the Elimination of All Forms of Racial Discrimination, 1977).

12. Ibid., *Biblical and Theological Concerns*, 12.

13. Gabriel Habib, "A Statement," in Fleischner, *Auschwitz*, 417, 418, 419. George Khodr echoed these sentiments this time in reference to the Lebanese War. See his "Christians of the Orient: Witness and Future; The Case of Lebanon," *WSCF Journal* (May 1986): 35-42.

14. Naim Stifan Ateek, *Justice and Only Justice: A Palestinian Theology of Liberation* (Maryknoll, NY: Orbis, 1989), 9–10.

15. Ibid., 33–34, 48.

16. Ibid., 63–64, 66, 69, 77.

17. Ibid., 168, 170

18. Mubarak Awad, "Statement," Database Project on Palestinian Human Rights, Jerusalem, June 5, 1988. For a discussion of his understanding of nonviolence see Mubarak E. Awad, "Nonviolent Resistance: A Strategy for the Occupied Territories," *Journal of Palestine Studies* 13 (1984): 22-36.

19. For a typical, and unfortunately, superficial response to Christian liberation theology, see Leon Klenicki, "The Theology of Liberation: A Latin American Jewish Exploration," *American Jewish Archives* 35 (1983): 27–39.

20. For an example of an emphasis on the death of Jesus see Jon Sobrino, *Christology at the Crossroads: A Latin American Approach*, trans. *John Drury* (Maryknoll, NY: Orbis, 1978). For an overall discussion of contemporary Christian and Jewish perspectives on the trial and death of Jesus, see John T. Pawlikowski, "The Trial and Death of Jesus: Reflections in Light of a New Understanding of Judaism," *Chicago Studies* 25 (1986): 79–94.

21. Joan Casanas, "The Task of Making God Exist," in *The Idols of Death and the God of Life: A Theology*, ed. Pablo Richard et al., trans. Barbara E. Campbell and Bonnie Shepard (Maryknoll, NY: Orbis, 1983), 113, 114, 115.

22. Ibid., 115, 116. He writes, "I do not believe that the Omnipotent who, because he so chooses, shelves his omnipotence and allows

himself to be oppressed and massacred with the people for the alleged reason that it is love that must conquer has proven to be the type of God whom the most altruistic and heroic activists experience as an ultimate dimension and horizon of their struggle" (116).

23. Ibid., 133, 134.

24. The Attorney-General of the government of Israel v. Adolph Eichmann , in the District Court of Jerusalem, criminal case no. 40/61, minutes of session no. 30, pp. L1, M1, M2, N1.

25. Joyce Hollyday, "The Battle for Central America," *Sojourners* 11 (1982): 17.

26. Ernesto Cardenal, *The Gospel in Solentiname*, vol. 1, trans. Donald D. Walsh (Maryknoll, NY: Orbis, 1982), 255–56.

27. Quoted in Reuben Ainsztein, *Jewish Resistance in Nazi-Occupied Eastern Europe* (London: Paul Elek, 1974), 643, 644.

28. Eyewitness account quoted in Eliezer Berkovits, *With God in Hell: Judaism in the Ghettos and Deathcamps* (New York: Sanhedrin Press, 1979), 21, 22.

29. Quoted in Placido Erdozain, *Archbishop Romero: Martyr of Salvador*, trans. John McFadden and Ruth Warner (Maryknoll, NY: Orbis, 1981), 75–76.

30. Jane Hunter, "Links to Guatemala: Doomed by Democracy?" *Israeli Foreign Affairs* 2 (1986): 1. The documentation that Hunter, herself a Jew, uses throughout her newsletter is overwhelmingly from Jewish sources in Israel published in Israeli newspapers and periodicals.

31. Jane Hunter, "Reagan's Unseen Ally in Central America: Israel Sends Arms to the Contras but Won't Show Its Face," *Israeli Foreign Affairs* 1/1 (1984): 1, 2.

32. Jane Hunter, "The Relationship Between Israel and South Africa: How Close?" *Israeli Foreign Affairs* 1/3 (1985): 1. For a more detailed analysis of this relationship see Hunter, *Undercutting Sanctions— Israel, the U.S. and South Africa* (Washington, D.C.: Washington Middle East Associates, 1986). Also see James Adams, *The Unnatural Alliance* (London: Quartet Books, 1984).

33. Jane Hunter, "Tutu Abhors Holocaust Monopoly," *Israeli Foreign Affairs* 1/9 (1985): 1, 6. For those Israelis who do realize the connection regarding fascism and suffering see Hunter, "Israel and South Africa: In the Present Tense," *Israeli Foreign Affairs* 2 (1986): 5, 6. One of the reasons for supporting such foreign policy is the maintenance of a burgeoning military-industrial complex in Israel. Aaron Klieman, who teaches in the Political Science Department at Tel Aviv University, documents the Israeli arms industry in his book, *Israel's Global Reach*.

34. Pablo Richard, "Biblical Theology of Confrontation with Idols," in Casanas, *Idols of Death*, 7, 9, 15, 19.

35. Walter Benjamin, "Theses on the Philosophy of History," in *Illuminations*, ed. Hannah Arendt, trans. Harry Zohn (New York: Schocken, 1978), 255, 256, 257.

36. Etty Hillesum, *An Interrupted Life: The Diaries of Etty Hillesum 1941–43*, ed. J. G. Gaarlandt, trans. Jonathan Cape (New York: Pocket Books, 1985), ix.

37. Ibid., 194, 195.

38. Ibid., 255.

39. Ibid., 186, 187.

40. Ibid., 184, 185.

41. Ibid., 99–101.

42. Martin Buber, "The Meaning of Zionism," in *A Land of Two Peoples: Martin Buber on Jews and Arabs*, ed. Paul R. Mendes-Flohr (New York: Oxford University Press, 1983), 181.

43. Ibid., 183.

44. Ibid., 183, 184.

45. Ibid., "Zionism and 'Zionism'," 221.

46. Martin Buber, *Eclipse of God* (Atlantic Highlands, NJ: Humanities Press, 1979), 129.

47. See Gillian Rose, *The Broken Middle: Out of Our Ancient Society* (Oxford: Blackwell, 1992).

48. Azmi Bishara, "Bantustanisation or Bi-Nationalism?" *Race and Class* 37 (1995): 49. For Magnes's letter, see Goren, *Dissenter in Zion*, 279.

49. See Edward W. Said, *The End of the Peace Process: Oslo and After* (New York: Pantheon, 2000).

50. See Carter Heyward, *Revolutionary Forgiveness: Feminist Reflections on Nicaragua* (Maryknoll, NY: Orbis, 1987).

51. See Hannah Arendt, *The Human Condition*, 2d ed. (Chicago: University of Chicago Press, 1998), 236–47.

Chapter 7

1. As with any movement of dissent, the price to be paid is in the realm both of opportunity (speaking engagements and job possibilities, for example) and of psychology (the feeling of rejection and charges of traitorous activity, even consorting with the enemy). The most frequent accusation is that through dissent one is laying the groundwork for another Holocaust. The result is often self-censorship. Those who continue to speak realize that solidarity carries pain and sacrifice. Just as often, people of conscience drift away from identification with the Jewish community.

2. Perhaps this is the future of religious resistance: small groups within diverse communities who, while remaining rooted in their own

community, come into solidarity with each other. For an early approach to this question see, "The Prophetic Voice in the Twentieth Century" in Ellis, *Faithfulness in an Age of Holocaust*. A more recent understanding can be found in ibid., *Practicing Exile: The Religious Odyssey of an American Jew* (Minneapolis: Fortress, 2001).

3. The constant equation of Yassir Arafat with Adolf Hitler in Jewish writing and public discussion exemplifies the exaggeration and denigration of the Palestinian people. Most of the world, as well as many officials within the United States government, sees Arafat as a moderate. See Alan Hart, *Arafat: Terrorist or Peacemaker* (London: Sidgwick & Jackson, 1984). Clearly the September 11th event has raised these questions to another level. The prejudices against Palestinians and Arabs in general is as strong in the twenty-first century as it was in the twentiety.

4. See Rosemary Radford Ruether, *Faith and Fratricide: The Theological Roots of Anti-Semitism* (New York: Seabury, 1974) and Elisabeth Schussler Fiorenza, *In Memory of Her: A Feminist Theological Reconstruction of Christian Origins* (New York: Crossroad, 1983); Isabel Carter Heyward, *The Redemption of God: A Theology of Mutual Redemption* (New York: University Press of America, 1982). Ruether is exceptional because she has continued on in her analysis. See her book, co-authored with Herman J. Ruether, *The Wrath of Jonah: The Crisis of Religious Nationalism in the Israeli-Palestinian Conflict*, 2d ed. (Minneapolis: Fortress, 2002).

5. Attempts to heal the rift theologically often revolve around the person of Jesus. Two books by Jewish authors are interesting on this point. See Harvey Falk, *Jesus the Pharisee: A New Look at the Jewishness of Jesus* (New York: Paulist Press, 1985) and Pinchas Lapide, *The Sermon on the Mount: Utopia or Program for Action?* (Maryknoll, NY: Orbis, 1986). On Paul, see Alan F. Segal, *Paul the Convert: The Apostolate and Apostasy of Saul the Pharisee* (New Haven: Yale University Press, 1990) and Daniel Boyarin, *A Radical Jew: Paul and the Politics of Identity* (Berkeley: University of California Press, 1994).

Index

CPSIA information can be obtained at www.ICGtesting.com
Printed in the USA
BVOW01s1652231013

334420BV00001B/4/P